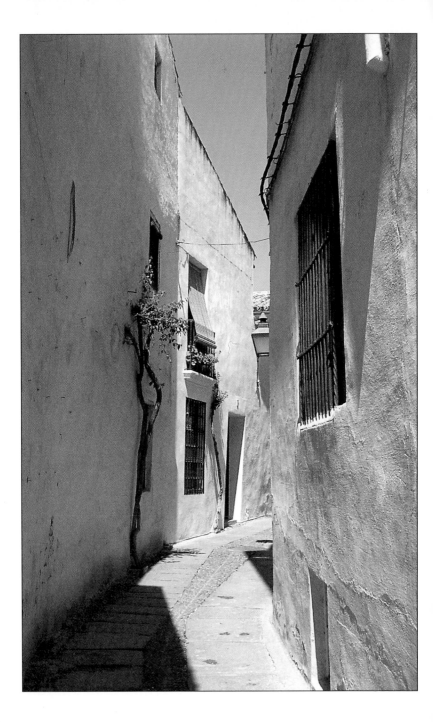

SPAIN

SOUTH

First Edition
1991

TABLE OF CONTENTS

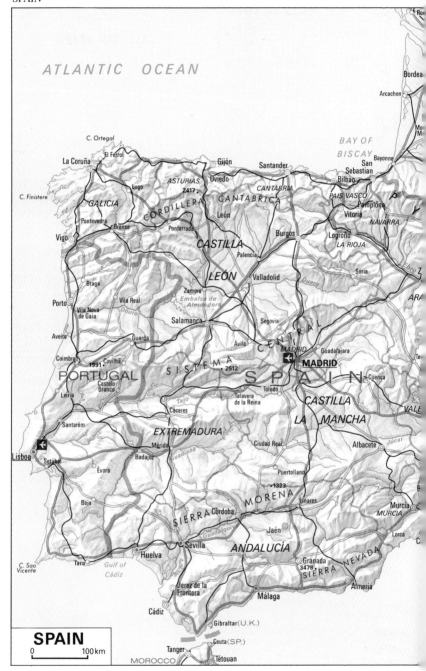

LIST OF MAPS

HISTORY AND CULTURE

The Mythical Origins

In the 6th century BC a seafarer from the Phoenician settlement of Massalia (Marseille), circumnavigated the Spanish coast. The written record he left was used centuries later by the Latin poet Avienus as the basis of his *Ora Maritima*. This is how we know of Tartessus, the mythical kingdom on the Spanish Atlantic coast which must have been situated about where the city of Huelva now is. Tartessus was a city-state which had an advanced form of social organisation and an abundance of gold, silver and copper. Its first ruler was Geryones, the owner of the red oxen which were stolen by Hercules as one of the twelve labors he had to endure. In order to accomplish this task he had to kill the king. On either side of the gateway to the sea he set a huge pillar. The Rocks of Gibraltar and Ceuta are what has remained of them as a warning that beyond them the sea ends and its waters pour into a bottomless abyss. Be that as it may, in the 6th century BC the last king of Tartessus maintained close trade links with Greece. However, the ancestors of the settlers at Tartessus came undoubtedly from Asia Minor and Egypt. From there they made sea voyages to seek for new markets. They proceeded to settle on the coast of Almería. At Los Millares, near what is now the town of Santa Fé de Mondújar (Almería), they

Preceding pages: Flamenco dancing needs practice. Alley in the Jewish Quarter of Córdoba. Olive trees as far as the eye can see. The Festival of Moors and Christians in Alcoy. The moment of truth at the tail end of a bullfight. Left: The "Lady of Elche". Above: The megalithic dolmen in Antequera.

founded a settlement of stone and clay dwellings which was surrounded by fortifications and, moreover, had an aqueduct and a necropolis.

From here these peoples spread all across Andalusia and the Levante. Halfway between Almería and the mining center at Tartessus, the megalithic dolmen of Antequera was found. In addition, the strange Balearic *taulas* and *talayots* date from this period.

Phoenicians, Greeks, Carthaginians

It can be safely assumed that trade links between the Phoenician cities of Tyre and Sidon on the coast of Asia Minor and Tartessus were formed about 1000 BC. Near their trading partners, the Phoenicians founded a settlement of their own. It was called Gadir and is today the modern city of Cádiz, which is Europe's oldest city. Later they established other centers for processing raw materials on the Mediterranean coast: Malaka (Málaga), Sexi (Almuñecar) and Abdera

15

(Adra). Carthage, which was founded about 800 BC on the coast of Tunisia was destined to attain great historical significance. Tartessus remained under Tyrian hegemony until 575 BC, when Nebuchadnezzar of Babylon destroyed Tyre. At that time Phocaean Greeks took advantage of the crisis to conquer the Phoenician trading colonies in Spain. In order to strengthen trade ties they founded Mainaké (Velez-Málaga), Hemeroscopeion (Denia), Akra Leuca (Alicante), Sagunto, Rhode (Rosas) and Emporion (Ampurias). During the same period, the Celts, who were an Indo-European nomadic people, settled the interior of the Iberian Peninsula. The Iberians came from Africa to settle in the south and east. In the central region they intermarried with the Celts to become the indigenous Celtiberians, although on the coasts they came under Hellenic hegemony. The Iberians were farmers and herdsmen. Their settlements, such as Iponuma (Córdoba) or Ilduro (Mataró), were fortified. The Iberian sculpture which has been found is exquisite. Good examples of it are the Ladies of Elche (3rd century BC) and Baza and the mythical beast of Bazalote, which had the body of a bull and a human head.

As soon as it had assumed the hegemony formerly exercised by Tyre, Carthage extended its influence in the Mediterranean. It proceeded to destroy Tartessus. Then it seized the Straits of Gibraltar, founded the city of Ibiza, took Sicily and Corsica, and ultimately established its center of operations on Sardinia. It was not long before the trading powers Rome and Carthage clashed. The Punic Wars were the most extensive armed conflict in antiquity. The first of these wars saw Carthage lose her colonies on Sicily, Corsica and Sardinia. The Carthaginians subsequently fled to the coast of Andalusia,

where they founded New Carthage, which is now Cartagena, under Hamilcar Barca. From there they advanced northward along the coast. The Greeks, who had settlements there, reacted by allying themselves with Rome. The Second Punic War began in 219 BC, when Hannibal, Hamilcar's son, attacked Sagunto. Remaining loyal to her allies, the city withstood the siege until there was nothing left for its citizens to do but commit collective suicide. Then it was that Hannibal set out on his legendary and fateful march on Rome.

The Romans

While Hannibal was campaigning in Italy, the Romans attacked the troops he had left in Spain. Thus the Punic Wars spread to Spain. In 210 BC, Scipio made Emporion his headquarters, recapturing Sagunto and taking all of southern Spain. The ancient Phoenician settlement of Gadir, which was the last stronghold of Carthage on the Peninsula, fell to Rome in 205 BC. The Romans decided on continuing to exploit the mines and agriculture as sources of raw materials. 40,000 slaves worked the mines of Carthago Nova, which had been devastated. The upshot of all this was that tribute soared to 2,400,000 sesterces in 179 BC. Settlers were sent from Rome to cultivate the land. In addition, Roman traders soon established themselves. Their particular strongholds were in the Guadalquivir Valley and the mining regions.

It was the Romans who founded most of modern Spain's cities, not only as military bases but also as market towns where the grid of roads which crisscrossed the country intersected. Therefore, their settlements were culturally homogeneous to an unprecedented degree. Even previous settlements became Roman. This entailed assuming the Roman life style, which had become a status symbol.

Right: The Romans created intricate mosaics, here an example in Italica.

16

In the age of the Emperor Augustus there were three Spanish provinces: Provincia Baetica with Córdoba as its capital, Provincia Tarraconensis (Tarragona) and Lusitania with its capital at Mérida. This last was founded as a spa for elderly and deserving legionaries. Lucius Cornelius Balbo was the first consul of non-Italian origin. The Emperors Trajan, Hadrian and Theodosius were Spaniards by birth. The rhetorician Seneca the Elder and Seneca the Younger, the philosopher, were from Córdoba. In the early centuries AD about a quarter of the Roman Senate came from Hispania.

The Romans left so many architectural monuments that the modern mind boggles. They built roads and massive bridges, enormous stone structures, elevated in the middle, with arches and buttressed piers and a small temple for show. The aqueducts were built on similarly sophisticated lines (Mérida, Puente del Diabolo in Tarragon, Los Caños de Carmona near Sevilla). Theaters and circuses were built everywhere for mass entertainment. Remains of these have been preserved in Tarragona, Mérida, Itálica, Ronda and Sagunto. In the museums there, mosaics which adorned these structures have been restored.

Christianity reached Spain in the 3rd century. Since the 7th century, texts have referred to the legends of the missions of St Jacob, patron saint of Santiago, and St Paul, who is said to have been a missionary in Lusitania. Since the 6th century, there have been tales of the seven apostolic *varones* (men) who preached in the south. However, Christianity is much more likely to have been brought to Spain by traders and soldiers. The new religion spread so rapidly that the Visigoths found a completely Christianised country.

The Visigoths

In the 4th century the Huns invaded Central Europe from Central Asia, expelling the Germanic tribes who subsequently migrated to France and Spain. While the Suebi settled in what became

Galicia, the Alani migrated as far as Lusitania (Portugal) and the Vandals went as far as Andalusia and North Africa. As allies of Rome, the Visigoths occupied Southern France. Toulouse was their capital. After being expelled by the Franks, in 507, they too retreated to the Iberian Peninsula. There they established Toledo as their capital. Despite this burst of expansive drives, the Visigoths can hardly have numbered much more than 100,000. They settled several regions of the central Meseta, and managed to consolidate their hegemony from Toledo. The 3 - 4 million Roman Spaniards living on the Mediterranean littoral were at any rate safe from the "barbarian" threat because they were under Eastern Roman protection. Justinian attempted to revive the Roman Empire from there. Consequently, the Spanish Levante coast was Byzantine for 70 years (549-620) after that.

The Visigoth King Leovigildo managed to unite the remaining German tribes and, in emulation of Rome, he made himself the ruler of a great empire. Religious homogeneity stabilised Visigoth hegemony. What is significant here is that the Visigoths brought with them the Arian form of Christianity which they had adhered to since the 4th century. The doctrine of the Alexandrian missionary Arius denied that Christ was the Son of God, but instead proclaimed him as merely "godlike". The ensuing conflicts made Roman Christians in particular oppose the doctrine of Arianism. Leovigildo attempted to convert the Spanish Christians to Arianism while his son, Hermenegildo, converted at Sevilla to Roman Catholicism. When Leovigildo took Sevilla, he had his son executed. The Roman Christians responded by declaring him a martyr and a saint. The

Right: The Moorish baths were a considerable improvement in general level of hygiene in medieval Spain.

martyr's brother Recaredo, also a convert to Roman Catholicism, ascended the throne a year later after their father's death. At the 3rd Council of Toledo (587), he proclaimed Roman Catholicism the national doctrine.

The Visigoth Empire did not, however, prove very stable. The kings, who were appointed by generals and bishops at councils, often reigned only a short time. Intrigues and power struggles were rife. The last king of the Goths, Don Rodrigo, was elected in the face of dogged resistance on the part of the nobility. Those opposing him sought Arab aid. The Arabs had in the meantime swept across North Africa spreading Islam. This brought about the downfall of the Visigoths, for the Arabs came, contriving to take advantage of their victory over Don Rodrigo as a pretext for establishing themselves on the Iberian Peninsula.

The Arabs

In 711, Tarik the Moor landed at Gibraltar ("Tarik's Mountain"). He had been sent by the North African governor of Damascus, Muza Ben Musayr. After defeating the Visigoth King Rodrigo at Guadalete, he advanced in a few months' time as far as Toledo. Muza followed him with reinforcements to take Sevilla and Mérida. In an unprecedented campaign they conquered Spain in the following years with the exception of spots in the Pyrenees and the mountains of Asturias. It was from here that the Christian forces were to launch their ultimate campaign of reconquest, the *Reconquista*. For the first 40 years Spain, as Al-Andalus, remained a province of Damascus. The Syrians, Arabs and Berbers who had made up the earliest occupation forces contented themselves with retaining military control of the country and with confiscating the riches of the Visigoth nobility. Naturally this caused various clashes to flare up. In 755, a scion of the Umayyads ar-

rived from Baghdad who had managed to escape the slaughter wrought there by the Abbasids upon his clan. This scion of the Umayyads, Abd ar - Rahman I (756-788), and his followers assumed power in Al-Andalus and founded an independent emirate at Córdoba.

Although Islam was now the official religion, Jews and Christians were still permitted to practice their rites undisturbed if they were willing to pay land tax. For this reason many Christian peasants converted to Islam and were known as *Muladíes*. However, Christian artisans who lived in the cities retained their faith and came to be known as *Mozárabes*. In the mid 9th century there was a sort of mystic revolution among the Mozarabs at Córdoba which culminated in acts of provocation. Many sought martyrdom. Although they had been tolerated hitherto, Mozarab rites turned into a vehicle for political dissidence. The heretic Omar Ben Hafsum, who was a *Muladí* of Visigoth descent, led the Mozarabs to rebellion in the mountains of Ronda. As a consequence, large groups of Mozarabs had to emigrate to the north at the close of the 9th century. The front of Christian reconquest had by then advanced south to the Duero. The Mozarabs settled in reconquered Christian Spain, bringing with them their religion, which had stagnated in 200 years of Arab predominance and the benefits of the sophisticated Arab civilisation.

The Caliphate of Córdoba

In the early 10th century Al-Andalus was at its political and cultural zenith. The introduction of new farming methods and the improvement of the Roman irrigation system had turned the Guadalquivir Valley, the *vega* (wetlands), of the Genil and the *huertas*, fluvial plains of the Mediterranean coast, into lush fertile orchards and fields. Citrus fruits, fruit trees, rice, sugar cane and cotton were introduced and cultivated. In the cities, and above all Córdoba, Sevilla and Málaga, craftsmanship flourished. Silk

weaving, metalworking and pottery not only covered local needs but met the demands of the entire European feudal aristocracy. Almería was one of the richest ports in the West. It functioned as a bridgehead between the Emirate of Córdoba and the Caliphate of Baghdad. Córdoba, the capital, was aglitter with affluence, culture and elegance.

It was this affluence which enabled Abderramán III, the half-breed son of a slave from Navarre and the Emir, to assert his right to the Umayyad legacy. He proclaimed himself Caliph, which meant that he was the spiritual leader of Hispanic Muslims. While the Caliphate of Córdoba (912-1031) lasted, the Moorish Kingdom attained its greatest extent. At that time it covered three quarters of the Iberian Peninsula as well as Tanger and North Morocco.

Above: The mosque in Córdoba exemplifies a style that pervades much of Spain. Right: Maimonides, the philosopher, was one of the scholars at the university of Córdoba.

The young Caliph Abderramán III pacified the whole kingdom, secured the borders threatened by the Christians and enlarged the capital. Inside the walled city was the mosque which he had had enlarged. It had been built in the reign of Abderramán I to hold 5000 worshippers. The most recent renovation, which it underwent in the reign of Almanzor, enlarged it to hold 25,000. In the *medina* were the *alcázar* of the governor and the bazaar. By the end of the 10th century, Córdoba had a population of a million as well as 80,000 shops and workshops. At the same time, León, the important Christian capital to the north, had only 7000 inhabitants, and hardly more than a dozen shops.

At the then famous university of Córdoba the sciences of astronomy, botany, mathematics and medicine were at an advanced level. Furthermore, the library of Alhaquén II comprised over 400,000 volumes. This necessitated an army of scribes who were officially employed to copy texts.

At this time relations between Muslims and their Christian neighbours were good. A queen of Navarre, Doña Toda, came to Abd ar Rahman's court seeking a cure for the obesity of her son, Sancho the Fat. She remained for two years at the Córdoban court until physicians had cured her son and he could ascend the throne. Ordoño IV of León and the Court of Barcelona also sought the Caliph's friendship. It is difficult to imagine what sort of impression the Caliph's court must have made on such relatively primitive rulers, accustomed as they were to rustic forts and encampments. They, like all visitors, were received in the famous and sumptuous palace of Medina Azahara which had been built by Abderramán III outside the city. After passing numerous guards and going through countless doors, visitors reached the throne room to be ultimately received by a godlike being, detached and sublime, who already seemed to be in bliss at the gates of paradise. The audience hall was indeed meant to impress, with walls of marble and gilt and a central fountain filled with mercury reflecting an unearthly light when the sun shone. When it was agitated, the quicksilver shot out rays like lightning, as if the entire hall shivered. Only ruins remain of this palace, which was in the end destroyed by the Almoravids due to their dislike of splendour. But records bring the lavish sophistication of the until then matchless buildings to life.

The last Caliph of Córdoba was Almanzor (Al-Mansur), who was actually the military governor. He sent the young Caliph Hishem II slaves and concubines. In this way he contrived to induce him to leave Medina Azahara only rarely. Almanzor established what was really a military dictatorship and went on rapid raid-like campaigns into Christian territory. In 987, he reached Barcelona. By 997, he was at Santiago de Compostela where he stole the cathedral bells, which he then hung in the mosque at Córdoba as

a provocation. There they remained until Ferdinand III took them back 200 years later. Almanzor willed that his son should succeed him but the Arab kingdom fragmented into many dynastic entities or *taifas*: Sevilla, Huelva, Granada, Niebla, Valencia, Badajoz, Málaga, etc.

The Almoravids and Almohads

After Alfonso VI had advanced the Reconquista by 1085 as far as the Tajo River and had also taken Toledo, the *taifas* were forced to summon the aid of the Almoravids. They were a Berber dynasty that controlled large areas of North Africa and the Gold Route to the Sudan. Led by Yusuf Ben Tasfin, the Almoravids crossed to Gibraltar, defeated Alfonso VI and began to reunify the *taifas*. They accomplished this by taking the cities of Granada, Málaga and Sevilla. Since they were adherents of orthodox Islam, a rigid political and cultural regimen prevailed. High-ranking officers held the major offices under the suzerainty of Marrakesh.

The people soon rose up against this un-accustomed rule. The Almoravids were threatened elsewhere, too. In the south they were attacked by the Almohads, who took the Gold Route in the Sudan and all of Morocco in 1147.

The only *taifas* to remain independent were Badajoz and Zaragoza. Valencia was taken by *El Cid Campeador*, a Mozarab noble banished by his king, Alfonso VI. He was the hero of the epic *El Cantar de Mío Cid* as well as of many medieval legends and romances. After his death Valencia again fell to the Arabs until it was finally liberated 100 years later by Jaime I, the Conqueror.

The Almohads ruled Al-Andalus and North Africa for almost a century. From Morocco they rapidly took Tarifa and Algeciras. They then proceeded to establish Marrakesh as their capital and Sevilla as their cultural and administrative center. They not only were able to withstand the advance of the Christian armies to the south but they also attacked Castile and Navarra.

The Almohads made Sevilla into a real capital. They built the mosque and the Giralda, which is a minaret strikingly similar to the Koutubía at Marrakesh. Apart from the tower, only the Orange Court remains of the mosque complex. The Torre del Oro and the Alcázar were part of the city fortifications. These buildings are what may be regarded as an unsuccessful attempt at emulating the splendour of the Caliphate of Córdoba.

The Beginnings of Catalonia

After the 8th century Arab invasion the Visigoth state fragmented. Only small enclaves in the northern mountains remained free of Muslim influence. After 722 the Asturians expanded southwards, making León their capital in 910. Castile,

Right: Another great creation of Moorish architects, the Alcázar of Sevilla.

one of the counties of this kingdom, split off from it in 961. The other peoples in the Pyrenees were supported by the troops of Charlemagne, who also took part in an attempt to liberate Zaragoza. As dramatically recounted in the *Chanson de Roland,* Charlemagne's retreating rear-guard was decisively defeated in the Pyrenees. He did manage to integrate the Catalonian counties into his empire, however, uniting them with Roussillon to form the Spanish March. The Catalonian counties remained French for 100 years until Wilfried the Hairy became the first independent Count of Barcelona in 874. Aragón ultimately split off from the Kingdom of Navarre. In the south it spread as far as Zaragoza and to the Río Jalón. In the east it was united with Catalonia in 1137 by marriage.

After Almanzor's raids (985), Catalonia was widely settled and building commenced in earnest. In this region of Spain the Romanesque style emulated French and Lombard architecture. It was austere with flat stones imitating bricks. Blind arcades were a distinctive feature of the apse. Belfries stood apart from churches and had several tiers of windows.

Moorish raids were what showed the importance of fortifications. San Pére de Roda (1022) was built as a fortified monastery. The Romanesque part of the monastery of Sant Cúgat del Vallés is strategically located on what was once the site of a Roman *castrum*. It is important to remember that monasteries provided protection for the peasants working their lands. Church sculpture and painting, on the other hand, were not primarily aesthetic exercises but were instead devoted to disseminating biblical history in graphic anecdotes made drastically simple for the common man.

At the close of the century, building increased with the concomitant growth of Catalonia. The cloisters of the cathedrals at Gerona and Poblet, the Cathedral of

Tarragona and Sant Cúgat are also from this period.

The Reconquista

In the face of Almohad incursions on their territory, the kingdoms Castile, Navarra and Aragón united against the enemy. In 1212 a decisive battle was fought at Las Navas de Tolosa (Jaén Province). There, victorious Christians beat the Almohads back beyond the Sierra Morena. With this victory the ideal of Christian reconquest as a sacred mission was born. What had been campaigns of conquest now received legitimation on a higher spiritual plane. What was left of the Arab kingdom, on the other hand, again fragmented into *taifas* of which only Granada lasted until the late 15th century.

Ferdinand III of Castile took the cities of Córdoba, Jaén and Sevilla and made the region of Murcia a Castilian protectorate in 1244. But along the border, where the names of villages are still written with the addition of "de la Frontera", the skirmishes continued. At that time towns changed hands frequently. Ferdinand III divided the lands conquered in Andalusia among the loyal paladins who had supported him on his campaigns. The borders of the old *taifas* were redrawn. A brief rising of the remaining Moorish peasants in 1263 ended with their banishment.

This drastic measure brought in yet more land to be distributed and was of course, to have serious future consequences. Vast tracts of land were reallocated to the northern aristocracy. These doughty nobles were a force to be reckoned with, and they were without a bourgeoisie to keep them in check.

The Mediterranean in the Middle Ages

The united counties of Aragón and Catalonia grew into a great power in the 13th century. The possession of major ports, as well as trade and the consistent

The kingdom attacked Tunis with an army of legionaries, intervened in Sicily and arrogated power over Corsica and Sardinia. In addition it fought, allied with Venice, against Pisa and Genoa and even took part of Greece and Byzantium. This expansionist drive formed the basis of Spanish claims to Naples and Italy well into the 18th century.

The great number of municipal buildings extant today indicates the prosperity of the era. The hall where the "Council of One Hundred" convened and the Exchange, the docks, the royal palace with Tinell Hall and the Santa Creu Hospital are merely the most important buildings in the Barcelona Barrio Gotico. Gothic sacred architecture was more austere, characterised by dignity, beauty and elegance. The best examples of it are Sta. María del Mar and the Monastery of Pedralbes in Barcelona, as well as the cathedrals at Barcelona, Gerona and Palma de Mallorca.

policies pursued by eight kings in the years between 1213 and 1410 resulted in enormous growth in the region.

Jaime I conquered Valencia and Játiva in 1236. While the mountainous regions bordering Aragón, through which the Wool Route led from the Pyrenees to the Mediterranean, was being divided among the Aragónese aristocracy, the coast was settled by Catalan nobles. They remained in the cities to pursue agriculture from there all the while, retaining the Arab system of cultivation. Arab farm hands, known as *Moriscos,* were not banished from the region. Moreover, Catalonia had a powerful merchant fleet at its disposal so that in Valencia the commercial outlook was favorable. The Balearic Islands, taken in 1229, were colonised in a similar manner. Farm labor from Empurdá was settled there. Mallorca became a major island trading port.

But, unfortunately, the splendor was not to last. Between the rural aristocracy and the urban mercantile class tension had been mounting since the migration of farm labor into the cities had begun to increase. Moreover, the country had been weakened by wars, the incursions of pirates and plague epidemics. Domestic anger focused on the Jews. By the 13th century drastic pogroms had started. By the late 14th century Mallorca had lost nearly all its mercantile houses and most of its fleet. Barcelona had now only about 20,000 inhabitants.

The resulting loss of political power is revealed in the Compromise of Caspe. When Martin the Good died in 1410 without an heir, there were five contenders for the throne. After an interregnum, nine representatives from Aragón, Catalonia and Valencia met at Caspe for consultation. After tough negotiations a Castilian of the line of Trastamara was made king. Fifty-seven years later, in 1469, two young contenders for the

Above: The cathedral of Barcelona. Right: Intricate carvings on the portal of the Palacio del Marqués de dos Aguas in Valencia.

throne, both of the Trastamara line, married secretly at Valladolid. They were, of course, Isabella of Castile and Ferdinand of Aragón, later to go down in history as the Catholic Kings.

The committed preacher Vicente Ferrer and the "Papa Luna" had taken a particularly active part in ensuring the election of the Castilian candidate. The latter, the Aragónese Pedro de Luna, Pope Benedict XIII at Avignon, hoped that the affluent Castilian would help to resolve the issue of schism among Catholics.

Although the Bank of Catalonia recorded its greatest gains between 1420 and 1435, the general economy was in decline. By 1450 it had stagnated. Since the Jews were expelled by the Inquisition in 1484, commerce was sluggish. The discovery of America and the subsequent shift in the handling of overseas trade to the Atlantic coast ports only deepened the crisis.

Much of the country's wealth was transferred to Valencia in those years. With its 75,000 inhabitants it was the largest city in 15th century Spain. The Aragonese Borjas of Gandía, who had settled the fertile *huerta* after the Reconquista, were among the most influential families in the region. Two popes were members of this prominent clan. One of them, Alexander VI, italianized their name to the more familiar "Borgia". He was on intimate terms with Ferdinand and Isabella, and issued the bull dividing the Atlantic Ocean between Spain and Portugal in the interest of the two monarchs. It was also he who bestowed upon them the title „the Catholic Kings".

The entire correspondence of the Borjas has been preserved. It is in pure Catalan, at that time at its sophisticated acme. The first author generally known to have written in Catalan was Raimundo Llull (1235-1315), a Mallorcan poet and philosopher. Ausias March and Jeanot Martorell were to follow. But economic decline brought about cultural stagnation.

Consequently, Catalan as language of letters was in eclipse from the 16th to the mid 19th centuries.

The End of the Reconquista

Since the 13th century, only Castile – weakened by disputes over the succession to the throne and in the face of aristocratic revolt – had been advancing the cause of the Reconquista. Yet economic developments had begun which guaranteed Castilian prosperity for two centuries. Alfonso X founded the Mesta in 1273 to promote the development of vast areas of the country. This was an association uniting herd owners and governing *transhumance*, a nomadic grazing system providing for adequate summer and winter pasturage. The Mesta regulated drovers' routes, *cañadas*, as well as tax levies and the export of wool to England and Flanders. This trade was so lucrative that it was for centuries the chief source of Castilian wealth. Most Mesta members belonged to the nobility, the militant orders of knights or the clergy. Overseas trade and cotton imports in time reduced the value of wool and, consequently, the Mesta. Castile afterwards declined economically until in the 19th century the Mesta was forbidden by the *Cortes* at Cádiz.

The marriage of Isabella of Castile and Ferdinand of Aragón was not the work of diplomats. Isabella's claims to the throne were at first not assured since her brother's daughter disputed them. The latter, however, was rumored to be the bastard daughter of Don Beltrán de la Cueva. At the Battle of Toro (1474), Isabella's faction stood up to the "Beltraneja" and won. The resulting union of the kingdoms of Castile and Aragón marked the beginning of national unity and the ultimate rise of Spain as a global power.

The Siege of Granada

Since being expelled from Jaén in the 13th century the Nasrid dynasty had ruled in Granada. Their kingdom, comprising the modern provinces of Almería, Granada and Málaga, had a population of about 300,000. The Nasrids, like the *taifas* before them, paid tribute for the protection of the king of Castile. In the 14th century they built the Alhambra at Granada, a marvellous complex of palaces, fortifications and baths. Designed to harmonize with its surroundings the structure was a skillful blend of empty spaces, inner courtyards, and the interplay of light and water. Gardens were as important as buildings. The hill on which the complex is situated is laced with water conduits. A sophisticated hydraulic system feeds a multitude of fountains. The airiness of the structure, which was built of relatively fragile materials, belies the tremendous effort that went into its construction. The motto inscribed on a wall "May the beholder be struck dumb with amazement and his judgement be

confounded" sums it all up. Somehow the complex has miraculously survived. Washington Irving's tales made it world famous in the early 19th century.

When the Catholic Kings first attempted to take Granada, the Moorish kingdom was in a state of internecine war. The ruling Nasrid dynasty had split into two factions. The romances, songs of the period in a frequently melodramatic vein, tell of the ruler Muley Hassan, who was enamoured of the *Muladí* Zoraya. He made her his queen instead of his spouse, Aixa. Fleeing to Guadix, Aixa contrived to have her son Boabdil, not yet of age, made king. He was recognized by Granada, and Muley Hassan and his brother El Zagal fled to Málaga. Taking advantage of the situation, Ferdinand Catholic demanded tribute of Boabdil for his support in resisting the latter's family. Thus began the Siege of Granada which was to last ten years. The Catholic Kings first assaulted the region which was under El Zagal's sway. They only managed to take Ronda, Loja, Baza and Málaga after a long siege. At one point they miraculously escaped assassination at Málaga. However, the Moor who was to murder them during their siesta mistakenly stabbed a count.

After the Catholic Kings were sure that Granada was theirs in 1490, Boabdil unexpectedly mounted resistance. Settling down at Sta. Fé, the Catholic Kings began a siege that did not end until the city surrendered two years later. But Boabdil remained ruler of the Alpujarras. This region retained its property, laws, religion, customs and taxes despite the conquest of Granada. After the war about 150,000 Moriscos remained in the country. More importantly 40,000 settlers from Andalusia and Murcia were given land. But peace was short-lived. The Moriscos revolted against Christian oppression. In 1499 Cardinal Cisneros visited Granada, bringing a new plan for forced conversion of the remaining

Year of Conquest
- No Moorish occupation
- Reconquest 10th century
- Reconquest 11th century: I.
- Reconquest 11th century: II.
- Reconquest 13th century
- Reconquest 15th century

THE RECONQUISTA

Moriscos. The plan was rejected. In the Alpujarras, rebellion flared up. Ferdinand the Catholic finally banished the Moriscos, with a noticeable deleterious effect on agriculture. Many were willing to convert, thus remaining in the country.

Christopher Columbus

During the 15th century Genoa and Turkey prevailed as great powers in the Mediterranean. Spain and Portugal, on the other hand, were forced to venture on to the Atlantic for slaves, sugar and gold. The two Iberian nations competed in the search for a new route to Africa and the Orient. Portugal occupied the Azores, Madeira, the Sahara and Guinea. Castile, tied down by the Reconquista, took only the Canary Isles. At loggerheads over the political issue of the Beltraneja, the two kingdoms entered into treaty sealed by a papal bull granting Portugal the sole right to advance south of the Canaries. The only direction in which Spain could expand was westward.

Christopher Columbus (1451-1506), an experienced Genoese seaman, was forced to convalesce at Lisbon from a shipwreck. In the port there he must have conceived the idea of seeking an Atlantic route to India. He presented his plan to King John II of Portugal, but the monarch was preoccupied with exploring the coast of Africa and therefore not interested. Yet King John of Portugal wanted to keep the plans from falling into the hands of his arch-enemies, the Catholic Kings.

Widowed by 1485, Columbus and his seven-year-old son went secretly to relatives at Huelva. Lodged in La Rábida monastery there, he spoke to a monk who was father confessor to Isabella the Catholic. The monk gave him a letter of recommendation to the court. The Catholic Kings did not have a settled court, since they had become accustomed during the war years to travelling with a mobile retinue between the cities Valladolid, Salamanca, Segovia and the front, wherever it happened to be. Columbus managed to join their train as a

27

travelling merchant. Although his project interested the Kings, the coffers of state were empty and he was repeatedly put off with promises. He was compelled to wait for seven years. During that time he had his brother present his plans to the kings of England and France, but they too paid little heed. However, he was able to induce the Dukes of Medina Sidonia, who where resident in the region of Huelva, to put in a good word with the Catholic Kings. They were willing to give him enough money to make a longer wait worth his while.

After Granada finally surrendered on 2 January 1492, Columbus' project could be discussed by the Crown Council. Two crucial issues remained unresolved. First, Columbus demanded the title of viceroy of the lands he should discover as well as the title of admiral "ad perpetuum", i.e. as

Above: The Moors giving the Catholic Kings the keys to the city, a depiction on a choir stall in Toledo. Right: Isabel the Catholic dictating her testament.

a hereditary title. He also demanded a tenth of all booty he might capture and an eighth of the revenue from the expected volume of trade. These demands seemed exorbitant to the Catholic Kings. Columbus left the court without having achieved anything. Nonetheless, a messenger from the Kings caught up with him at Santa Fé. In the "Capitulations of Santa Fé" the Catholic Kings acceded unexpectedly to his demands. The second pressing problem was how to raise the 2 million maravedis needed. This was resolved in a circuitous manner. Legend has it that Isabella the Catholic pawned her jewels with one Luis Santángel, whom she charged with financing Columbus' project. A Jew from Valencia and Treasurer of the kingdom of Aragón, Santángel managed to divert part of his fortune, which had been confiscated by the Inquisition, for the purpose of raising the necessary funds. The Italian colony at Sevilla raised other funds. The richest Florentine and Genoese merchants and bankers resided in Calle de las Sierpes,

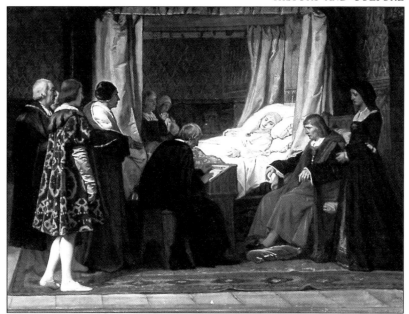

the "Wall Street" of the time. One of the Italians, Giovanni Pinelli, Juan Pinello in Spanish, lent the expedition money and persuaded the Dukes of Medina Sidonia to contribute. It was Pinello who grabbed exclusive shipping rights to the New World after the voyages proved successful. A total of 1,640,000 maravedis was raised. The rest was a forced contribution from the world-famous seamen of the port of Moguer, where the expedition was fitted out. On 3 August 1492, Columbus set out with three caravels and accompanied by the Pinzón brothers and the cartographer Juan de la Cosa. On the first voyage they discovered the islands of Guanahaní, Cuba and Haiti and on the second the Lesser Antilles. It was not until the third voyage that he reached the continent of South America. He took it for India and sailed along the coast. On his last voyage he discovered Honduras, Nicaragua, Costa Rica and Panama. He sailed home in 1504 when Isabella the Catholic was dying. King Ferdinand did not keep to the terms of the "Capitula-

tions of Santa Fé". Columbus died at Valladolid in 1506 without realising the significance of his discoveries. Up to his death the voyages had made debts. However, if Philip II had later been bound by the contract, he would have had to pay the equivalent of 10 tons of gold.

In the decades that followed, every adventurer and naval officer aspired to leading an expedition and discovering and subduing unknown lands. From 1519 to 1521, Hernán Cortés conducted his famous Aztec campaign. Twelve years later Francisco Pizarro subdued the Inca kingdom. In 1541, Francisco de Orellana explored the Amazon. By the close of the 16th century, Spain as a global power embraced all of western South America, vast tracts of the Caribbean, Mexico and the Philippines as well as Spain itself, Portugal and parts of Italy and Flanders.

Jews and Inquisition

In Roman times, the first Semites had migrated to Spain. In Catalonia and

29

Aragón in particular there were large Jewish communities which contributed greatly to the economic life of the cities. But even under the relatively tolerant Visigoths, discrimination set in, leaving the Jews at times the only ethnic group without any rights at all. Therefore it is quite certain that Arab settlement was strongly promoted by the Jewish community. Moorish rule was considered the Golden Age of Jewery in Spain. To the Jews is owed in part the glory of Córdoba. However, in the 13th century European pogroms against Jews spread to Spain.

The Catholic Kings needed the gold of Jewish bankers to finance the Siege of Granada. When this was no longer necessary, they issued an edict in March 1492 allowing the Jews three months' time to liquidate their possessions and leave the country. Of the over 400,000 Jews living in Spain, 160,000 emigrated to Portugal, Turkey, North Africa, Italy and Romania. Called Sephardim and highly educated, they founded communities abroad.

In some of them, 15th century Castilian is still spoken. 50,000 Jews preferred baptism to exile, joining the 200,000 who had already converted. The national economy was even more seriously affected by the host of artisans' workshops and businesses being left derelict than by the capital drain due to Jewish emigration.

Since 1231 the Inquisition had existed as an institution in Europe. This was the ecclesiastical court set up by Rome to check heresy. In 1478 the Spanish kings were granted jurisdiction over this court and the right to appoint the Grand Inquisitor. The first Court of the Inquisition was established at Sevilla. Soon it had turned into a ruthlessly effective police force in the service of Spanish absolut-

ism. After the expulsion of the Jews the Inquisition took over the surveillance of converts to punish clandestine retention of their former rites. Intellectuals and merchants, traditionally Jews, were objects of suspicion on principle. Only farmers and herdsmen remained free of surveillance. Thus one can say that the notion of racial purity advocated 500 years later by Hitler was born in 15th century Spain. If one aspired to public office, one's racial purity had to be proved. Treachery and secret denunciation were rife. The Inquisition held secret trials but celebrated monstrous public executions, or autos-da-fé. The consequences of such practices soon became manifest. Spanish society congealed to inertia. All energies were focused on the one outlet permitted, religion. Consequently, sacred art was powerful and enormously expressive.

In the 16th and 17th centuries thousands of heretics were tortured and burnt at the stake. From the 18th century, the Court of the Inquisition tended to concentrate on censoring books. The *Cortes* at Cádiz banned it and secularization finally abolished it.

Society in the Reign of the Catholic Kings

During the reign of the Catholic Kings the intellectual movement known as Humanism grew. Based on the study of the Classics, it was to influence all of Europe. The Castilian and the Aragonese courts were both interested in Latin letters. In 1474 the art of printing reached Valencia from Italy.

Architecture underwent a renascence in this period. The Diputation and the Silk Exchange at Valencia, as well as the city hall and the palace of the Regional Government at Barcelona, are all exuberantly High Gothic, a style which lasted into the 16th century. The cathedral which was built into the mosque at Córdoba in the reign of Charles V was also in

Right: Francisco Goya painted this strikingly vivid portrayal of a court session of the infamous Spanish Inquisition.

this style. The building of the period blends traditional *Mudéjar* elements, as the style employed by Arab architects in Spain is called, the lavish ornateness of Late Gothic and the emphasis on revealing structure characteristic of the Italian Renaissance, in fashion at the time. Such riotously comprehensive eclecticism is called "Isabellinic" since it was the style preferred by Isabella the Catholic. Artisans from all over Europe – Castilians, Flemish, Bretons and Germans – worked on major buildings such as the cathedral of Sevilla, each one of them contributing to the stylistic blend.

Enrique Egas was one of the major artisans of the period. Primarily a sculptor, he also devoted his energies to architecture, which he always saw as sculpture. It was he who added Italian convex stone moulding to the Gothic architectural repertoire. After the death of Juan Guas, he completed the church of San Juan de los Reyes at Toledo and built the Sta. Cruz Hospitals at Granada, Toledo and Santiago.

The Habsburgs

The Catholic Kings involved their offspring in strategic marriages intended to resolve all outstanding Iberian problems with Europe, but without much success. In England, which was a potential ally against France, the union of Henry VIII with Catherine of Aragón proved to be problematic. Their daughter María, who was married to the king of Portugal, died, whereupon her sister Isabella married the widower. Juan, heir to the throne of the United Kingdoms of Castile and Aragón, died young, so that Isabella the Catholic was forced to name her daughter Juana to succeed her on her death (1504). She was married to the son of Maximilian of Austria, Philip the Fair. Ferdinand the Catholic was to be regent during his lifetime, but Philip contested the regency. Ferdinand retired to his estates in Aragón. Philip I died in 1506, leaving his wife insane with grief. She was known as Juana the Mad. After Ferdinand also died in 1516, his grandson, Charles V, who had grown up in Flanders, became heir to the throne. The interregnum was administered by cardinal Cisneros. In 1517, the 17-year-old sovereign arrived with a retinue of Flemish advisers. He did not know a word of Spanish. After a short stay he was forced to return to Germany to be crowned Emperor of Germany as heir to his other grandfather, Maximilian I. He left the task of governing Spain to his confidant, Adrian of Utrecht. The Castilian aristocracy disliked having a foreign governor and a Flemish court, which was the status aspired to by Charles' following. Consequently, in the young Emperor's absence the *Comuneros* uprisings (1520/21) broke out in the Castilian cities, but were soon crushed.

Valencia was the richest city in southern Spain at the time. However, it suffered from social unrest and was continually threatened by pirates. Therefore the guilds took up arms. They used their new authority to rise against the ruling class, taking over the city and sending their own representatives to the city council. When the viceroy of Valencia objected, a popular uprising broke out. It subsequently spread to the entire Levante and the Balearic Islands. Immediately after the imperial troops had managed to subdue the rebellious *Comuneros* in the north, they intervened here, too, in 1521. They crushed the artisans' rising in a pitched battle and summarily executed the instigators.

Charles V, Charles I of Spain, returned there in 1523. Throughout his reign he was compelled to fight on several fronts, and at times it seemed on more than one at once. There were several clashes with Francis I of France over conflicts of interest in Italy. In 1530 Charles was crowned king of Bologna. In the Mediterranean there were continual skirmishes with Turkish pirates who harried the coasts of Italy and Spain. In 1535 Charles V captured Tunis, but the pirates continued to operate from Algiers which he was unable to take. In Germany he was embroiled for years in wars against the Protestants.

In 1526, Charles V married his cousin, Isabella of Portugal, at Sevilla. The nuptials were celebrated in the Palace of Pilate. The pair tarried at Granada for some months. There Charles had his own palace built in the Alhambra precincts. The empress died 13 years later in childbirth and was buried at Granada.

During the reign of Charles V, Spain grew to be the greatest power in Europe. After the discovery of America, most trade was carried on from the ports on the Atlantic coasts. Vast wealth came into the country to be deposited with the bankers. Due to the number of wars he fought, the emperor was heavily in debt to them. After the Peace of Augsburg, Charles V abdicated in favour of his son, Philip II, and retired to Yuste monastery in 1556 where he died two years later.

The Renaissance

In the 16th century, Italian architectural influence grew. Buildings were now structurally different. What is today known as Plateresque architecture became popular. An entirely decorative style incorporating Mudéjar elements, the Plateresque style made austere Renaissance forms lavishly ornate. The center of this architectural style, which is named after the chased forms of silversmithing, was Salamanca. It spread from there. The Kings' Chapel in the cathedral of Sevilla and the cathedrals of the Extremadura in Plasencia, Coria, Cáceres and Trujillo show obvious Salamancan influence. The facade of the Sevilla city hall, however, incorporates classical elements such as the base, medallions, convex stone moulding and applied decorative elements.

Right: The Giralda, at one time a minaret, has presided Sevilla since the 16th century.

The classical revival movement came from Italy. Buildings were ordered spatially on classical lines. Fussy ornaments were dropped so that the aesthetic quality of a building lay not in details but in the harmonious ordering of the whole. Facades were austere since they were no longer condemned to conceal what was behind. The great architects of the period were Diego de Siloe, Pedro Machuca and Gil de Ontaño.

The Late Gothic - Plateresque architect Diego de Siloe worked in his late phase on the cathedral of Granada, which was also classical in style. The center of the cathedral, the high altar, is round, 22m (72ft) in diameter and 44m (144ft) high. The dome has semi-circular openings to admit light. The apses of the cathedrals at Málaga and Guadix and the sacristy of the cathedral in Sevilla are from the same phase of this architect's work.

One of his pupils was Andrés de Vandelvira. It was he who made Siloe's work known in Andalusia. The domical vaulting which he designed has Gothic fans branching into exuberant profusion. Regarded as the major architect of Jaén Province, Vandelvira left important buildings in Ubeda, Baeza and Jaén.

Even sculpture was under Italian influence. The Hurtado de Mendoza tomb in the cathedral at Sevilla is the work of Domenico Fancelli. The Entombment in San Jerónimo at Granada was executed by Jacobo Florentino. The sculpture on the catafalque of the Catholic Kings at Granada is the work of the Burgundian artisan Felipe Bigarny. Bartolomé Ordoñez, indebted to Michelangelo, executed the chancel of the cathedral at Barcelona and the funerary statues of Philip the Fair and Juana the Mad at Granada.

Philip II

Charles V left the Austro-German part of his empire to his brother Ferdinand, and Spain, Burgundy and the Netherlands to his son Philip. The latter inherited 15 million maravedis in debts as

well as the task of defending the Catholic religion on the continent. When, in the second year of his reign, Philip II decisively defeated the French at San Quentin, he did not even have the money to pay his troops. This was to be the only battle in which he himself fought. He actually preferred to rule his vast realm from his desk, and often worked at this monumental life's work to the point of exhaustion. In monastic seclusion he devoted himself to the task of ruling. In 1581 he inherited Portugal and its overseas possessions through the maternal line. It was said that the sun never set on his empire.

In Europe, two separate developments prompted Philip to intervene. Spanish troops under the Duke of Alba fought to crush the uprising in the Netherlands until the Protestant north finally declared

Above: Don Juan of Austria is presented to his father, Charles V. Right: A modern representation of Don Quixote, the satirical brainchild of the 16th-century writer Cervantes.

its independence. After conquering the Portuguese colonies, the Dutch transferred some of their overseas trade from Sevilla and Lisbon to Antwerp. Moreover, Philip dispatched the Armada against Protestant England in retaliation for Francis Drake's raids. In 1588, 130 ships with 20,000 men left Lisbon Harbor. 30,000 joined the fleet from Flanders. But due to the lack of naval experience displayed by the Duke of Medina Sidonia and the rough seas about England, half the fleet was wrecked before the enemy hove in sight.

On the domestic front, Philip's main concern was to extend the influence of Catholicism. Led by Captain Valór, the Moriscos remaining in the Alpujarras rose up against Philip's repressive rule. After reconquering the region, they summoned the Turks to their aid. Philip in turn sent his stepbrother, John of Austria, who crushed the rebellion in 1570 and expelled the Moriscos. It was John of Austria who, commissioned by the Holy League formed by Philip II, Venice and the Pope, finally defeated the Turks in 1571 at the sea battle of Lepanto. Philip II died in 1598 in the hermitage of the monastery of El Escorial.

Culture in the Reign of Philip II – Mannerism –

Rigidly ascetic, Philip II asserted his moral principles, using the Inquisition in absolutist fashion to implement them. In this period the renascence of classicism reached its zenith in architecture. Philip II commissioned Juan de Herrera to build the colossal and austerely rectilineal Escorial. This austere style was known as the Herrera Style after its creator. In the south, Herrera also designed the Exchange at Sevilla.

With science and philosophy stagnating, art remained the only public form of expression. The Counter-Reformation affected even the religious institutions. Teresa of Avila and Juan de la Cruz led reforms of the Carmelite Order, preaching against the moral decline of the clergy. Their writings are masterpieces of erotic mysticism on the human soul's union with Christ.

Miguel Cervantes Saavedra (1547-1616), the most famous name in Spanish literature, participated in many events of his times. He did so with great gusto but was a perpetual failure at everything he put his hand to. His life was so eventful that he was never at a loss for subject matter for his greatest work. A native of Alcalá of convert descent, he fought in the Battle of Lepanto where he lost an arm. Captured by Algerian pirates, he was rescued by Knights Hospitallers. Later a tax official, he was arrested for embezzlement. His universal character, Don Quixote, has much in common with Philip II. With his medieval notions of imperial grandeur, the king seemed as anachronistic as the literary character. The impoverished *hidalgo* spent his time with romances instead of working, an oc-

cupation he considered fit only for Jews. He was under the delusion that he belonged to a medieval order of knights like his ancestors 300 years before. In *Don Quixote* Cervantes reflects on his times with the entire arsenal of Mannerist literary devices. Crazily exaggerated, the character of Don Quixote is idealism personified while Sancho Pansa, his servant and companion, is earthy and mundane. The two adventurers wander through the deserted countryside of La Mancha seeking adventure as if they were on a medieval crusade. The charm of the language, the situational comedy, the irony and the latent criticism of the times, which are all truly universal in character, make the novel a philosophical work. Don Quixote as a symbolic representation of Philip II and his anachronistic Spain became the bestseller of its era.

Mannerism gained ground in painting too. El Greco at Toledo and Morales in southern Spain are representative of this stylistic movement so popular at the time. In contrast to it, Renaissance formal aus-

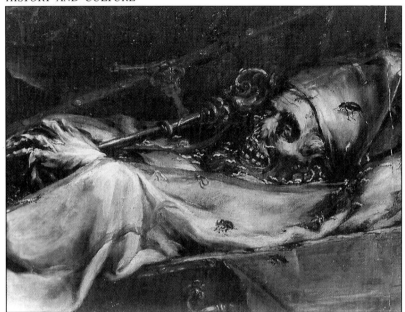

terity had yielded to the subjective view-point. The clear ordering of structures which was its hallmark began to dissolve, proliferating a profusion of forms, natural exuberance and glowing colours.

Luis Morales, called the Divine (1520-86), deserved this accolade not only for the subject matter of his paintings but also for the painterly perfection of his execution. Born in Badajoz, he studied in Italy and lived in Sevilla. The churches of the Extremadura (Badajoz, Alcántara and Arroyo de la Luz) contain retables which he painted. He was extraordinarily popular, perhaps partly because of the anecdotal content of many of his pictures, but also because of their aura of mysticism. This dichotomy is characteristic of devoutly Counter-Reformation Spain. On the one hand there are long sermons, which are nothing if not anecdotal, sentimental and populist; on the other, there is definitely a strain of abstract mysticism

Above: The transiency of earthly life in Finis Gloriae Mundi, painted by Valdés Leal.

appealing to the middle classes. Morales' figures are stylized. They employ expressive gestures and, of course, they are highlighted and enlarged. Finally, they are without plasticity yet realistic in detail. A notable characteristic of these figures, as with those of El Greco, is their extreme elongation, suggesting the emaciation of martyrdom, sadness and tears. Such elements were familiar to the ordinary viewer of the time.

The Baroque Era

Three Habsburgs left their stamp on the 17th century. Politically incompetent rulers, they tended to trust the reins of power to aristocratic favorites who brought the country to the brink of ruin. Among the royal decisions to have the most disastrous economic consequences was the expulsion of the Moriscos in 1610 by Philip III and the Duke of Lerma. Agriculture in Aragón and Valencia, both depopulated by epidemics, received a further setback when 500,000

Morisco farm laborers left the country all at once. In addition, Philip IV and the Conde Duque de Olivares allowed Portugal to separate from Spain while France supported separatist movements in Catalonia. The peasants there rose up in arms. On Corpus Christi Day, "Corpus sangre", they assaulted members of the central government in Barcelona. This marked the beginning of the "Reapers' War" ("dels segadors"). It lasted 12 years, ending with the secession of Roussillon. The last of the Habsburgs, Charles II, called "the Bewitched", was sickly and degenerate and died in 1700 without an heir. In his will he entrusted Felipe d'Anjou, the grandson of his sister and the Sun King, Louis XIV, with securing the succession.

But, as if all this was merely fat on the fire, the chaotic century nevertheless proved to be the Golden Age of Spanish art. The richness and diversity of the Baroque with its capricious use of formal elements produced artists whose fame knew no bounds. In the field of literature alone, Cervantes was succeeded by the great playwrights Lope de Vega, Calderón and Tirso de Molina as well as the poets Quevedo and Góngora. Then too, in the visual arts, Baroque architects produced buildings of impressive scope. Structural elements varied in significance, some being clearly emphasised. Alonso Cano designed the façade of the cathedral at Granada and Francisco Hurtado the tabernacle for it, as well as that of the Cartuja at Granada. Leonardo de Figueroa designed the presbytery of the cathedral at Sevilla. The façade of the Palacio del Marqués de Dos Aguas at Valencia was the work of Rovira.

The painting of the period was dominated by what is known as Tenebrism, facilitating the representation of religious ecstasy and fervor in naturalistic nudity. Saints were portrayed with the features of people from off the streets. Ribalta (1564-1628) and Ribera (1591-1652)

gave expression to commonplace fears, reproducing such moods by employing the shadowy illumination prevalent in churches. Both painters worked in Italy. José Ribera, affectionately known in Italy as "Spagnoletto", was a pupil of Francisco Ribalta's and was in contact with Caravaggio. In his early phase he painted pictures of saints and martyrs only. *St Andrew, The Crucifiction* and *The Martyrdom of St Barnabas* are representative works of this phase. At the same time, Ribera began to paint mythological and classical subjects. In *Jacob's Dream* he is mainly concerned with the atmosphere of the picture, achieved through depth and unexpected gradations of color.

Andalusian painting, also displaying elements of Tenebrism, has four famous representatives: Zurbarán, Alonso Cano, Murillo and Valdés Leal. They worked primarily on altarpieces and were thus, artistically speaking, at a far remove from mundane reality. In contrast, Velázquez – another contemporary Andalusian painter – spent most of his working life at the royal court in Madrid.

Francisco de Zurbarán (1598 - 1664) is known as the painter of monks, whom he portrayed with religious fervor. Their habits, which he painted in great detail, have little to do with the Tenebrist mania for showing the ravages of time on naked bodies although he does employ a technique similar to that employed in tenebrist painting.

Zurbarán, on the other hand, reduced anecdotal content to a minimum. The key to his works is the light which seems to radiate from the figures themselves. Faces and hands are executed with great precision. Background objects have been cut off so that they appear to continue outside the picture-plane. Caravaggio was actually the first to handle the picture-space in this manner. Zurbáran studied in Sevilla and was intrigued by Tenebrism early on. Success came early to him. In fact, by the time he was 28, he had had quite a few commissions from monasteries. He also executed the retable in the chapel of San Pedro in the cathedral at Sevilla as well as a series for the monastery of Guadalupe. Unfortunately for Spanish art, in 1640 he went through a personal crisis which crippled his creative genius. He died in 1664.

Alonso Cano (1601-67) was a painter, sculptor and architect. He was not only the universal artist par excellence; his life can be said to read like a novel. He was a pupil of Velázquez at Sevilla, where he married the daughter of the Sevillan painter Juan de Uceda. At some point his wife's corpse was found and he was suspected of the murder. He went to Valencia and Granada where he became cathedral almoner. Strangely enough, his major works date from this period. One of his most famous pupils was Pedro de Mena (1628-88), who painted mystical, almost ecstatic figures.

Bartolomé Esteban Murillo (1618-82) spent his whole life in Sevilla. Highly esteemed as a painter, he had the great good fortune of being able to live a pleasant life with his nine children. Murillo's early works are Tenebrist and are his most interesting. Although his subject matter was mainly religious, the daily life of the neighbourhood poured into pictures like *The Holy Family with a Little Bird*. From 1640, Murillo accepted commissions from the monasteries which had employed Zurbarán. This was the period of those representations of the Virgin for which he is justly renowned. The creative talent Murillo had displayed in more realistic works was, unfortunately, neglected during this time.

Juan de Valdés Leal (1622-90) is considered the leading Spanish painter of dramatic scenes. His still lifes with skulls, skeletons and decaying corpses are related to the spiritual regimen of St Ignatius of Loyola. His two masterpieces, *In ictu occuli* and *Finis gloriae mundi,* hang in the church of the Hospital de la Caridad at Sevilla. His friend and colleague Murillo is said to have exclaimed on seeing how perfectly they were executed by Leal: "These pictures even smell."

With Valladolid, Sevilla was the second major center of Spanish Baroque sculpture. The School of Sevilla followed painting in using ordinary people as models for the saints and altarpiece figures they executed on commission. The use of simple tricks like expressive eyes or glass tears gave such portrait sculpture the desired expression. The founder of this group was Martínez Montañés (1568-1649), who shunned the excesses of the Castilian school. He gave his figures bodily plasticity to offset the pain-racked expression often required by the stylistic canon prevalent at the time. Works of his are in the cathedral at Sevilla and the churches of Santa Clara and El Salvador. Among his pupils, the most distinguished were Juan de Arce, Pedro Roldán and his daughter Luisa, *La Roldana.*

The Bourbons

After the last Habsburg was dead, the War of the Spanish Succession broke out in 1701. All of Europe was involved. The two factions were headed by Felipe d'Anjou, representing the dreaded interests of Louis XIV, on whose side Castile was; and Archduke Carl of Austria, supported by Aragón and the Grand Alliance. The heir apparent to the Austrian throne withdrew his claim in 1713 when he became Emperor on the death of his brother. Fearing a powerful new Hispano-Austrian alliance, Europe acquiesced in the Treaty of Utrecht after Philip V became king of Spain. Its terms were that he should not enter into a political union with France. Further more, Naples, Milan and Flanders were to be ceded to

Right: Godoy, one of the first politicians in modern style, viewed by Francisco Goya.

Austria; Menorca, Gibraltar and the slave-trade monopoly to England.

The Bourbons brought with them not only the centralist principle by which the Sun King reigned but also, and equally characteristic of the period, the Rococo style currently in vogue at the French court. The 18th century can be considered the century of three kings. Each in his own way wrought radical social change. Philip V subdued the Levante and Catalonia, which had supported his adversaries, and built a fortress at Barcelona. Moreover, he revoked regional privileges by decree.

Charles III brought the Enlightenment to Spain. By and large his ministers were progressive intellectuals. They established the first public banks, improved the infrastructure and roads, modernized the ports and agriculture, and embarked on early industrialisation in the form of cotton and silk factories. His minister Olavide limited the powers of the Court of Inquisition and the 500-year-old sheepowners' association, the Mesta.

Concerned about Jesuit influence in the Paraguay missions, he banished the religious order while admitting, at the same time, the Free Masons.

Charles IV was ruled by his wife, María Luisa de Parma, as Goya's portraits show only too clearly. Carlos' (the Bourbons in Spain are usually known in English by the Spanish form of their names) favorite was Manuel Godoy, a handsome young man from the Extremadura. He came to court as a stable lad and his rise must have been due to his relations with the queen. The king left the fate of the country in the hands of this ill-starred favorite. Events were accelerated by developments in France. Godoy tried in vain to save the lives of Louis XVI and Marie Antoinette. Then he fought a religious war against France which ended with the Peace of Basel, giving Menorca to Spain and conferring the title of Prince of Peace on Godoy. He employed all the means of censorship and isolation available to prevent revolutionary ideas from spreading to Spain. He went so far as to

39

sign a pact with Napoleon committing his support in Portugal against England. After invading Portugal, Godoy took the lands about Olivenza. As a battle trophy he sent his queen an orange twig, after which the campaign was known as the "Orange War".

The mutual assistance pact between France and Spain gave Napoleon a pretext for invading Spain in 1808. But his allies, Godoy and Carlos IV, had by then been deposed by rebels, and Ferdinand VII had ascended the throne.

The War of Independence

Desirous of blockading England, Napoleon had to control all ports, particularly those of Portugal. Therefore he invaded the Iberian Peninsula. The Spanish royal family had supported him. They offered no resistance whatever to the un-

Above: French troops executing rebellious Madrileñas as seen by Goya. Right: Farmers still constitute the poorest class.

expected usurpation of power by the French. The king went into French exile and Joseph Bonaparte, Napoleon's brother, ascended the Spanish throne as José I. Because of his fondness for the bottle, he was known in Madrid as "Pepe Botellas". On 2 May 1808 a popular uprising in Madrid against the French occupation sparked off the War of Independence. The socio-economic problems of the country and the differences between the liberal adherents of the French Revolution and the monarchists were overshadowed by the romantic aspect of a people united against an invader. A French general is said to have boasted that his army would take Spain as easily as eating breakfast; but just as they were preparing to swallow up Sevilla, his troops were defeated by allied Spanish and English forces at Bailén (Jaén).

Napoleon personally pursued the English army with 120,000 troops, devastating half the country in the process. Difficulties in Central Europe demanded his presence and he left part of his troops in

Spain under the command of his generals. However, they were not able to make any headway against the guerilleros of the popular resistance.

Cádiz, being surrounded by swamps in which Napoleon's cannons became mired, and, in addition, impregnable from the coast, remained free of French occupation. A liberal government in exile established itself there in 1812, drawing up a constitution modelled on the French Revolution. After the French were driven from the country in 1814, Ferdinand VII became king again amid general rejoicing.

The 19th Century

Nonetheless, the regime of Ferdinand VII was repressive. This state of affairs fostered the developments that ultimately led to the loss of the colonies and the national crisis of 1898. Spanish society was stirred up enough to take progress in hand in various regions. The Carlist Wars in the north, the Catalan Renaixença,

secularisation, the brief intermezzo of the first republic and the beginnings of a labor movement all ensured a stirring century in the reigns of Fredinand VII, Isabella II and Alfonso XII.

The Salic law excluding females from dynastic succession had been introduced by Philip V, only to be revoked by Carlos IV. On the death of Ferdinand VII, his brother, Carlos María Isidro, appealed on the grounds of a technical flaw against repeal of the Salic law to prevent the accession of Isabella II, the legitimate heir to the throne. The Carlist Movement grew out of this to instigate several civil wars during the 19th century. In 1936 the Carlists sided with Franco. Later, in the Montejurra (Navarra) there were bloody clashes until Fraga, the Minister of the Interior, put an end to their political influence.

At the same time a nationalist movement was gaining ground in Catalonia. It began with the revival of the language, which had been neglected since the 15th century. The first work to be published in

modern Catalan was Carles Aribau's *Ode to my Native Land*, a tribute in the newspaper *El Vapor* to a Catalan industrialist. Poetry competitions were a forum of expression for the revived urban bourgeoisie, which did not exist in the rest of Spain and which, in Catalonia at least, sought its identity in the lost grandeur of Gothic Catalonia. The literary works and historical research of Milá i Fontanals made the Catalan past a popular subject in 1850. Poets like Verdaguer and Maragall wrote in Catalan and their works were eagerly received by the theatre, the press and the cultural associations.

The Labor Movement

Like industrialisation, the labor movement came later to Spain than to the rest of Europe. The entirely agricultural economy had produced a proletariat of farm laborers without land and leasehold

Above: Retired farm laborers in Andalusia. Right: Pablo Picasso at the age of 52.

living from seasonal work. The sheer numbers of unemployed in the cities, where the free market of early industrialisation was indeed a free-for-all, caused wages to drop to the point where union organisation was essential. In 1879 the Socialist Workers' Party (PSOE) was founded and in 1880 its union, the UGT. Ten years later the party was winning a good percentage of the vote at municipal elections. From 1910 it had seats in the Congress where it made a stand against moderate republicans.

The Spanish anarchist tradition goes back farther. It was introduced in Spain by Fanelli, an Italian friend of Bakunin's. The anarchist movement grew underground, finding many adherents in Catalonia, the Levante, Andalusia and Aragón. When it went public in 1881, two currents emerged. The Anarcho-Communists, influenced by Kropotkin and Malatesta, considered the trades unions overly bureaucratic. Their stronghold was rural Andalusia. There the legendary "Black Hand" sprang up, a secret organisation accused of various crimes and strongly suppressed by the government. In 1883 the court at Jerez condemned 15 members to death for murder. The Anarcho-Collectivists, on the other hand, aspired to a classless society without private ownership of property, which was to be achieved through syndicates. They managed to make their weight felt. In 1910 they founded their union, the CNT. After World War I it attracted attention through a series of strikes in Catalonia.

The Generation of '98

Since the mid 19th century, independence movements had been gaining ground in the Spanish colonies. Backed by the US, Cuba embarked on a war with Spain which ended with the loss of her colonies (Cuba, Puerto Rico, and the Philippines). Without colonial resources for the first time in 400 years, Spain suffered a national crisis. It proved to be the raw material for an entire generation of writers. The works of Azorín, Valle Inclan, Machado, Pérez Galdós, Unamuno, Pío Baroja, Ortega y Gasset, Jiménez and Blasco Ibánez are full of the themes of Spain's political decadence and its contrasting natural beauty in the country. Joaquín Costa fought for radical reforms to end the imbalance between Spanish and European economic development. He was committed to abolishing illiteracy and the *Cacique*, the institutionalised use of local political influence and landowner manipulation of indentured farm laborers' votes to form power blocks.

The 20th Century

The new century faced social unrest on two fronts in Spain – the traditional peasant class preserving the medieval legacy and the modern society of the Industrial Revolution. Agriculture's shaky foundations were the exaggerated subdivision of land in the north and vast land-

holdings in the south. Apart from mining in the Cantabrian mountains and the Catalonian textile industry, industrial development was minor.

At the turn of the century, Spain was held back by the crisis of 1898. However, it was soon embroiled in a war again, this time in Morocco, in an attempt to assert colonial claims. The terrible battlefield conditions and heavy losses sustained by Spanish troops gave rise to increasing protest on the home front. In 1909 there was a general strike in all of Catalonia. Government intervention took a toll of 100 in the Tragic Week at Barcelona.

Spain's political neutrality in World War I opened new markets, a development particularly favorable to the cities. The large number of new buildings going up in Barcelona and Madrid was a sign of this temporary prosperity.

Modernism

Since the last third of the 19th century, the Catalan bourgeoisie had, when commissioning buildings, promoted a style emulating the Central European Jugendstil and Art Nouveau. Known as *Modernismo*, it embraced the traditional fine arts as well as architecture, interior decoration and furnishing, advertising, graphic design and literature.

The architect Antoní Gaudí (1852-1926) is considered the founder of Modernism. His first work, the Casa Vicens (1880), displayed obvious Mudéjar influence. Over the years, Gaudí's style began to consist of structurally integrating decorative elements. The Palacio Güell (1889), Casa Batlló (1906), Casa Milá or the Pedrera (1910) and Güell Park (1915) are consummate works of art. The even now unfinished cathedral of the Sagrada Familia, begun in 1883, proved to be too much for one lifetime. Gaudí died in anonymous poverty in a traffic accident.

Domènech i Montaner, a contemporary of Gaudí's, designed his first Modernist buildings for the Barcelona World Exposition in 1888. Although some of these were torn down, the restaurant is today a zoological museum. The exposition made Modernism widely popular. The Palau de la Música Catalana at Barcelona is considered to be the architect's masterpiece.

Josep Puig i Cadafalch was an exponent of Neo-Gothic. His Casa Martí houses the Café Els Cuatre Gats, the favorite haunt of Modernist bohemiens. Picasso, Pablo Gargallo, Ramón Casas and Santiago Russinol used to meet there.

Pablo Picasso (1881-1973) came to Barcelona in 1895. His father had been appointed professor at the art academy there. In 1897 he painted *Science and Compassion,* which was sent to the exhibition at Madrid. The time which he spent in Barcelona was his Blue Period. In 1904 he went to Paris. Many years later,

Right: The furrows he drew in the earth seem to have become imprinted on his face.

while the Republic lasted, he was appointed director of the Prado (in absentia) although his mature work was done in France.

Vicente Ferrer and Demetrio Ribes are at the center of Valencian Modernism, both influenced by the Viennese Secession. The major building by the former is 31 Cirillo Amorós at Valencia, and by the latter, the North Station.

The Generation of '27

Unrest among urban and rural laborers continued throughout the 1920s. Governments fell, until General Primo de Rivera came to power with the king's blessing. During the seven years of his dictatorship, intellectuals were exiled and corporatist industrial concerns were founded. This was the time when a group of young poets, most of them Andalusian, met in the student hostel in Madrid in 1927 where Dalí, Miró and Buñuel had lodged before them, to celebrate the 300th anniversary of the death of the Córdoban Baroque poet Góngora. Among them were García Lorca, Alberti, Salinas, Cernuda, Alonso, Aleixandre (Nobel Prize 1977) and Guillén (Nobel Prize 1986). From this purely symbolic act grew one of the major European poetry movements. The writers began by admiring the pure poetry, highly stylized and remote, characteristic of the Modernist period. Later they were attracted by Surrealism, which appealed to the dark layers of the subconscious. On the founding of the Republic, they began to concern themselves with politics. All of them suffered during the Civil War and spent the Franco era in exile, where many of them died.

Federico García Lorca (1899-1936) was perhaps the most famous of the Generation of '27. Among his many interests was a love of both classical and folk music. In 1929 he went to New York. His Surrealist work *A Poet in New York*

grew out of the impression made by the city during the Depression. His *Gypsy Ballads* were very popular. Indeed they soon became a modern oral tradition *(The Unfaithful Wife, The Death of Antoñito Camborio, The Ballad of the Sleep-walker)*. He was particularly well known for his *Elegy on the Death of Ignacio Sánchez Mejías*, an educated torero and a friend of the poet's. This is definitely one of the major elegies of Spanish literature. The following tragedies are the best known of his plays: *Blood Wedding* and *The House of Bernarda Alba*. In them the sufferings of the Andalusian *campesiños* are depicted. At the beginning of the Civil War, the 38-year-old García Lorca was shot by the Guardia Civil at Viznar.

Salvador Dalí turned early to Surrealism. Influenced by Freudian psychoanalytic theory, he approached the portrayal of people in a new way. The Surrealist films he made together with *Luis Buñuel* scandalized the public. His right-wing leanings saved him from exile and led to a commission to paint portraits of the Franco family. After a period of sacred art he increasingly indulged in bizarre effects in his work, as amusingly presented in his museum at Figueras.

The Second Republic

Increasingly faced with the economic failure, Primo de Rivera resigned in 1930. The Republican movement had gained so much ground that Alfonso XIII also abdicated in 1931 and went into exile. The economic situation, already shaky due to the 1929 Depression, rapidly deteriorated. Capital drained from the country because agrarian reform, nationalisation of industry and financial reform loomed large. The climate of political instability with stagnating investment and labor conflicts resulted in a sharp drop in productivity, which in turn led to increased unemployment.

After the dissolution of the monarchy, a provisional coalition government was formed by Republicans and Socialists. It won the election two months later. The

45

constitution, passed at the end of the year, guaranteed the separation of Church and State and universal suffrage.

Azaña, an intellectual lawyer and staunch democrat, headed the government. He wanted to break the power of the Church and the military, promote education on a broad basis and improve social conditions. A decree released the military from the loyalty oath to the monarchy and suggested that soldiers unwilling to serve the Republic should retire. The army consisted of 105,000 troops and 195 generals at the time. About 10,000 left but most of the commanders remained. The military coup of 1932, which was suppressed, indicated that Azaña's attempts to make the army unpolitical had failed.

The religious issue was also touchy. Anti-clericalism dominated the most influential political groups. The government had not intervened when unruly crowds in Madrid set fire to churches and monasteries in May 1931. The constitution provided for the secularization of the religious orders and the power of Rome was ruled to be unconstitutional. The property of the Church was nationalized. Religious communities camouflaged themselves as educational associations, since there was a sad lack of schools. Only 10,000 schools had already been provided, but this still left 350,000 children of school age without schooling.

The agrarian sector was also in urgent need of reform. The smallholdings in the north consisted of 0.42 ha on an average. In Andalusia, La Mancha and the Extremadura on the other hand, there were 12,500 estates of over 250 ha each. Many of these were in the possession of aristocratic families and some even comprised up to 80,000 ha. On these vast estates most of the arable land lay fallow or served as hunting preserves for the owners. Against these vast landholdings were arrayed 10 million *fincas* of fewer than 10 ha and a horde of *campesinos*

living from seasonal work. The Agrarian Reform Act passed in 1932 provided for the expropriation of 6 million properties and for aid to 930,000 peasant families. But a year later it had brought effective changes to only 12,500 families and had effected the transfer of only 110,000 ha to new owners.

The Anarchists had been against the government from its inception. After numerous demonstrations all over Spain, the villages of the Catalonian mining region proclaimed a spontaneous form of Anarcho-Communism without any program. Needless to say, they were rapidly and harshly suppressed. In 1933 unrest spread to the Levante and Andalusia, but risings were quelled at once. Only at Casas Viejas (Cádiz) was there a major rising. Government troops massacred the rebels and expunged the village from the map. A scapegoat was found who had ordered this act and could be called to account for it but criticism of the government continued to mount. In 1933 the Socialists left the government, forcing Azaña to resign. The Radical Centrist Party won the election with a high turnout. Lerroux formed a government supported by the Confederation of Spanish Rightist Parties (CEDA). In two years this government undid what the previous one had achieved in the same time, while both right- and left-wing parties became extremist.

In 1933 the son of the former dictator Primo de Rivera founded the Falange Española. Inspired by German and Italian Fascism, José Antonio proclaimed the ideal of national unity, calling for the use of force against separatists, Marxists and the parties. The dialectic of fists and pistols made the group, which consisted mainly of students, notorious. On 5 October 1934 the Socialists, together with the Communists and Anarchists, called for a revolutionary strike. In Madrid, Barcelona and the mining regions over 40,000 strikers were arrested. For ten

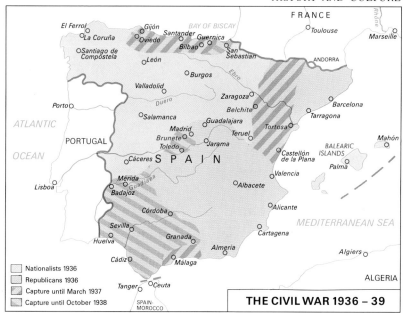

Nationalists 1936
Republicans 1936
Capture until March 1937
Capture until October 1938

THE CIVIL WAR 1936 – 39

days workers transformed Oviedo into a Soviet Republic. From Madrid, General Franco commanded the troops that crushed them, leaving 1300 dead. Franco was subsequently proclaimed Generalissimo. An Anti-Republican Union was formed in the army. The monarchists, too, closed ranks in exile and began to procure weapons for the battle against the Republic.

When Lerroux had to resign following a scandal in 1935, another election was held. The Labour Parties and the Republicans united to form a Popular Front. Their program called for a general amnesty, rehiring of those dismissed after the October Rising, readmission of Catalan special status and the revival of agrarian reform. The Anarchists supported the Popular Front and its program. The 1936 election was a clear victory for the Popular Front. Azaña formed a government and began to implement his campaign promises. But throughout the country there were violent clashes. A Communist, Dolores Ibarrui, was elected to a parliamentary seat in 1936. Her devotion to the common cause of the workers earned her the sobriquet of *La Pasionaria*. Born in 1895 in Vizcaya, she was far more popular than historians have been willing to admit. After the Civil War she went to Moscow, where she was head of the Spanish Communist Party until 1978. On her return to Spain in 1977, she was re-elected as Member for Asturias as a symbolic act in the first democratic election. Her death in 1989 closed a chapter of Communist Party history. The memorial ceremony was a demonstration confirming how popular she was.

The Civil War

On 17 July 1936, the Spanish troops stationed in Morocco revolted, to be followed a day later by the garrisons on the Balearic Islands and the Canaries. The military coup led by General Mola was supported by the Church, which regarded it as a sort of crusade. The Carlists in Navarra and the Falange declared their

solidarity with the rising. The Left reacted quickly to thwart the immediate seizure of power by the Junta. Although the military took Zaragoza, Sevilla, Granada and Cádiz in a short time, large parts of Andalusia and the Extremadura, Catalonia and the Levante remained loyal to the Republican government. The rebels united as the Nationalist Forces. They were led in the various regions by generals of whom General Franco, commander of the Moroccan troops, particularly distinguished himself.

Of course, Hitler and Mussolini supported the rebels from the beginning. They provided aircraft to transport the Moroccan troops to the mainland. France and England, however, showed an ambivalent attitude. In Paris, for instance, the orders issued by the Republican government for weapons procurement

Above left: Franco, dictator in the name of nationalism. Above right: Federico García Lorca, a poet killed in the name of nationalism. Right: Sunday morning.

were suppressed by embassy employees who secretly sympathised with the rebels. The right-wing press and the British government were naturally only concerned with protecting British interests, particularly in the Andalusian mining region. They were of the opinion that these interests were better safeguarded by a right-wing government.

Terrified of Hitler, the Western powers signed a non-intervention pact in August. The totalitarian governments, on the other hand, regarded the Spanish Civil War as an ideal opportunity for testing their weapons since world war was imminent. On the other side, Russia sent weapons and supplies to the Republicans. The Italians furnished the Nationalists with submarines, aircraft and a large volunteer legion. The Germans tried out their aircraft and tanks and sent an elite troop, the *Condor Legion.*

In the democratic countries, the war provoked protests from intellectuals in particular. Appealing for support for the Republic, the Communist International

formed international brigades. 40,000 romantic idealists volunteered of their own good will to reinforce the Republican troops with the combat experience they had gained in World War I. They served mainly on the Madrid and Catalan fronts.

The strategic balance which had prevailed at the beginning of hostilities was destroyed when Málaga fell in 1937. The Nationalists proceeded ruthlessly against the population. The Basque Country fell the same year. The bombardment of Guernica by the German *Condor Legion* caused worldwide concern. A series of battles in Asturias, Madrid and Zaragoza left the entire north, apart from Madrid, in the hands of the Nationalists. Late in 1937 the Nationalists launched a powerful drive against southern Aragón, Catalonia and the Levante. A year later they had reached Castellón on the Mediterranean, where they succeeded in driving a wedge into Republican territory between Catalonia and Valencia. To save Valencia, where the government had sought refuge, the Republicans concentrated all their remaining energies on the Ebro offensive.

A peace plan and even the pointed disbanding of the International Brigades in 1938 were to no avail. Confident of victory, General Franco marched on Barcelona. Early in 1939, the government fled to France seeking asylum together with 300,000 refugees. The Civil War ended on 1 April 1939.

The Franco Era

Franco had founded the Nationalist movement while the Civil War was going on. This front united various rightist factions, the Falange and the Carlists. In the early postwar period, a Nationalist purge of the democratic opposition took a toll of 200,000. Regional special status and public use of the Catalan, Basque and Galician languages were forbidden. All her ancient prerogatives were restored to the Church. Since Catholicism was again the state religion, the Spanish state, of course, had a say in the appointment of bishops. Civil divorce was naturally no longer allowed.

The Franco regime was based on a "constitution" only made up of individual basic laws, such as the *fuero* regulating working conditions and establishing vertically organised unions which represented both employers and employees. In 1942 the *Cortes*, the Spanish parliament, reconvened, but only 103 of the 564 representatives had actually been elected.

Spain remained officially neutral during World War II. Nonetheless, she sent 47,000 "Blue Division" volunteers to the aid of the Axis Powers in Russia. After the war, for understandable reasons, Spain was refused admittance to the UN. This form of political quarantine led to a phase of extreme economic and political isolation. But with the advent of the Cold War, the US changed its tactics. It used all available means of securing military bases in the western Mediterranean. Spain was able to sign a Concordat with the Vatican and treaties with the US which brought loans and, ultimately, UN membership in 1953. For whatever reason, in the 40 years his regime lasted, Franco made no state visits. Apart from US presidents Eisenhower (1959) and Nixon (1970), he entertained no foreign heads of state.

Isolation forced Spain to adopt a strategy of economic self-sufficiency after the Civil War. To support primary industry, the National Industry Institute (INI) was founded. It subsidized coal and steel. Agriculture, which was stagnating and largely incapacitated because of ruined machinery, took years to regain full production capacity. Things got so bad that food had to be rationed and famine lasted until 1951. In 1953 Marshall Plan aid was forthcoming.

In the 1960s, an economic upswing took off, but it did not include the agrar-

ian sector. Under ministers recruited from the influential Catholic lay brotherhood of Opus Dei, two new sources of hard currency were tapped: tourism and labor emigration. From 1966, however, foreign pressure forced the regime to become more moderate. Minister of the Interior Fraga authorised a Press Act which went so far as to substitute post-publication for pre-publication censorship. During these years, however, opposition to the regime was growing, even from within the Church. In regions with a separatist past, violent organisations gained ground. The ETA (*Euskadi ta askatasuna*, For a Free Basque Country) in particular became notorious. A trial at Burgos in 1970 with 16 defendants from the ETA turned into an anti-Franco demonstration. On the day in 1973, on which the trial of the undercover trade union began, the ETA blew up Franco's probable successor, Carrero Blanco, in his car. The murdered man's successor was Arias Navarro, who had taken up the cause of moderation. Nevertheless, while Franco was being kept alive by life support systems in 1975, five more political prisoners were condemned to death for show. Franco died on 20 November 1975 and was buried in the Basilica of the Valle de los Caidos which he had had erected to himself and to the victims of the Civil War.

The Transition to Democracy

On 22 November, Juan Carlos I, grandson of Alfonso XIII, ascended the throne as Franco had intended. The opposition sat down to a round-table conference at which they demanded the democratisation of the country. Juan Carlos managed to engineer the resignation of Arias Navarro. Then he selected Suarez out of three proposed candidates as his successor. The next step soon followed. In April 1977 the Communist Party was legalized. Two months later, the first democratic election was held. An attempted coup by

Right: Spanish society has changed with the times, even regarding the status of women.

the Guardia Civil, which was able to hold the entire parliament hostage for a terrible day in 1981, was aborted, although the written assent of the bishops to action by this arm of the executive had been obtained. Suarez resigned. His successor, Calvo Sotelo, signed Spain's entry into NATO. The Social Democrats (PSOE) won the 1982 general election on the campaign promise that Spain would leave NATO. After a plebiscite in 1985, the government took back this promise.

Modern Spain really had its inception as a democratic state in the constitution of 1978 and the Statute of Autonomy of 1983, which divides the 50 provinces of the country into 17 autonomous regions. Plebiscites produced universal approval of this form of federalism according the regions of Galicia, the Basque Country and Catalonia, which have their own languages, special status as distinctive ethnic groups. Since it seemed certain that Spain would become a member of the EC, the world market, which was becoming thoroughly convinced that demo-

cracy would last, began to invest in Spain. For the conurbations of Barcelona, Madrid and Valencia, the 1980s were a period of enormous growth in the industrial and service sectors, in international investment and in population growth. The agrarian regions, on the other hand, drained by emigration in the '60s and '70s, suffered from rising prices, continued emigration and unemployment. The crisis in the regions traditionally dependent on mining and textiles was an additional factor. While the large cities, the coastal reigons with agricultural exports and the border regions seemed to be keeping abreast of European development, an army of poverty-stricken unemployed industrial workers has in the meantime grown up in the small towns and the satellite towns surrounding the metropolitan conurbations.

However, with the Olympics at Barcelona, the World's Fair at Sevilla, and Madrid as cultural capital of Europe, 1992 is rightly regarded as marking a new beginning for modern Spain.

CATALONIA

COSTA BRAVA
GERONA
COSTA DORADA
TARRAGONA

The scenery of Catalonia, the northeastern part of Spain, is highly diverse in all respects. This region reaches from the rocky coast of the Costa Brava south past the densely populated area around Barcelona to the damp, fertile plains of the Ebro Delta and west to the highest peaks of the Pyrenees.

COSTA BRAVA

The section of coast between the border and Blanes has long been known to travellers as the Costa Brava. The name comes from the Tramontana wind which blows in all seasons of the year from the north to lash the sea. Apart from some sandy river deltas, the coast in this region is extremely rocky. Steep cliffs curve into romantic bays where the pine forests often extend to the edge of the sea. Although domestic and foreign tourism discovered the area long ago, the coast is for the most part so inaccessible that basically only small holiday resorts have managed to develop. These look like red and white dots scattered about the blue-green landscape.

Preceding pages: Sweeping views in the Sierra Morena. Taking it easy after retirement. Left: The simple fishing boat is often a key to family subsistence.

Figueres is the center of Alt Empordà. The old city is on a hill. In the *rambla* is the Gothic parish church of Sant Pere. On the city hall square, which is surrounded by arcades, are the **Casa de la Vila** and a tower which is all that remains here of the old city walls. The **Teatro Principal** (1826) was transformed into the spectacular **Dalí Museum** in 1974. The slab covering the artist's grave is embedded in the heart of the fantastic museum. The **Museo del Empordà** exhibits regional culture, sculpture and painting. While Iberian and Roman artifacts have been discovered in the Aigueta district, the present town dates back to the founding of the monastery of **Sant Pere de Rodes** in the Port de la Selva hills on the coast above Llancá. The 10th century building, consecrated in 1022, underwent a period of such prosperity in the 11th and 12th centuries that extensive renovation and additions could be carried out. They produced what is still standing: a three-aisled basilica with a lofty central nave covered by barrel vaulting. The twin rows of piers stand on high bases and the pier arches rest on capitals decorated with stylized foliage. Unfortunately, not much is left of the cloister and the main portal. Nevertheless, what does remain clearly represents Catalan Romanesque at its most impressive.

The coast near Figueres falls into two very different-looking sections. The first is the strip round the **Cabo de Creus** peninsula, linked to the mainland by the Sierra de Rodes, the most easterly point of the Iberian peninsula. Three fishing villages nestle on the almost inaccessible coast: **Port de la Selva**, Cadaqués and Rosas. The first town has an attractive fishing port and marina, which serves as a haven from storms. Due to its inaccessibility, **Cadaqués** long remained a refuge for intellectuals and artists. The small village with its bookshops, art galleries and tradition of jazz is in an incomparable setting. The spirit of Dalí, the genius loci of Empordà, still seems to be breezing through the alleys. His mysterious house on the neighbouring harbor of Port Lligat – easy to spot with those gigantic eggs crowning the garden fence – is simply a must for visitors. Finally there is **Rosas,** which is also the name of the superb bay stretching as far as **L' Escala**. The latter fishing village is famous for its tinned anchovies, which are a staple at meals. Beyond the resort cottages and broad beaches of Rosas is the national park at Aigüamolls de l'Empordà. The medieval old town core of **Castelló de Empúries** is well preserved. The 14th century Gothic church of Sta. María is particularly noteworthy. **Ampuriabrava,** which is the town's port, has an extensive network of canals and an airfield for amateur pilots. Finally, just outside L'Escala are the archaeological excavations at **Empuries.** Systematic excavation has gone on here since 1908. Remains of both the first Greek settlement of *Emporion* and Roman *Emporiae* have been found on the site. A museum at the site exhibits art treasures and mosaics.

Not far north of Figueres is **Perelada.** The core of the old town is dominated by the large **Castillo de Rocabertí,** an impressive structure with an interesting Renaissance façade. The whole complex is surrounded by a spacious park. It serves as a casino and in summer is host to a music festival.

The main town of Lower *(baix)* Empordà is **Bisbal d'Empordà**, east of Gerona. Its episcopal palace gave rise to its name, for this was the seat of the bishops of Gerona. The city is, in addition, the seat of the regional government. It looks back on a long tradition of pottery-making. In the vicinity are pretty villages like **Vulpellac,** with its Gothic and Renaissance castle, and **Cruïlles**, which still has parts of the old fortress as well as Miquel monastery. **Peratallada** stands on a rocky eminence cleft by ravines. Three precincts can still be distinguished around the fortress and the castle. The latter is on the atrium plan with Gothic and Romanesque elements. The narrow alleys all converge on the square, the Plaza Mayor. The parish church and the church of Canapost are Romanesque and the church of St Julià de Boada is even pre-Romanesque. In **Ullastret**, a walled 4th and 3rd century BC Iberian settlement has been excavated. It must have been situated on an island in a lake that has long since been drained and must surely has maintained ties with the Greek colonies. The towns of **Foixà**, with its large medieval fort, and **Verges**, which is famous for its ancient "Danse Macabre", a sort of dance in the Maundy Thursday procession, are almost on the banks of the Río Ter.

Torroella de Montgrí is the first river port on the Ter River. Its 14th century fort was rebuilt in the 19th century. The city walls, the old town square with its arbours, and several town residences of the aristocracy are all in a good state of preservation. Above the town the bleak remains of the Gothic fort of Montgrí, which was never completed, crown a bare hillside. From here it is not far to **Estartit,** with its fishing port and marina. The incomparably lovely coast and the area around the **Medes Islands** just offshore are favorite haunts of divers and

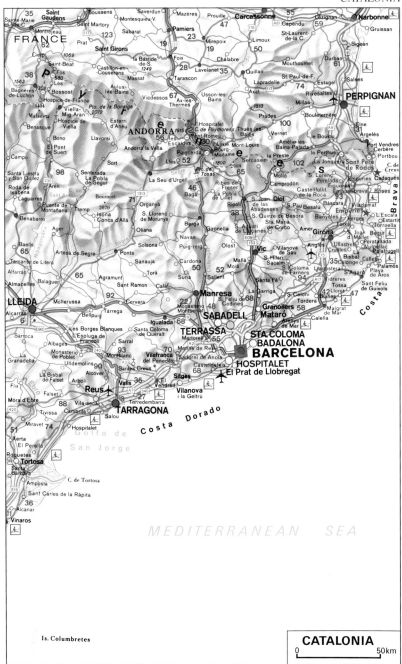

CATALONIA

0   50km

spear fishermen. To the south, the beach at **Pals** extends on both sides of the Ter delta. The Pals golf club is considered one of the country's best. Behind it rises the steep Begur Range. It drops sheer to the sea, forming the loveliest of coves and secluded spots. **Begur,** with the remains of its fort, the five massive towers of its city walls, the villas of the *indianos* (affluent former colonists), and its vernacular architecture, has retained its charm although the old fishermen's quarters have been completely taken over by tourists: Aiguablava with its *parador,* Fornells de Mar, Sa Tuna, Aiguafreda, Capsasal and Sa Riera.

The village of **Palafrugell** near the coast has a long tradition of industrial cork processing. Its varying periods of prosperity are reflected in the handsome 18th century buildings and turn-of-the-century *Modernismo* it boasts. Between it and the coast are the attractive resort

Above: Cadaqués, where Dali lived, is still a place for real and fraudulent artists.

towns of Aiguaxelida, Tamariu, Llafranc and **Calella de Palafrugell,** which is known for its vernacular architecture and its habaneras. These were the doleful laments of the soldiers who went off to war in Cuba. Here one can enjoy a traditional *cremat*, coffee flambé with rum. A lighthouse at **Cap San Sebastián** shows the way to a vantage point not far from **Cap Roig,** with its terraced botanical gardens full of exotic plants overlooking the sea.

Palamós, at the head of the bay of the same name, has a bustling fishing port and marina, the home port of major regattas. Founded in 1279 by Pere II the Great, the town looks just as it might have been then, with its old city on a jutting promontory. The medieval town core of **Calonge de Mar,** known as La Vila, is also intact. Its massively defiant fort is largely Gothic. The beaches of the bay and the town of **Playa de Aros** are among the most popular resort areas on the Costa Brava. A marina and the Mas Nou Golf Club are just two of the many recreational facilities offered. **S'Agaró,** on the rocky headland south of the bay, was founded in 1924. A luxury hotel, splendid villas and imposing summer residences make it one of the most exclusive spots on the entire Catalan coast.

The port of **Sant Feliu de Guíxols,** on the other hand, looks back on a long shipbuilding tradition. From the rocky promontory of San Telmo one has a view over the entire bay, the coastal boulevard Paseo del Mar with its Modernist houses, and the Gothic church of the old Benedictine monastery. Only the pre-Romanesque forecourt of the monastery, the famous Porta Ferrada, is extant.

The medieval city walls of **Tossa de Mar,** which can be walked on by adventurous visitors with enough time to do it, cling to a cliff rising from the sea. Seven towers enclose the old city, the Vila Vella, with what is left of the Gothic church and the 15th century governor's palace. The modern town extends along the beach. The museum houses an interesting collection of the works of artists at some time connected with the town (e.g. Marc Chagall and Joaquín Sunyer) as well as archaeological finds from the Roman settlement at **Ametllers.**

Just before **Lloret de Mar** the coast suddenly ceases to be steep. The winding mountain road descends quite abruptly to the broad coastal plain. Here there was room enough indeed for the large hotels which have made the city the most frequented spot on the Costa Brava. The promenade reflects past glories: Modernist houses and 18th century buildings. A touching monument honors seamen's wives. On 24 July a procession, *Sa Relíquia,* takes place along the sea. **Blanes** is the last town on the Costa Brava. It nestles at the foot of the hill on which ruins of the fortress of Sant Joan overlook the bay and the harbor. Gothic buildings give the old town core its character: the church, remains of the old manor house, the fountain on Calle Ample. Flora enthusiasts are surprised to find two botanical gardens at once: **Mar i Mutra** in Sa Forcanera Bay and **Pinya de Rosa**, specializing in tropical flora. A monument on the Paseo del Mar leading to San Roque promontory honors the writer Joaquim Ruyra. Many of his works deal with the lives of local seamen.

GERONA

Gerona, the "city of four rivers", is situated at the confluence of the Ter, Güell, Galligant and Onyar Rivers. Originally a Roman *municipium*, it has been the bishop's seat since the 5th century and has in its long history withstood countless sieges. The resistance offered by the city to Napoleon's troops has become the stuff of legend. The city's greatest treasure is its cathedral, which has a Romanesque bell-tower and cloister, a single nave with the broadest span of Gothic vaulting in all medieval European architecture (23 m/75 ft), a Baroque facade and wide front steps. The museum contains an astonishing 11th century tapestry of the Creation. The art museum in the episcopal palace contains a further treasure trove of Romanesque and Gothic art. The church of San Feliu is a blend of Romanesque, Gothic and Baroque elements. Moreover, there are early Christian tombs in the presbytery. Other buildings certainly worth taking a look at are the 12th century Arab baths, the Gothic monastery of Sant Domènec, the Renaissance Aligues palace and the Baroque Jesuit seminar of Sant Martí Sacosta.

The Onyar River bisects the city. On the right is the old city, to the left is the modern town, extending to Devesa Park. Narrow alleys run through the old Jewish quarter in which one of the country's largest Jewish communities lived in the late Middle Ages. The Cabbalist school here was renowned.

The lake at **Bañyoles** dominates a wide plain which is intensively cultivated and has long been densely settled. It is

bounded on the west by the Sierra de Rocacorba. The lake, fed by underground springs, is figure eight-shaped, 2 km (1.2 mi) long and 235 m (770 ft) across. Five streams flow out of the lake, crossing the town of Bañyoles and ultimately flowing together to form the Terri. The serene beauty of the landscape is reflected in the calm waters of the lake, which is a popular spot for bathing, rowing, canoeing and water-skiing. This is where the trial heats for the '92 Olympic rowing championships will take place. The town of Bañyoles itself is at the center of the district of Pla de l'Estany. It grew up around the Benedictine monastery of Sant Esteve, which was rebuilt in neo-classical style from ruins in the 19th century. Since the 11th century, Bañyoles has been registered as a market town, to which status the Old Exchange, Llotja del Tint, testifies. The Gothic church of Sta. María dels

Above: In Gerona, colorful houses reflect in the river's peaceful waters. Right: Farmers sell their produce at local markets.

Turers, the Darder Natural History Museum and the plaza with its arcades are all places well worth looking out for. The 15th century **Pia Almoina** houses the archaeological museum boasting what is scientifically and popularly known as the "Bañyoles Jaw", which is presumed to have been part of a Palaeolithic human being.

Besalú, with its Romanesque churches and massive fortified bridge, is the gateway to the volcanic hill country this side of the Pyrenees. **Olot,** the capital of Garrotxa, was destroyed by an earthquake in 1428. The old town core is dominated by the Neoclassical church of San Esteban. The sacristy museum contains Gothic panel paintings as well as a painting by El Greco. The residential area of Malagrida southeast of Clarà Park is noteworthy for imposing turn-of-the-century buildings like the Torre Malagrida, the Can Vayreda or the Can Masramon. On the other side of the river, the Torre Castany houses a museum of modern art with works by the "Olot School", which included artists like Galwey, Masriera, Urgell, Casas and Rusiñol. The 16th century Convent del Carmen, with its Renaissance cloister, has housed the local art academy since 1783. The above painters belonged to its tradition. It is pleasant to find that the scenery which inspired the artists is still spectacular. About 40 volcanic peaks rise from the surrounding region. Among the best known of these are Croscat and Sta. María. The crater of the latter harbors a chapel. Near Sta. María is the town of **Sant Pau**, with an old fort, city walls and a church which has a remarkable alabaster retable (1340) with Passion scenes. If one visits the area in autumn, one should definitely not miss the beech wood of Fageda d'en Jordà. It still seems to breathe the enchantment, which enthralled many a Catalan poet like Jacint Verdaguer.

The monastery at **Ripoll** was one of the major spiritual centers of medieval Catalonia. However, the town owes its growth over a long period of time to metalworking. The Benedictine monastery at Ripoll was founded by Count Guifré el Pelós during the Christian resettlement of the Pyrenees in 879. Its acme was under Abbot Oliba from 1008. He enlarged the church, adding two bell-towers, and led the monastery to a cultural renewal. The exquisitely worked Romanesque portal was completed by the mid 12th century. Unfortunately, the earthquake of 1428 damaged the building so severely that the Romanesque vaulting had to be replaced by Gothic vaulting and one of the towers even had to be taken down. In the 19th century, however, worse damage was caused by disastrous renovation which reduced the number of aisles from five to three and covered the interior walls with plaster to suit neo-classical taste. A fire as well as 19th century secularisation combined to destroy parts of the enormous monastery archives. What survived has been preserved in the archives of the Crown of Aragón at Barcelona.

Through the hauntingly beautiful valley of the Río Ter one reaches **Vic,** situated on a plain between the Montseny mountains and the foothills of the Pyrenees. Here the air is crisp and bracing. Frequently, there is a cold inversion weather here, which brings mist or days of rain. Vic is a bustling trade and commercial center. Tuesday is local market day and Saturday is regional market. On All Saints' Day, Christmas, the beginning of Lent and in Holy Week there are large markets which profer produce from the entire country. These are actually small trade fairs. The townspeople of Vic are known nationwide as shopkeepers and merchants. The town began on a small hill above the confluence of the Méder and Gurri Rivers. Above it was a Roman temple and, later, the three-storeyed fort, the 19th century **Castillo de Montcada**. The temple walls were incorporated in the fort as its inner court. From the 15th century it was used as a prison and granary. When the Roman temple was rediscovered in 1882, parts of the fort were torn down in a flurry of archaeological enthusiasm. A second historical core formed around the cathedral, a Neoclassical structure with a Romanesque belltower. Frescoes by Sert adorn its interior. He painstakingly restored them himself after they were destroyed in the Civil War. The centers of the town converge on the **Plaza del Mercadal**, the market place. Gothic and Modernist buildings surround it. Typical streets run through the old town, opening out into charming plazas. The **Paseo** and the **Ramblas** follow the course of the old walls, of which very little is left. The streets are elegant and lined with aristocratic residences, although sacred architecture sets the keynote here. The churches of La Piedad, San Justo, El Carmen and the monastic buildings of Sant Felipe Neri, Sta. Teresa and Sant Domènec are only the major buildings. Particularly noteworthy is the episcopal palace, which houses the **Museo Episcopal** and its large collections of regional Romanesque and Gothic art.

Between the plain of Vic and the Vallés reservoir rises the imposing **Montseny Massif.** Since the end of the 19th century the whole region has grown into a popular resort area. The villages of Viladrau and Arbúcies and the Santa Fé and Sant Bernat Hotels are particular magnets for those seeking solitude in hauntingly beautiful surroundings. Many mountain paths lead through the coolness of oak, holm oak, pine and chestnut woods up to the highest peaks, El Turó de l'Home (1707 m/5600 ft) and El Matagalls. The Sierra was densely settled in the Middle Ages. One comes across numerous old farms, many of them deserted, and some small Romanesque churches: El Brull, La Castanya, Cerdans, Montseny, La Móra, Sant Cristòfol de Monteugues, Sant Marçal and Tagamanent.

Right: Fishing also means long hours spent repairing nets in the blazing sun.

COSTA DORADA

Its golden beaches gave the southern part of the Catalan coast its name. The fertile coastal plain extends to the sea, where many fishing villages have grown into seaside resorts.

Arenys de Mar looks back on a long tradition of shipbuilding. In the 16th century it had no fewer than four docks and in the 18th it commanded an impressive overseas fleet of 45 ships. However, decline set in with the loss of the colonies, the invention of the steamship and Barcelona's supremacy as a port in the 19th century. The fishing port is still important nonetheless. It is crowded with an ever increasing number of sailboats and yachts. No slight is meant to the town's better restaurants, but the canteen of the fishermen's guild (*cofradía*) is absolutely a must. There the best *tapas* of all are served, prepared from the fresh catch just brought to market on the mole. Giant burnt almonds and *Calisay,* an orange liqueur, are unforgettable specialties.

Like every other town on the coast, Arenys was continually menaced by pirates. Of ten large fortified towers built in the 16th century, two still stand. The parish church of Sta. María boasts a fine Baroque altar by Pau Costa (1704). A museum is informative on the history of seafaring. The bustling town inspired Salvador Espriu to write his famous poem *Cementiri de Sinera.*

Mataró is at the heart of the Maresme, the fertile region known as Barcelona's vegetable garden. The town used to be a fishing village, but owes its growth to the textile industry, which achieved major importance in the 17th century. The center of town is the Plaza de Santa Ana. Young and old meet in the course of an evening stroll down the Rambla or Riera. At Whitsun a regional fair is held here and July 27 is the feast of the patron saint. The 17th century basilica of Sta. María is entirely Baroque. The Altar of the Rosary

and the Chapel of the Mater Dolorosa with paintings by Viladomat are among its greatest treasures. The other churches and several noteworthy examples of profane architecture – such as the town hall, the museum, and the Hospital de San Jaime – are also Baroque.

The golden strip of coast extends past the conurbation of Barcelona. Not far to the south, in the fertile plain of the Llobregat delta, begin the beaches of **Castelldefels.** They too are extremely popular with city-dwellers.

In the early years of the century, the Catalonian administration, the *mancomunitat*, drained the marshes, planted pines to fix the dunes and began to build a resort town which was destroyed in the Civil War. The beach is bounded on the south by the Garraf Range, which abruptly alters the coastal landscape. The road winds through arid, rugged terrain. The coast is steep as far as **Sitges,** which is a tourist resort with cosmopolitan flair. The old town extends on the la Punta promontory, crowned by the 18th century church with its seven Baroque altars. The town hall is Modernist, as is the **El Cau Ferrat Museum**, built early in the century by Santiago Rusiñol. The adjacent Museo Maricel, a rebuilt hospital, was fitted up by Charles Deering. The museums house important collections of Spanish and Catalan wrought-iron work, paintings by El Greco, Rusiñol, Utrillo, Casas, Sert and Picasso, as well as pottery and sculpture. The collections of the **Museo Romantico** in the Baroque Casa Llopis include a curious doll collection. The modern part of the town extends along the Paseo Maritimo to a modern hotel complex with a golf course. On Corpus Christi Day the entire town is a sea of carnations which form carpets for the procession to pass over. The spring rally from Pl. Catalunya in Barcelona to this attractive seaside resort is another important local event.

Turning off from the coast, one is soon in the heart of the wine-growing region of Penedés. *Cava* wines are its specialty. The wine-growers of **Sant Sadurní de**

Anoia introduced the *méthode champenoise* in 1872 to compensate for the ravages of phylloxera, the vine-pest, which destroyed the roots and leaves of grape vines. The first Spanish sparkling wines were an instant success. Today *Cava del Penedés* can easily hold its own on the international market with French champagne. It is drunk with pleasure wherever a party is going on. The town of **Villafranca del Penedés** is the capital of the wine-growing region. Its *Fiesta San Félix* is regarded as one of Catalonia's most characteristic festivals. Here the tradition of *castellers* thrives. These are living pyramids of acrobatic young men piled up on each other. The town has several Romanesque and Gothic churches, of which Sta. María is the most notable. Its façade may be Neo-Gothic, yet it has a Romanesque portal and interesting frescoes. The *castellers* tradition is also alive and

Above: The summer heat draws capacity crowds to Catalonian beaches. Right: The Cistercian monastery in Poblet.

flourishing at **Valls,** which has a well-preserved medieval old town. The Gothic church of San Juan with its Renaissance façade and Neo-Gothic bell-tower dominate the skyline. In one of the side chapels, the sea battle of Lepanto is commemorated on 17th century tiles. Valls is the centre of the Alt Camp region, known for a delicious simple dish, *calçotades,* made of braised onions.

The Large Monasteries

To the northeast and northwest of Valls are two of the most magisterial monasteries in Catalonia. The city walls and towers of medieval **Montblanc** can be seen from far away. Near it, in the lush green country on the north slope of the Sierra de Prades, is the Cistercian monastery of **Santa María de Poblet**. Its name derives from the Latin for "poplar meadow". Poblet is an impressive site. In addition to the church and monastery, it has buildings used by the confederation of Catalonia and Aragón since King

Pedro III the Ceremonious chose this as the place for royal interment.

Founded in the 12th century, the complex was added to until the 18th century. A hundred years of neglect and decay followed on 19th century secularisation. Not until the 1940s was the monastery restored and reopened. Inside the thick outer wall there are three precincts. The central one is the monastery proper with its spacious cloister.

The outer precinct, reached by the **Puerta de Prades**, the meadow gate, was reserved for farming and maintenance purposes. In this precinct is the Gothic chapel of Sant Jordi. Adjacent to it, the fortified 15th century **Puerta Dorada** leads to the second precinct with its spacious Plaza Mayor, where the ruins of the old almshouse and the Romanesque chapel of Santa Catalina await the traveller. At the center of the square stands an austere Gothic cross. The Kings' Gate, **Puerta Real**, flanked by two large turrets, is the entrance to the third precinct, which is old and enclosed

by strong walls built by Pere III in 1366. The 12th century church, built in the reign of Alfonso I, has three aisles. The central nave and one of the side aisles have even retained the Romanesque barrel vaulting. Five chapels radiate from the apse. The ground plan is clearly a departure from austere Cistercian architectural principles. The seven chapels off the side aisle are 14th century. The high altar is dominated by an alabaster retable by Damiá Forment (1527-29). On both sides of the crossing are the supports of the royal tombs, which were restored after 1940 by Frederic Marés. Eight kings of the House of Catalonia and Aragón are buried here with their wives. The spacious cloister, in Romanesque-Gothic transitional style, frames a central lustral fountain under a Romanesque "temple". The fountain was used by the Cistercians, traditionally active farmers. The depiction of the royal palace above the west wing of the cloister is in magnificent Flamboyant style. The Romanesque cloister and the chapel of San Esteban are together the oldest part of the complex. Today about 30 monks dwell in this venerable monastery, preserving Cistercian tradition.

The **Santes Creus** monastery lies in a small valley planted with poplars and hazel bushes with a superb mountain backdrop. The bucolic setting of vineyards, almond and olive orchards is characteristically Mediterranean. Farmers now live in many of the old monastic buildings. In style and by tradition, the monastery resembles Poblet. Building began here, too, in the 12th century. Here there are also three walled precincts, although the fortifications of this monastery are less massive. In the first precinct with its austere portal is the Baroque church of Santa Lucía, which had a Romanesque predecessor. The royal portal, which is also Baroque, leads to San Bernardo Square in the second precinct and a fountain consecrated to San Bernat Calbó. The abbot's palatial quarters replaced an almshouse here in the 17th century. Of the latter, only the cloister was incorporated into the new structure. Today the village town hall is on this spot. The church, consecrated in 1211, is on the plan of a simple Latin cross. The apse chapel is flanked by two radiating chapels on each side. The west façade elegantly manages to unite a Romanesque portal with a 13th century Gothic rose window. In the interior the 14th century Gothic royal tombs are noteworthy. The Gothic cloister dates from 1313. The English artisan Reinard Fonoll, an inspired master mason, worked on it together with Guillem Seguer, who executed the Flamboyant window decoration. The chapter house, linked to the cloister by a Romanesque portal, contains several 16th century abbots' tombs. The monks' dormitory is now used for concerts.

Right: Some things are sacred, such as serious talk during the cooler evening hours.

The monastery dates back to 1150, when Barcelona nobles gave land near Barcelona to the French abbey of Grand Selva in Languedoc. By 1158 the monks were looking for a more tranquil location and moved to Santes Creus. In the 13th century the monastery prospered enormously under two abbots. The abbot San Bernat Calbó was adviser to King Jaime I, whom he accompanied when Valencia and Mallorca were taken. Abbot Gener founded a school of chroniclers. Santes Creus played a major role in the founding of the Montesa order of knights in 1319. They accomplished missions for the Crown of Catalonia and Aragón comparable to those undertaken by the Templars in North Africa. Although Poblet was more important, the abbots of Santes Creus had a decisive political influence. Humanist studies and a comprehensive library made the monastery culturally significant. Decline set in with the war against France, when the monastery was forced to its doors and to auction off its possessions. Restoration work has been promoted in recent decades by the regional government, which has founded bibliographical archives, sponsors classical concerts courses in Gregorian chant.

TARRAGONA

At **Tarragona,** the Río Francolí flows into the sea. Except for the side traversed by the Rambla, the old city is still entirely enclosed by Roman walls. The original Roman settlement of Tarraco has left its stamp on the city. The great cathedral crowns its highest point. An early Christian basilica and a Visigoth church which became a mosque under the Arabs are presumed to have previously occupied the site. The present building was not begun until the mid 12th century. The original plan provided for five Romanesque aisles, but when the style changed to Gothic they were reduced to three. The main facade with its Gothic

central portal and two Romanesque side portals was never completed. The high altar retable by Pere Johan (15th century) is one of the cathedral's greatest treasures. The Gothic side chapel of **Santa María de los Sastres** is considered a masterpiece of its period. The central apse contains the 14th century funerary statue of Archbishop Juan de Aragón.

In the vicinity of the cathedral there are several more recent churches in a jumble of Roman and medieval ruins. At the centre is **Plaza de la Font**, where once Roman circus races were run. The Rambla bisects the modern part of the city. It ends at what is known as the "Balcony of the Mediterranean", a promenade overlooking the sea. From there one has a view over the terraced coast, the Roman amphitheatre, the beach and the port. The **Praetor's Palace** houses the archaeological museum with the finds from the Roman excavations. The interesting **Diocese Museum** contains a unique collection of 15th - 17th century tapestries. On the outskirts of town are a well-pre-

served aqueduct, known as "the devil's bridge", and the Roman necropolis.

The petrochemicals industry has encroached on the environs of Tarragona. Nonetheless, there are still numerous clean sandy beaches. **Altafulla**, **Torredembarra** and particularly **Salou** are great favorites with swimmers.

Tortosa was founded to guard the Ebro crossing and it also lived on the proceeds. The old city is guarded by the Arab fort of **San Juan**, the *Zuda*. Taken in 1149, it became a royal residence. Today it houses a *parador*. Above the Roman river port are the cathedral and the episcopal palace. The elegant Gothic inner courtyard and the colourful painted facade were recently renovated. The Renaissance college of San Luis houses the Open University.

The **Ebro delta** is the largest wetlands area in Catalonia and, with 320 sq km (124 sq mi), the second most important habitat of this kind on the western Mediterranean. Widespread and intensive cultivation of this land is irreconcilable with

the needs of its indigenous flora and fauna. In order to find a balance between conservation and agriculture, parts of the area were designated a national park by the regional government in 1983, an action warmly welcomed by international environmental organisations. The park comprises an area of 7736 ha including various lakes, canals, the islands of Buda, San Antonio and Sapinya, and the Punta de la Banya and Punta del Fangar peninsulas. The very flatness of the delta gives it a charm all its own. The interior, where the countryside is cultivated with vegetables, orchards and extensive rice-fields, is particularly attractive. The rice-fields change completely with the seasons: In winter they are ploughed, in spring flooded, and in summer lush green. This coastal wetlands area is among the most beautiful in the Mediterranean. Ponds fringed with willows and reeds alternate with beaches and dunes.

Above: Tarragona, on the Costa Dorada, has a beautiful old section.

PROVINCE GERONA
(Telephone area code: 972-)
Accommodation
FIGUERES: *LUXURY:* **Ampurdán**, Ctra. Madrid – France at km 763, Tel: 500562. *MODERATE:* **Pirineos**, Ronda de Barcelona 1, Tel: 500312. *BUDGET:* **Hostal España**, C/ La Junquera 26, Tel: 500869.
BEGUR: *LUXURY:* **Aiguablava**, Playa de Fornells, Tel: 622058. *MODERATE:* **Begur**, C/ Comas i Ros 8, Tel: 622207.
BANYOLES: *MODERATE:* **Hostal L'Ast**, Paseo Dalmau, Tel: 570414. *BUDGET:* **Victoria**, C/ Dr. Hysern 22, Tel: 571279.
OLOT: *MODERATE:* **Montsacopa**, C/ Mulleres, Tel: 260762. *BUDGET:* **La Perla**, Ctra. de la Deu, Tel: 262326.
SANTA PAU: **Hostal Bellavista**, Ctra. San Martí, Tel: 680103.
PALAFRUGELL: *LUXURY:* **Mas de Torrent** (5 km outside of town) Tel: 303292.
RIPOLL: *MODERATE:* **Solana del Ter**, Ctra. Barcelona – Ripoll, Tel: 701062. *BUDGET:* **Hostal Canaulas**, Puente de Olot 1, Tel: 700254.
GERONA: *LUXURY:* **Ultonia**, Av. Jaime I. 22, Tel: 203850. *MODERATE:* **Inmortal Gerona**, Ctra. Barcelona 31, Tel: 207900. *BUDGET:* **Hostal del Centro**, C/ Ciudadanos 4.
Museums / Sightseeing
FIGUERES: **Museu Dalí**, Pl. de Salvador Dalí i Gala, 9 a.m.–8.30 p.m., Oct – June 11.30 a.m.–5.30 p.m., closed Mon. **Museu de l'Empordá**, 11 a.m.–1 p.m. and 3.30–7 p.m.
BANYOLES: **Museu Darder de Historia Natural**, Pl. de Estudis 2, 11 a.m.–1 p.m. (in summer 10 a.m.–1 p.m.) and 5–8 p.m., closed Mon. **Museu Arqueologico**: 10 a.m.–1 p.m. and 4–6.30 p.m., closed Mon.
OLOT: **Museu Casal dels Volcans**, Av. de Santa Coloma, 10 a.m.–2 p.m. and 4 p.m.–6 p.m., in summer 5–7 p.m., Sun 10 a.m.–2 p.m.
RIPOLL: **Basilica**, 9 a.m.–1 p.m. and 3–8 p.m. Museum and cloisters: 9 a.m.–1 p.m. and 3–7 p.m., closed Mon. **Muso-Archivo Folclórico**, 9 a.m.–1 p.m. and 3–7 p.m., Mon 9 a.m.–1 p.m.
ARBÚCIES: **Museo Etnológico del Montseny**, C/ Mayor 3: 12 noon–2 p.m. and 5–8 p.m. Sun 12 noon–2 p.m.; in winter 6–8 p.m., Sat 12 noon–2 p.m. and 5–8 p.m., Sun 12 noon–2 p.m.
GERONA: **Museo de Arte**, Pujada de la Catedral 12 and **Museo Arqueologico de Sant Pere de Galligants**, C/ Santa Llúcia 1: 10 a.m.–1 p.m., 4.30–7 p.m., Sun 10 a.m.–1 p.m. **Museo Capitular de la Catedral**, 10 a.m.–1 p.m. and 3–6 p.m.

PERELADA: **Casino**, 6 p.m.–3 a.m., on weekends 5 p.m.–4 a.m.
Information / Oficina de Turismo
FIGUERES: Pl. del Sol, Tel: 503155.
OLOT: C/ Mulleres, Tel: 260141.
SANTA PAU: Can Vayreda, Tel: 680349.
RIPOLL: Pl. del Abat Oliba 3, Tel: 702351.
GERONA: Rambla Llibertat 1, Tel: 202679.

PROVINCE BARCELONA
(Telephone area code: 93-)
Accommodation
VIC: *LUXURY:* **Parador Nacional** (outside of town), Tel: 8887211. *MODERATE:* **Ausa**, Pl. Mayor 3, Tel: 8855311.
FOGAS DE MONCLUS (Montseny): *MODERATE:* **Santa Fe**, in the Santa Fe village, Tel: 8475011.
MONTSENY: *LUXURY:* **San Bernat**, Finca el Cot, Tel: 8473011.
ARENYS DE MAR: *MODERATE:* **Raymond**, Paseo Xifré 1, Tel: 7921700. **Carlos I.**, Paseo Catalunya 10, Tel: 7920383.
MATARÓ: *MODERATE:* **Castell de la Mata**, Ctra. Nacional at km 656, Tel: 7905807. *BUDGET:* Cerdanyola, Pl. Isla Cristina 1, Tel: 7982045.
CASTELLDEFELS: *LUXURY:* **Mediterraneo**, Paseo Marítimo 294, Tel: 6652100. *MODERATE:* **Hostal Flora Parc**, Av. Constitución, Tel: 6651847. **Fuentes Carrionas**, Passeig dels Tarongers 40, Tel: 6643461.
SITGES: *LUXURY:* Calípolis, Paseo Marítimo, Tel: 8941500. **Hostal Helvética**, Paseo Marítimo 21, Tel: 8941279. *MODERATE:* **Romantic**, C/ San Isidro 23, Tel: 8940643. **La Reserva**, Passeig Maritim 62, Tel : 8941833. *BUDGET:* **Hostal Continental**, C/ Villanueva, Tel: 8940957.
VILAFRANCA DEL PENEDÉS: *MODERATE:* **Pedro III el Grande**, Pl. Penedés 2, Tel: 8903100.
Musums / Sightseeing
VIC: **Museo Episcopal**, Pl. Bisbe Oliba 3: 10 a.m.–1 p.m. and 4–6 p.m., Sun 10 a.m.–1 p.m.; closed on weekdays in winter. **Museo Arqueologico**: 10 a.m.–1 p.m. and 4–6 p.m. (in winter 10 a.m.–1 p.m.), Sun 10 a.m.–1 p.m.
ARENYS DE MAR: **Museo Marés de la Punta**, weekdays 6–8 p.m., Sat 11 a.m.–1 p.m. and 6–8 p.m., Sun 11 a.m.–2 p.m., closed Mon.
SITGES: **Museu Cau Ferrat** and **Museu Maricel**: 10 a.m.–1 p.m. and 5–7 p.m. (in winter 4–6 p.m.), Sun 10 a.m.–2 p.m., closed Mon. **Museo Romantico**, 9.30 a.m.–2 p.m. and 4–6 p.m., Sun 9.30 a.m.–2 p.m., closed Mon.

VILAFRANCA: **Museo de Vilafranca**: 10 a.m.–2 p.m. and 4–7 p.m., Sun 10 a.m.–2 p.m.
Information – Oficina de Turismo
VIC: C/ Ciutat 1, Tel: 8862091.
MONTSENY: Ctra. de Brull, Tel: 8473003.
ARENYS DE MAR: Riera Bisbe Pol 8, Tel: 7920242.
MATARÓ: Riera 48, Tel: 7960808
CASTELLDEFELS: Pl. Iglesia, Tel: 6651150
SITGES: C/ Vilafranca, Tel: 8944700
VILAFRANCA: Cort 14, Tel: 8920358

PROVINCE TARRAGONA
(Telephone area code: 977-)
Accommodation
TARRAGONA: *LUXURY:* **Imperial Tarraco**, Paseo Palmeras, Tel: 233040. *MODERATE:* **Lauria**, Rambla Vova 20, Tel: 236712. **Hostal Viña del Mar**, Vía Augusta 137, Tel: 232029. *BUDGET:* **Hostal El Callejón**, Vía Augusta 213, Tel: 236380.
SALOU: *MODERATE:* **Cala Font**, Cala de la Font, Tel: 370454. **Caspel**, Av. Alfons el Magnanim 9, Tel: 380207. **Los Angeles**, Tel: 381466. *BUDGET:* **El Reco**, Carrer del Vaporet 8, Tel: 370216.
VALLS: *MODERATE:* **Casa Félix**, Ctra. de Tarragona, Tel: 606082
POBLET: *BUDGET:* **Hostal Fonoll**, C/ Ramon Berenguer IV. 2, Tel: 870333
SANTES CREUS: *BUDGET:* **Hostal Grau**, C/ San Pedro III. 3, Tel: 638311.
TORTOSA: *LUXURY:* **Parador Castillo de Zuda**, Tel: 444450. *BUDGET:* **Tortosa Park**, Av. Conde Bañuelos 1, Tel: 446112.
Museums / Sightseeing
TARRAGONA: **Museo de Historia de Tarragona**, Escaleras de San Ermenegildo; **Museo y Necrópolis Paleocristianos**, Paseo de la Independencia; **Museo Nacional Arqueologico**, Pl. del Rei; Opening times for all three museums: 10 a.m.–1.30 p.m. and 4.30–8 p.m. (in winter 4–7 p.m.), Sun 10 a.m.–2 p.m., closed Mon. **Museo Diocesano de la Catedral**: weekdays 10 a.m.–1 p.m. and 4–7 p.m.
POBLET: Museum opens 10 a.m.–12.30 p.m. and 3–6 p.m., in winter until 5.30 p.m.
SANTES CREUS: Museum opens 10 a.m.–1 p.m. and 3.30–7 p.m., in winter until 6 p.m.
Information – Oficina de Turismo
TARRAGONA: Rambla Nova 46, Tel: 232143.
VALLS: Pl. Blat 1, Tel: 601043.
TORTOSA: , Pl. España 1, Tel: 442567.
DELTEBRE: Delta de Ebro – Nature Reserve: Centro de Recepción y Documentación, Pl. 20 de Mayo, Tel: 489511

BARCELONA
Pride of the Catalans

Barcelona was founded as the Roman colony of *Barcino* in the reign of the Emperor Augustus on the plain between the Llobregat and Besós rivers. The original Roman settlement on *Mons Taber* hill was laid out according to the plan common to the time. This meant that it was rectangular and the forum was at the intersection of the axes. Still the heart of the city and the seat of city government, this spatial arrangement is now Pl. de Sant Jaume. Above it on the hill was the temple of Augustus, of which four columns now stand in the Centre Excursionista de Catalunya.

What remains of the Roman walls formed part of the 3rd and 4th century fortifications which were strong enough to withstand the first Frankish invasion. Despite a period in which it was capital city in the reign of Ataulfo, the city declined under the Visigoths. In Moorish hands for a brief period only, it was recaptured by the Franks in 801. Barcelona then became an outpost of the Carolingian realm south of the Pyrenees and seat of the County of Barcelona.

In 988, in the reign of Borell II, the county became independent of France

Left: An interesting view of Gaudi' s cathedral Sagrada Família in Barcelona, an unfinished masterwork.

and adopted the role of political leader of all the Catalan counties. Until the 15th century, Barcelona remained the capital of the Confederation of Catalonia and Aragón. A sharp upturn in maritime trade at that time made it one of the most important economic powers in the Mediterranean region.

This distant and glorious past was played out against the backdrop of the medieval part of the city. Its center, with the most important administrative buildings, was what is now usually known as the **Barrio Gótico,** although of course a great deal of Gothic architecture has survived in other parts of the city too.

The Medieval City

The **Pl. del Rei** in front of the royal residence is dominated by the **Palau Reial Major,** a mainly 14th-century complex where the kings resided. The 16th-century tower is locally known as the **Mirador del Rei Martí.** A stair winds up to the **Saló del Tinell,** which is a magnificent ceremonial hall with wide stone arches supporting the ceiling, and the small chapel of Sta. Ágata. It is Gothic too, and contains a superb Condestable retable by Jaume Huguet. On the other side the Plaza is bounded by the Lloctinent Palace, a truly splendid Re-

Through the cloister one reaches the entirely Romanesque chapel of Sta. Lucia. The episcopal palace and the Gothic chapter house, the **Cases del Canonges,** have become the residence of the regional President. The **Casa del Ardiaca,** which was actually built on ancient Roman walls, has become the city's historical archives. The modern college, audaciously decorated in interesting sgraffito style by no lesser artistic luminary than Picasso, contrasts sharply with the cathedral.

Sant Jaume Square is where everything important happens in Barcelona. Each weekend, city residents meet here to dance the *sardana*. The Plaza is framed by the seat of the regional government and the city hall. The Catalan institution of the *cortes*, essentially a parliamentary form of government even then, dates back to the 13th century.

The portal of the residence, the inner courtyards and the chapel of Sant Jordi (St George) are prime examples of the Gothic Flamboyant style in Catalonia. The ordered Renaissance façade of the palace was completed in the 16th century. The city hall also proudly illustrates a long tradition of parliamentary government. Until the 18th century, the **Consell de Cent,** the Council of 100, met in the hall of the same name. Although the side façade of the city hall is Gothic, it presents a Neo-classical front to the square.

The 14th-century church of **Sta. María del Mar** is in the old **Barrio de Ribera** section, where merchants, aristocrats and seafarers lived at the time of the maritime trade boom. The church's austerity of line and harmonious proportions are considered to represent the best of Catalan Gothic. It used to be on the waterfront until the coastline gradually began to advance.

Montcada Street, lined with the residences of Barcelona's wealthiest and by extension most powerful families, is in the same quarter. Many of these have re-

naissance building housing the Aragón Crown Archives. Finally, there is the **Casa Clariana Padellás,** which houses the city historical museum. Its basement is fascinating as the site of an important excavation of the original Roman city.

The **cathedral,** a large three-aisled church on austere Gothic lines, is an interesting example of Catalan eclecticism. It can be regarded as essentially 13th and 14th century since only the main façade is 18th century. Although the two octagonal towers above the transept are typical of Catalan Romanesque, the 19th-century tower is, not so unbelievably perhaps, more typical of the French-inspired High Gothic. The tomb of Sta. Eulalia is in the crypt. The Gothic choir was decorated in 1519 with the coat of arms of Juan de Borgoña. It was in fact he who commissioned the construction of the choir to mark the occasion of a session of the Order of the Golden Fleece.

Above: Barcelona, a great gathering point for the architectural and artistic scene.

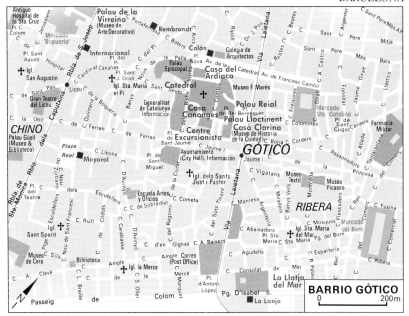

tained all the characteristic features of Gothic palaces. Invariably, entrances conceal arcaded courtyards from which stairs lead up to the *belle étage*. Two such palaces, the Palau Aguilar and the Palau del Baró del Castellet, together house the **Picasso Museum**, which exhibits important early works as well as some of the prolific artist's most famous paintings and a series of studies of *Las Meninas* by Velázquez. Other palaces house the **Textile Museum** and the **Maeght Art Gallery**. The Palau Dalmases, another of those ancient dwellings, is still in its original condition.

The complex of the old **Hospital de la Santa Creu,** built in 1410 to unite various dispensaries scattered throughout the city, is in the **Barrio del Raval** on the other side of the Ramblas. The superb Gothic halls house the Library of Catalonia. The Baroque House of Convalescence, with its tiled inner courtyard, and the old Neoclassical Surgeons' College (which, by the way, is still in use as the Academy of Medicine), are definitely noteworthy. This quarter has preserved the tradition of **Sant Ponç Market**, where a number of rare plants, including various teas and medicinal herbs, are sold. The **Casa de la Caritat,** which is to house the new museum of contemporary art, is being renovated by the English architect Richard Meyer. The Gothic **Convent Los Angeles** serves as the library of Barcelona's museums. In the southernmost part of the quarter, right where all the bars are (this of course means in the Barrio Chino), one may be surprised to find the handsome church of **Sant Pau del Camp.** It is pure Romanesque in style and has been part of a Benedictine abbey since the 10th century.

The little Gothic church of **Sta. María del Pi** with its lovely rose window is in the thick of yet another quarter of the old city. The picturesque Petritxol Street is nearby, where one of the city's oldest art galleries, the **Sala Parés**, is located. La Palla Street, which is lined with antique shops and second-hand bookshops, leads to the cathedral. Not far from the Bene-

77

dictine Monastery of **Sant Pere de les Puelles** is the first of the Modernist houses for which Barcelona is deservedly famous, the **Palau de la Música Cata-lána,** which is bursting with utterly amazing ceramic and sculptural decor. Completed in the year 1908 it is without any doubt Domènech i Montaner's masterpiece.

The Ramblas, Heart of the City

The Ramblas, or Las Ramblas, form without doubt the liveliest part of the whole city and thus the best place to get to know it. This great avenue, colorful, bustling, spectacular as it is, runs all the way from the Plaza de Catalunya to the harbor. It was originally the bed of a stream running along the 13th-century city wall. The walls gradually became too confining for the growing city and their scope was widened to include the area up

Above: Gypsies provide skillful entertainment for the meanderers on the Ramblas.

to what is now the central ring road. The Ramblas was suddenly inside the city limits.

The monastic and academic buildings lining it were built from the 15th to the 17th centuries. Down the middle ran a broad promenade, which was later planted with trees. The section of the Ramblas immediately following the Pl. Catalunya is named after the fountain which is so rich in tradition, **Rambla de Canaletas.** It is said that whoever drinks from this particular fountain will return to the city. Football fans tend to gather here. The newspaper kiosks, always surrounded by curious onlookers, are characteristic of this section of the Ramblas.

The next is called **Rambla dels Estudis,** since the University of Barcelona, the Estudi General, was here until 1714. However, it is now usually called the Rambla dels Ocells because of the stalls selling songbirds and other small pets which now make it so lively. Standing on the far side are the Baroque Bethlehem Church, which belonged to the Jesuits, and the 18th century **Palau Moja.** In its great hall are important murals by Francesc Pla el Vigatá. Jacint Verdaguer, the great *Renaixença* poet, lived here when he was father confessor to the Marquis Comilla. The Renaixença was the important 19th-century Catalan cultural renewal movement.

The next section, the **Rambla de les Flors,** is a riot of color, with its multitude of little flower stands. Ponteferissa Street turns off to the left. It is an important commercial thoroughfare and fashion center. On the right is the Palace of the Vicereine (when it was built, the widow of the Viceroy of Peru), **Palau de la Virreina.** Set back from the street, it is a unique 18th-century Rococo building flanked by proud equestrian statues by Gargallo. An active cultural center, it mounts exhibitions regularly.

Beyond it is Sant Josep's Market, which is now popularly known as the **Boquería.** It is by far the most traditional and best stocked market in Barcelona. Here, at the head of the **Rambla dels Caputxins,** a large mosaic by Joan Miró is embedded in the paving. Café terraces, restaurants and hotels jostle for place here. Here, too, is the **Gran Teatre del Liceu,** in which mostly operas are performed. All the great stars of Italian and Wagnerian opera, the two most popular operatic genres in Barcelona, have sung here at some stage in their careers. After it, streets lead off to the right into the **Barrio Chino,** where Bohemia meets the underworld as described in several literary works notably by the French writer Jean Genet. A few paces farther down a side street, Nou de la Rambla, is the **Palau Güell,** which is a small residence built in 1888 by Gaudí. Nowadays it houses the theatre museum.

On the other side of this Rambla, the **Pl. Reial** was laid out in the mid 19th century in what were once the grounds of a Capuchin monastery. Uniform in style and framed by arcades, the square is decorated with lanterns by Gaudí and motifs of seafarers and explorers. Bars and tables in front of restaurants make it a popular venue. Sunday is stamp and coin market day on this square. Calle Avinyó is not far from the square. There Picasso found the inspiration for his famous *Girls from Avignon* (1907), painted at the beginning of his Cubist period. One finally reaches the sea by continuing along the Rambla Santa Monica and across Pla del Teatre, where the **Teatre Principal** and the monument to the composer Padre Frederic Soler are. The **Palau Marc,** housing the regional ministry of culture, is noteworthy in this section. The statue of Columbus closes the Ramblas, marking off the maritime section of the city.

Harbors and Beaches

On returning from his first voyage of discovery to the Americas in 1493, Columbus was received by the Catholic Monarchs in Barcelona. His statue on a 5-meter high column is the work of Gaietà Buïgas (1886). It has become an important city landmark. At its foot the *golondrinas*, "swallow boats", glide continually between the quay and the mole. The very lifeblood of the city pulses in this maritime section between Montjuic and the traditional fishermen's quarter of Barceloneta, which extends in the opposite direction as far as the beaches at Poble Nou and the mouth of the Besós.

The **Drassanes,** the original 14th century docks, are the most monumental relic of the grandeur of the medieval maritime power that once was Barcelona. Their size and state of preservation are unique in the world. There surely could be no more appropriate setting for the Maritime Museum. Behind them is what remains of the old city walls. The restored **Moll de la Fusta** area, with its bars and restaurants overlooking yacht clubs and marinas, represents an enterprising first step towards remaking the

old harbor section into a leisure area. By crossing tranquil Duc de Medinaceli Square, one reaches the **Basílica de la Mercè,** the Baroque shrine of seafarers consecrated to the city's patron saint. Beyond the Vía Laietana, the main thoroughfare of the old city, is the **Llotja** on Antonio López Square. This is the Old Exchange. Behind its Neoclassical façade, the 14th-century Gothic hall with its dividing arches still houses the Exchange. Across from it are buildings with handsome arbors, known as *porxos d'en Xifré.* Josep Xifré, who laid them out in 1836, was an *indiano,* a rich colonist who returned home. Near this square, the harbor bazaar sprawls as far as Plaza de Palau, where the new customs building, the **Duana Nova,** stands. It is actually not all that new, for it is a rococo building which has housed the civil administration since the early years of the century.

La Barceloneta is a quarter of the city which, like Venus, emerged from the waves. It is on a triangular spit of land drained in the 17th century while the harbor was being dug. Laid out on a uniform plan in the mid-18th century by the military engineer Juan Martín, it is a prime example of Baroque town planning. At the heart of the quarter are the square, the market, and the church of Sant Miquel del Port. Fishermen and seamen have always lived in this quarter. But because of its beaches, seafood restaurants, taverns and swimming baths, La Barceloneta has also always been popular with the city's residents as the ideal area to engage in leisurely activities.

Quite a few sports clubs have moved in, such as the Club Natación Barcelona. One of this club's members invented *patín* sailing. Neither rudders nor masts are needed for this ultra-modern sport, which is fast becoming all the rage on the Catalan coast. Paseo Maritimo runs from here right up to the Olympic Village at Poble Nou.

Above: Cranes waiting for floating prey in the harbor of Barcelona. Right: Tools of street performers' trade in the Barrio Gótico.

A large part of the city's seafront is, of course, taken up by moles and docks. In the Barceloneta next to the old mole, Muelle del Reloj, is the fishing port, a picturesque spot adjacent to the yacht basin. It looks especially impressive from above when one takes the cable car, the *teleférico*, from the iron tower of San Sebastià at the head of the harbor mole. One floats to the tower of Jaume I, over the berths of the passenger ships, to reach the Miramar look-out platform at the top of Montjuic.

The **Ciutadella Park** extends between the Barceloneta and Ribera quarters. It was named after fortifications built by Philip V during his campaign to subdue the city, which had sided with the Habsburgs in the War of the Spanish Succession. The fortifications were torn down in 1869, but the governor's palace, the chapel and the arsenal remain. The last, a handsome Baroque building, is now the Catalonian parliament. Part of it houses the Museum of Modern Art, with works by Dalí, Miró, Fortuny, Regollos and Sert. The park in its present form was laid out by Josep Fontseré for the World Exposition of 1888. The triumphal arch was then the entrance. Many of the early Modernist buildings built for the Exposition have since been torn down. What remains is considered seminal *Modernismo*: the **Castell dels tres Dragons** by Domènech i Montaner, which is now a natural history museum; the **Hivernacle,** a glass and iron construction by Josep Amargós, which has been converted into a cultural center, and the Umbracle.

The Barcelona **zoo** is also in the park. Surprisingly, it houses some astonishing sculpture: Roig Solé's *Woman with a Umbrella* and a fine work of Llimona's. The old market, the **Mercado del Born,** is adjacent to the park. It too has been converted into a multi-purpose cultural center.

The Eixample: the Ascendancy Years

The growth of commerce in the 19th century made it necessary by 1854 that the city tear down the old walls because they stood in the way of expansion. Adjacent areas had been kept free of housing until that time. Then, in 1860, the zone around the old city was developed as planned by the engineer Ildefonso Cerdá. A simple grid of streets running parallel to the sea formed the ground plan. At intersections, corners were cut across diagonally. The plan proved sensible and progressive although Cerdá's park projects were, unfortunately, not carried out at the same time. All this activity focused on enlarging the city (Ensanche, Eixample) coincided with the period of Barcelona's cultural ascendancy. Commercial and industrial growth had made its citizens prosperous. Their affluence was reflected in the way the city was beginning to look. The Renaixença movement was the expression of this political and cultural ascendancy. It manifested itself in the visual arts as *Modernismo.* The Eixample is among the most interesting examples of 19th-century European urban planning. Strolling through its streets means continually discovering superbly imaginative architectural detail. *Modernismo* sought and employed entirely new decorative materials with consummate artistry. They can be spotted on the façades of monumental buildings as well as in the entrances and porter's lodges of apartment blocks and even on shops.

The old city and the Eixample coalesce at **Plaza de Catalunya**. Laid out in 1927, it is adorned with interesting sculptures by Josep Llimona, Eusebi Arnau, Pau Gargallo and Josep Clarà. The **Paseig de Gràcia**, the central thoroughfare of the Eixample, begins here. It has broad pavements lined with exclusive commercial establishments: jewelers, banks, art galleries, cinemas, hotels, restaurants and booksellers. Pere Falqués' lamps and

Right: The spires of Gaudi's Sagrada Familia, which can be seen from many miles around, dominate the entire city.

Gaudí's paving are regarded as the hallmarks of the boulevard.

Among the many eclectic, neo-medieval or simply Modernist buildings, Gaudí's **Casa Milà** stands out. Each of its apartments is unique. Not one is like any other in the building. Casa Milà is popularly known as La Pedrera. The block between Carrer de Aragó and Carrer del Consell de Cent is known as the "apple of discord". This is a reference to the mythical judgement of Paris. The "three graces" are Gaudí's **Casa Batlló,** Puig i Cadafalch's Casa **Amatller** and Domènech i Montaner's **Casa Lleó Morera.** The Neo-Gothic buildings of Enric Sagnier as well as the Cases Rocamora of the Bassegoda brothers on a level with the Carrer de Casp, are further outstanding examples of this style.

Parallel to the Paseig de Gràcia, the Rambla de Catalunya, a continuation of the Ramblas, traverses the Eixample with an inviting green strip down the middle, so that the whole is in effect a roofed avenue of linden trees. Here, too, turn-of-the-century architects placed imaginative Modernist buildings. Of these we mention only Puig i Cadafalch's **Casa Serra,** currently housing the provincial administration. In the Carrer de Aragó nearby is the old Montaner i Simon publishing house built by Domènech i Montaner. It houses the **Tàpies Modern Art Foundation.** Not far from it are the neo-medieval university buildings.

The broad **Avenida Diagonal** severs the city diagonally from Pedralbes, the university quarter, to **Plaza de las Glòries Catalanes.** The latter was intended by Cerdá to be Barcelona's new center. Now, finally, two new cultural centers all at once are being built there: a municipal auditorium with halls seating 2300 and 700, designed by Rafael Moneo; and a regional theater with halls seating 1000 and 400. The plans are by Ricard Bofill. He has undertaken to build a glass-fronted classical temple made up of metal struc-

tural elements. Works by the American sculptress Beverly Pepper are being set up in the vicinity of the North Station as a tribute to Gaudí and Miró: The *Fallen-in Sky* and *Spirals Branching Out*. The middle section of the Av. Diagonal is a busy commercial and shopping thorough fare. Distinguished Modernist buildings can be seen here too: Puig i Cadafalch's **Casa de les Punxes and Casa Quadras,** which houses the Music Museum. The later (1937) Rationalist building by Ricardo de Churruca on a level with Enrique Granados Street is also noteworthy.

North of the Av. Diagonal the Avenida Gaudí runs diagonally to it. At both ends of the avenue named for Barcelona's best known architect are the most important buildings of the Modernist period that played such an important part in the esthetic evolution of the city. The **Sagrada Familia,** the vast temple of atonement which was Gaudí's masterpiece, gave his architectural genius scope for expression in complex religious symbolism. It was begun in 1882 by the diocesan architect

Villar as the "Cathedral of the 20th century". Gaudí then took over the project and began to pour all his creative energies into it from 1883 until his death in 1926. Consecrated to the Holy Family, the immense building with its 12 soaring towers has become the most striking feature of the cityscape.

Although it was, and understandably so, left unfinished, it is still under construction with the aid of donations despite repeated protests against the completion. Foreign and Spanish artisans are trying to complete Gaudí's work. Subirach's contribution to the recently finished western façade has, however, met with considerable acclaim. At the other end of Av. Gaudí is Domènech i Montaner's **Hospital de Sant Pau.** Its tiled pavilions occupy spacious premises surrounded by lovely gardens.

The Leisure City

To the fortunate traveller who gets the chance to view the city from the water,

83

Barcelona seems to be enclosed by a natural barrier, the Sierra de Collserola. Its highest point, **Tibidabo** (512 m), is the focal point of the city. A tramline, **Tranvía Blau,** ends at the lower station of the funicular railway which takes passengers up the hill. The distinctive silhouette of the Neo-Gothic Sagrado Corazón Church, which is visible from a great distance, has also become an integral part of the cityscape. Next to it is an amusement park. The unforgettable view of the city it offers has made the hill a popular recreation spot. A 260 m (853 ft) high television tower is being built as if on purpose to dwarf the church and the Ferris wheel, which it does a like true sign of the times. The Carretera de Aigües winds along the Sierra halfway to the top, a paradise for joggers, cyclists and model plane enthusiasts.

Montjuic, altogether a less lofty eminence at 173 m (568 ft), constitutes an ac-

Above: The Parc de la Espanya Industrial, built on what was the grounds of a factory.

clivity on the water. Its strategic position directly above the city has made it ideal for military purposes since the Middle Ages. Preceded on the site by the Castillo del Puerto, the massive **Castell del Montjuic** was built as a star-shaped fortress fitted out with bulwarks and redoubts in the 18th century. After it had been for many years an infamous military prison and symbol of oppression, it was given to the city in 1960 and made into a military museum. The rest of the hill was landscaped to accommodate the 1929 World's Fair. Its barren slopes became luxuriantly planted gardens. A number of exhibition halls and sports facilities were built. They have been the starting point for the 1992 Olympic Park.

From the **Plaza de España** with its monumental fountain, one enters the Barcelona Trade Fair grounds through a semi-circular colonnade between twin towers. One recognizes immediately the origin: Indeed, they were inspired by the Campanile at Venice. The illuminated fountain, aflame with color on summer evenings, dominates a spacious plaza. Behind it is the German pavilion designed in 1929 by Mies van der Rohe. This is an exemplary piece of Rationalist modern architecture which, in addition, houses a sculpture by Georg Kolbe. A stair leads up to the **National Palace,** which housed the Catalan exhibition in 1929. It has been used to accommodate the Catalonian Art Museum since 1933. Among its many and varied exhibits are superb Romanesque and Gothic collections. Something which one should definitely not pass by are several frescoes removed from little Romanesque churches tucked away in the Pyrenees, and now displayed in an instructive manner.

The adjacent park contains many interesting sights. The **Poble Español** is a vast space in which replicas of vernacular architecture from all over Spain were built to form an entire village. With numerous bars and restaurants, it has be-

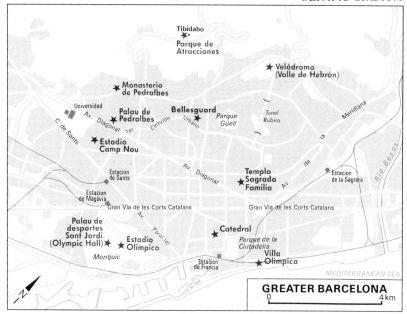

GREATER BARCELONA
0   4 km

come a theme park in which concerts and fiestas sometimes take place. In addition, model workshops demonstrate interesting crafts. The nearby equestrian statue of St George by Jordi Llimona offers a view of the whole town from its platform.

From here it is not far to the Olympic Ring. The **Olympic Stadium** itself is the joint work of Gregotti, Correa, Milà, Margarit and Buxadé. They have shown a feeling of continuity by retaining the 1929 stadium shell, in which they have incorporated a new interior. The **San Jordi Sports Palace**, the work of the Japanese architect Arata Isozaki, is the most distinctive feature of the Olympic grounds. Resembling a sculpture, it is an airy structure in the form of a huge drawn bow. The buildings which are to house the physical education college were designed by Bofill Associates.

Avenida del Estadio goes past **Palacete Albéniz,** decorated by Salvador Dalí, where important visitors to Barcelona reside. Then one comes to the **Fundació Miró,** a dynamic modern cul-

tural center endowed with an excellent selection of the artist's works. The building complex, which is full of light and sophisticated in style, is the work of J.L. Sert (1974). Parks lead travellers who might be in need of rest by this time to the open-air Grec theater where an annual summer festival is being held in July. The next stop on the way could be the Archaeological and Ethnological Museum, which not only has a good collection of Greek and Roman artifacts, but also provides insight into the fascinating megalithic culture. After the museum, for a change, one should wander on down to the old flower market, now a theater complex, at the foot of Montjuic.

The **Poble Sec** quarter sprawls between Plaza de España and the harbor. Distinctive chimneys are a reminder of the quarter's industrial past. Its main thoroughfare, Av. Paral.lel (the full stop in the word's midst is an aid to pronunciation), was so named after the astronomist Comas i Solà determined that it actually runs along 41.5 latitude. In the

early years of the century the entire quarter was known as Barcelona's Montmartre. Theaters, cabarets and light entertainment are concentrated here. Today El Molino and the Arnau Theater are particularly popular. If one feels venturesome, another funicular railway runs from the Paral.lel up Montjuic. From there a suspension railway runs to the amusement park and on to the fortress.

Barcelona by Night

In recent years Barcelona's nightlife has taken on an entirely different character. This is doubtless due to prosperity and the zest shown by the dynamic younger set among the city's residents. Whatever the reason, undreamt of creative energies have been let loose on planning and designing new night spots. The amazing thing is that tradition has not been ignored despite creative innovation.

Above: Cafés along the Ramblas welcome the post-opera crowds into the night.

Continuity is manifest in interior decoration as well as in graphic and industrial design. The various types of bars and pubs have brought new aesthetic and social perspectives to the fore which have played a part in transforming entire quarters. There are quite a few recreational establishments which promote cultural exchange between the city's residents. Some of them used to be factories, garages, co-operatives, warehouses, or businesses. Others are stylishly converted old buildings, former villas, or towers. Probably it is safe to assume that one can classify visitors according to the type of building housing their favorite haunts. Some, unconventional, or even rockers, prefer fringe aesthetics; others consider themselves as "modern". Making the rounds of Barcelona's night spots, one can glimpse the gamut of the city's life.

The 1992 Olympics

Four main areas of the city have been allocated for the 1992 Olympics sports events. The main infrastructure has been established well in advance of events. The most sweeping changes have resulted from the construction of the **Olympic Village** in Poble Nou beyond the suburb of Barceloneta. This has raised hopes of a restructuring of the entire waterfront.

The plans of architects Bohigas, Martorell and Mackay provide for a park, hotels, residential areas, a marina, protected beaches and a plaza on the waterfront where the Mediterranean Convention Centre will be built. The high-rise buildings which will go up here will be the city's tallest.

The entire **Montjuic** section has been transformed into the second major Olympic quarter. Accessibility to the area from all points has been improved and the Parc del Migdia has to this end been converted into an area for open-air concerts. In a broader sense it has been integrated as a recreational area into the neighbouring sections of the city and the Zona Franca to the south. Moreover, the areas where Olympic events will take place have been upgraded or built from scratch.

The **Valle Hebrón** section's most important building is the remarkable cycle-racing stadium, designed by Esteve Bonell and Francesc Rius. It is surrounded by lovely gardens in which the *Poema escultural* by Joan Brossa is exhibited. They merge imperceptibly with the **Parc del Laberint** belonging to the Neoclassical manor house (1799) of the Marquis Alfarras, which is almost hidden from view amid gardens full of mythical figures, a small temple, a pond and a labyrinth of pruned cypresses.

Finally, the facilities extant in the **Diagonal-Pedralbes** section are being integrated into the Olympic complex. First of all, the Camp Nou of Barcelona's home soccer team has a stadium seating 120,000 there. Then, of course, the university sports facilities and the Real Club de Polo are also in this section. And, as if all this were not enough, further sports facilities extend the area out beyond the city limits.

Outlying Areas

The quarter known as **Pedralbes** boasts the 14th-century convent of the same name. It was founded by Queen Elisenda de Montcada, who was the last wife of Jaume II. Its cloister and the chapel of Sant Miquel are the greatest treasures of this little-known Gothic gem at the edge of the city. In the Avenida de Pedralbes linking the convent with the Diagonal, no one should miss the **Pabellones Güell**. This building complex started as old stalls that were completely renovated, enlarged and decorated with an extraordinary wrought-iron dragon at the gate by Gaudí.

To the east is the fashionable **Barrio de Sarrià**. Its old core around the church of Sant Vicenç has retained its original character. Like the Barrio Sant Gervasi at the foot of Tibidabo, this quarter is first and foremost a residential area. The 15th-century country residence of King Martí, **Bellesgard,** was located in the former *barrio*. Gaudí completely rebuilt the residence. Farther to the east is **Parc Güell**, also by Gaudí. A riot of colour and bizarre forms, it was originally intended to be a garden city. Fortunately, it has been taken into the register of works under the protection of UNESCO.

The **Barrio Gràcia** extends between the residential areas in the foothills of the Sierra and the Eixample. Formerly a separate urban entity, it has retained more of its original character than many other sections of Barcelona. In the 19th century the Barrio Gràcia was known as a hotbed of liberal and republican convictions and a stronghold of the labor movement. It has its own celebrations and customs, such as Sant Medir, a pilgrimage on horseback to Sant Cugat del Vallés or the lively festival de la Mare de Déu d'Agost (15 August), for which the streets are roofed over with decorations. A walk through this quarter should include the church of Sant Josep from a 17th-century Carmelite convent, La Llibertat Market, which is an exciting cast-iron construction, and several Modernist buildings, among them **Casa Vicens,** one of Gaudí's earliest.

East of the Eixample is the **Barrio Sants.** Here the **Parc de la Espanya Industrial** commemorates its past as a quarter in which early industrialization occurred. Once the site of industrial premises, it is next to the modern train station. The Basque architect Ganchegui designed the park in the style of a Roman bath. Its central element is a pond surrounded by waterfalls and streams. In addition, ten look-out and lighting towers rise above the park. A slide ingeniously shaped like a dragon by Andrés Nagel is a further attraction for both children and architecture enthusiasts.

In front of the train station is the controversial ultra-modern Països Cataláns Square, designed by Helio Piñón and Albert Viaplana. Nearby is yet another imaginatively laid out park, **Parc Joan Miró,** popularly known as "Slaughterhouse Park" since there used to be one on the site. A spectacular Miró sculpture rises unexpectedly from the depths of a pond: *Woman with a Bird.* Palms, a children's playground, pergolas, pines and eucalyptus make the park a miniature oasis.

Recently quite a few such parks have been laid out to make life in the city more pleasant for residents, and to provide variety for visitors. The Creueta del Coll park is on one of the hills in the **Barrio de Horta.** It has a lake, suitable for swimming in the summer, and features artwork by Elsworth Kelly and Roy Lichtenstein. A sculpture by Chillida entitled *In Praise of Water* is also – appropriately enough – on display here.

Right: The Benedictine monastery of Montserrat, a Catalonian shrine etched in a cliff.

The park in the **Barrio Clot,** laid out according to plans by Daniel Freixens and Vicente Miranda, illustrates the consummate integration of railway tracks and an old factory chimney into garden landscaping. A sculpture by the modern American artist Bryant Hunt also enhances the premises.

Excursions

Sant Cugat del Vallès is on the other side of the Sierra, only twenty minutes by regional rapid-transit train from Pl. Catalunya. As a result of substantial population growth, it has developed into yet another suburb of Barcelona. The modern industrial park at Vallès has acquired an international reputation for research and high-tech production.

In this area is the Benedictine abbey after which the city was named. It was certainly once the most important monastery in the County of Barcelona. Nevertheless, not much is known about its beginnings in 878. It was built on the site of a Roman *castrum* on the Roman road between Barcelona and Egara (now Terrassa), on the spot where Cugat suffered martyrdom at the hands of Diocletian's soldiers in the early 4th century. By the 5th century a church had been built to commemorate the martyr. In the 7th century a polygonal apse was added. By then, monastic buildings had probably been erected. Between the 12th and 14th centuries the complex was rebuilt and enlarged, first in the Romanesque, and finally in the Gothic style. The 144 capitals of the cloister astonish anyone who has the time to take them one by one with the variety of themes portrayed. Three museums share the large number of art treasures found here: the Catalonian Art Museum, the Diocese Museum and the British Museum. In 1925 the monastery was declared a historic monument.

One really should not miss **Montserrat.** The quickest way to get there is the

motorway, but the regional rail service gets as far as Monistrol in the foothills of the Montserrat Massif. Its distinctive skyline of columnar, conical limestone formations extends over an area of about 50 square kilometres. Among the bizarre formations the highest peaks, Sant Jeroni (1224 m/4016 ft) and Los Ecos (1212 m/3976 ft) stand out. This fascinating landscape is made accessible by aerial cable cars and funicular railway. Footpaths lead into it, and at resting places near small chapels magnificent views open out over the plain. At 720 m one reaches the Benedictine monastery consecrated to the Virgin of Montserrat. Innumerable miracles are ascribed to the dark-skinned Virgin, called La Moreneta. The object of such widespread veneration is a small, painted, 12th century wooden figure which has survived untold fires and the looting of the monastery. Much of the complex was destroyed in 1811 by the invading troops of Napoleon. Inside there is still a handsome Gothic hall. A cloister built in the Gothic style in 1746

has survived. The Neo-Romanesque cloister, on the other hand, was designed in 1935 by Puig i Cadafalch. The library contains over 250,000 volumes, 400 incunabula, 200 Egyptian papyrus manuscripts with Greek and Coptic texts, and 2000 old manuscripts in Latin, Spanish, Hebrew, Arabic and Syriac.

The front, built in 1939, is the work of Francesc Folguera. Behind it an atrium formed by the cloister of Abbot Argeric (18th century) opens out in front of the basilica. The Romanesque entrance to the original 12th-century basilica is inconspicuously off to the side. Work went on for 32 years on the present church, consecrated in 1592. One of its most distinctive features is that it was constructed with Late Gothic rounded arches. The four prophets, on the other hand, are the work of Josep Llimona. The Virgin of Montserrat and Sant Jordi, one should remember, are the patron saints of Catalonia. Understandably, the monastery has always been a stronghold of Catalan tradition.

BARCELONA
(Telephone area code: 93-)
Accommodation
LUXURY: **Hesperia**, C/ Los Vergos 20, Tel: 2045551. **Ramada Renaissance Barcelona**, Ramblas 111, Tel: 3186200. **Colón**, Av. Catedral, 7, Tel: 3011404. **Meliá Barcelona Sarriá**, Av. Sarriá 50, Tel: 4106060. *MODERATE:* **Rey Don Jaime I.**, C/ Jaime I. 11, Tel: 3154161. **Mayoral**, Pl. Real 2, Tel: 3179534. **Montserrat**, Paseo de Gracia 115, Tel: 2172700. **Paseo de Gracia**, Paseo de Gracia 102, Tel: 2155824. **Montecarlo**, Ramblas dels Estudis 124, Tel: 3175800. **Gaudí**, C/ Nou de la Rambla 12, Tel: 3179032. **Astoria**, C/ Paris 203, Tel: 2098311. *BUDGET:* **Rembrandt**, Portaferrisa 23, Tel: 3181011. **Internacional**, Ramblas 78, Tel: 3022566. **La Lonja**, Paseo de Isabel II. 14, Tel: 3193032.

Information / Telecommunication
Oficina de Turismo: Aeropuerto del Prat: 8 a.m.-8 p.m., Sun and public holidays 8 a.m.-3 p.m. Ayuntamiento, Pl. de St. Jaume I, Mon–Fri 9 a.m.-9 p.m., Sat 9 a.m.-2 p.m., Tel: 3182525. Estación de Francia, Mon –Sat 8 a.m.-8 p.m., Tel: 3192791. Generalitat de Catalunya, Gran Vía de les Corts Catalanes 658, Mon – Fri 9 a.m.-1.30 p.m. and 4.30-8.30 p.m., Tel: 3017443. **Post offices:** 9 a.m.-1 p.m. and 5-7 p.m. Main post office: Pl. Antonio López, C/ Aragón 282. **Telefonica**: Pl. de Catalunya.

Transportation
Metro = Underground: Although underground-tickets are valid for travel throughout the underground-network, they don't cover travel on the suburban *Generalitat*trains. Multiple-ride tickets (10 rides on one ticket) are a good bargain. The **Tranvía Azul** (blue tram) departs every half hour from Av. Tibidabo, Balmes to Pl. Dr. Andreu. **Cable Cars**: Funicular Tibidabo, from Pl. Dr. Andreu, 7.30 a.m.–9.20 p.m. Funicular Montjuic, from Av. Parallel to Av. Miramar, 11 a.m.–8.15 p.m., Sundays from 12 noon to 2.45 p.m. and 4.30-9 p.m. Funicular de Vallvidrera, from Av. Vallvidrera to Pl. P. Ventura. Transbordador Aeri del Port (cable car across the harbor), leaves the harbor Torre Sant Sebastiá, glides over to Torre Jaume I. and to Jardins de Miramar, Montjuic, 11 a.m.-6.45 p.m., June to September 11 a.m.–10 p.m. Teleferico de Montjuic, from Av. Miramar on Montjuic to the Castell de Montjuic; runs druing summer weekends only, 11 a.m.-2.45 p.m. and 4–9 p.m. **Golondrinas**: the swallowtail boats flitting across the harbor deparat daily from the Columbus Monument, March – October 10 a.m.-8.30 p.m., and cross over to the jetty in 15 minutes only. **Rail Terminals**: Estación Central,

Barcelona Sants, Pl. Paisos Catalans. Estación de Francia, Paseig Nacional. Estación Cercanías (short-distance trains): Paseig Nacional. Suburban trains (Ferrocarriles de la Generalitat): see section on Pl. Catalunya. **Bus Terminals**: Julia (to Germany, France, Great Britain, Switzerland, Scandinavia, Italy and Portugal): Pl. Universitat 12; Tel: 3183895. Iberbus (France, Belgium, Netherlands, Italy): Av. Parallel 116, Tel: 3296406. Alsina i Graell (to Andorra): Rda. Universitat 4, Tel: 3026545. Les Courriers Catalans (Paris): C/ Pau Clarís 117, Tel: 3025875. **Airport**: 14 km outside of town in Prat de Llobregat. Flight information Tel: 3013993. Train connection from Barcelona Sants station to the airport every 20 minutes from 6 a.m. to 10 p.m. **Passenger Ships**: Estación Baleares, Moll de les Drassanes; Estación Internacional: end of Moll de Barcelona.

Rental Cars / Automobile Club
Avis, C/ Casanova 201; Tel: 2411476. **Hertz**, C/ Tuset 10; Tel: 2178076. **Regente Car**, C/ Aragón 382, Tel: 2452402. **Atesa**, C/ Balmes 141, Tel: 2378140. **Europcar**, C/ Consollde Cent 363, Tel: 2398403. **Rental Motorcycles**: Vanguard, C/ Londres 31, Tel: 2393880. **Real Automobil Club de España**: C/ Sataló 8, Tel: 2003311.

Museums
ON MONTJUIC: **Fundació de Joan Miró**, 11 a.m.-7 p.m.. Sun and public holidays 10.30 a.m. -2.30 p.m., closed Mon. **Museu d'Art de Catalunya** and **Museu de la Ceramica**, 9.30 a.m.-2 p.m., closed Mon. **Museu Arqueológico** and **Museu Etnológico**, 9.30 a.m.-1 p.m., 4-7 p.m., Sun. and public holidays 10 a.m.-2 p.m., closed Mon. **Museu Militar**, Castell de Montjuic, 9 a.m. -2 p.m., 4-7 p.m., Sun. and public holidays 10 a.m.-8 p.m., closed Mon.
MORE MUSEUMS: **Museo Picasso**, C/ Montcada 15-17, 9 a.m.-2 p.m., 4-7 p.m., Sun. and public holidays 9 a.m.-2 p.m., Mon 4-8.30 p.m. **Museu Textil i de L'Indumentaria** (national costumes): C/ Montcada 12, 9 a.m.-2 p.m., 4.30-7 p.m., Sun.and public holidays 9 a.m.-2 p.m., closed Mon. **Museu d'Art Modern**, Parc de la Ciutadella, 9 a.m.-7.30 p.m., Sun. and public holidays 9 a.m.-2 p.m., closed Mon. **Museu de la Ciéncia**, C/ Teodor Riviralta 55, 10 a.m.–8 p.m., closed Mon. **Casa Museu Gaudí**, C/ Olot (inside Parque Güell), 10 a.m.-2 p.m., 4-7 p.m.; closed Dec.-Feb. **Museu del Teatre**, Nou de la Rambla 3 (in the Gaudí-designed Palau Güell), 10 a.m.-1 p.m., 5-7 p.m., closed Sun and public holidays. **Museu de la Historia de la Ciutat**, Pl. del Rei, 9 a.m.-2 p.m., 3.30-8.30 p.m., Sun and public holidays 9 a.m.-2 p.m., Mon 3.30-8.30 p.m. (in

the 15th century Casa Padellas). **Museu Maritim**, Pl. Portal de la Pau 1, 10 a.m.-1.30 p.m., 4-7 p.m., closed Sun/Mon. **Museu de Artes Decorativas**, La Ramblas 99, 10 a.m.-1 p.m. and 4-6 p.m., Sat, Sun and public holidays 10 a.m.-2 p.m. **Museu de la Musica**, Av. Diagonal 373, 9 a.m.-2 p.m., closed Mon (in the modernistic building designed by Puig i Gadafalch). **Museu Clara**, C/ Calatrava 27-29, 9 a.m.-2 p.m., closed Mon. **Museu Frederic Marés**, C/ Comtes de Barcelona 10, 9 a.m.-2 p.m.; 4-7 p.m., closed Sun/Mon. **Museu del Perfum**, Paseig de Grácia 39, 10 a.m.-1.30 p.m. and 4-7 p.m., closed Sat/Sun. **Museu de Zoología** (in the "Expo 1888" exposition complex designed by Domènech i Montaner) Paseig del Tillers, 9 a.m.-2 p.m., closed Mon.

Sightseeing

Pavillon Mies van der Rohe (World Exposition 1929) in the exposition park in front of the Montjuic. **Acuario de la Barceloneta**, Paseig Nacional. **Casa de los Canónigos**, C/ del Bisbe. **Centro Excursionista de Catalunya**, C/ Paradís 10. **El Gran Teatre del Liceu**, Rambla de Caputxins, 61. **La Font Mágica** (fountain) Pl. Carles Buigas. Performance of waterworks Thur, Sat and Sun 9 p.m.-midnight, in winter Sat and Sun 8-11 p.m.**Llotja** (Lonja), Paseig de Isabel II. **Museu-Monestir de Pedralbes** (Monastery-Museum), Baixada del Monestir, 9: 9.30 a.m.-2 p.m., closed Mon; Metro: Palau Reial. **Museu Futbol Club Barcelona**, Arístides Maillol, Estadio C.F. Barcelona, 10 a.m.-1 p.m. and 4-6 p.m., Sun and public holidays 10 a.m.-1 p.m., closed Mon. **Palau (Palacio) de la Música Catalana**, C/ Amadeu Vives 1, modernistic building by Domènech i Montaner. **Palacio Real Mayor** and Salon de Tinell, 14th century. **Parque Güell**, by Antoní Gaudí, C/ Olot. **Planetarium de Barcelona**, C/ Escoles Pies 103, Demonstration 9.30, 10.30, 11 a.m., 3 and 5 p.m., Sun 12 noon, 1 and 6.30 p.m., closed Sat. **Poble Español**, Av. Marques de Comillas, Parc de Montjuic, 9 a.m.-8 p.m., in winter until 7 p.m. (Restaurants may close later). **Sagrada Familia**, Pl. de la Sagrada Familia. **Museum of Waxworks**, La Rambla 4-6. **Zoo**, Parc de la Ciutadella, 9.30 a.m.-7.30 p.m. *CHURCHES:* **Cathedral. Sta. María del Mar,** 14th century. **Sta. María del Pino**, 14th century, Pl. del Pi. **San Pablo** (Pau) del Campo 12th–14th century, C/ Huerto de San Pablo. **La Mercé**, 18th century, Pl. de la Mercé.

Restaurants

CATALAN: **Can Massana**, Pl. del Camp 6; **Agut**, C/ Gignás 16; **Agut d'Avignon**, C/ Trinitat, 3; **El Petit Dorado**, C/ Dolors Moncerdá 51; **Florian**, C/ Beltrand i Serra 20; **Gargantúa i**

Pantagruel, C/ Aragó 214; **Gran Colmado**, C/ Consell de Cent 318.
FISH: **Casa Chus**, Av. Diagonal 339; **Senyor Parellada**, C/ Argentería 37; **Can Majó**, C/ Almirante Aixada 23. For good restaurants also try the La Barceloneta quarter.
SPANISH: **Azulete**, Via Augusta 281; **La Balsa**, C/ Infanta Isabel 4; **Cas Isidro**, C/ Flors 12; **Tirton**, C/ Alfambra 16; **Botafumeiro** (Galician), C/ Gran de Grácia 81; **Elche** (Valentian), C/ Vila i Vilá 71; **Amaya** (Basque), **La Rambla**, 20; **Gorria** (Basque), C/ Diputacio 421; **La Troballa**, C/ Riera San Miguel 69.
VEGETARIAN: **Illa de Gracia**, Domenec 15; **Macrobiotico Zen**, Muntaner, 12; **Govinda**, Pl. Villa de Madrid 4-5;
DISCOTHEQUES: **Distrito Distinto**, Av. Meridiana, 104; **Studio 54**, Av. Parallel 54; **Up and Down**, C/ Numancia 179. *MUSIC BARS:* **Els Quatre Gats**, C/ Montsió 5 (Jazz); **Sisisi** (Jazz), Av. Diagonal 442; **Este Bar**, C/ Consell de Cent 257; **Frank Dube**, C/ Buscarons 24; **Humedad Relativa**, Pl. Mañe i Flaquer 9; **King Bar**, Av. Diagonal 618; **Mas i Mas**, C/ María Cubí 199 (St. Gervasi); **Metropol**, Passage Domingo 3; **Mirablau**, Pl. del Funicular, Mirasol, Pl. del Sol 3; **Nick Havanna**, C/ Roselló 208 (Eixample); **Particular**, Av. Tibidabo 61 (Sarriá-St. Gervasi); **Universal**, C/ María Cubí 182-184 (St. Gervasi); **Velvet**, C/ Balmes, 161 (Eixample); **Zig-Zag**, C/ Platón, 13 (Sarriá, St. Gervasi); **Boliche**, Av. Diagonal 508.
FLAMENCO BARS: **Bandolero**, C/ Muntaner 244; **El Patio Andaluz**, C/ Anibal 242; **El Cordobés**, Rambla Caputxins 35; **Blanca Paloma**, C/ Napols, 222.

Festivals / Public Holidays

April 23 *Sant Jordi* (St. George), patron saint of Catalonia; May 11 *Fiesta Sant Ponç*; market for herbs and health food in the C/ del Hospital; June 24 *San Juan*, street festival during the night from June 23 – 24. September 11 is the *Diada*, the Catalan national holiday; September 24 *Virgen de la Merced*, patron saint of Barcelona; Fiesta in the town quarter Gràcia around August 15. **Bullfights**, are not as common in Catalonia as in other parts of Spain. In Barcelona they take place on Sundays from April to October: Plaza de Toros Monumental, Gran Vía Corts Catalans, 747.

Shopping

Boutiques: Luxury fashion and jewellery shops offer their goods on the Paseig de Grácia between Pl. Cataluña and Av. Diagonal; **Antiques:** Centro de Anticuarios, Paseo de Grácia, 55. **Craft Shops:** Artespaña, Rambla de Cataluña, 75.

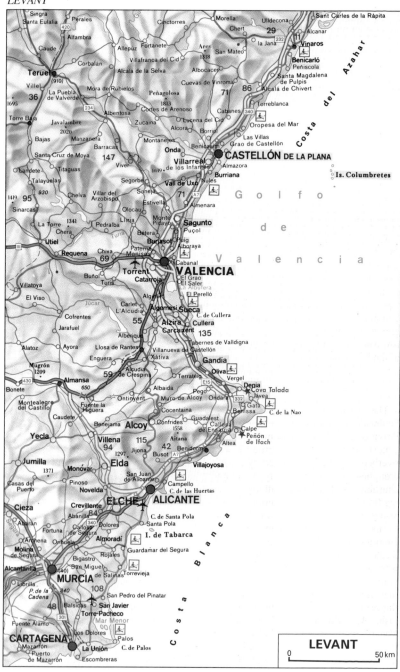

THE LEVANT

CASTELLÓN
VALENCIA
COSTA BLANCA

The region of Valencia begins south of the Ebro delta. It is a strip along the Mediterranean comprising three provinces: Castellón de la Plana, Valencia and Alicante. Despite its small size, however, the topography of the region is diverse, with a mountainous interior and a coastal region which industry, agriculture and tourism have made the most prosperous part of the Iberian Peninsula.

CASTELLÓN

The mountains framing the Iberian Peninsula run down to the coast in the Province of Castellón, leaving a deserted, almost arid landscape furrowed with riverbeds. Normally wracked by terrible droughts, they periodically turn into churning torrents after cloudbursts, causing flood disasters. This interior strip has always served to defend the rich coastal towns, as any number of forts (Biar, Villena) and fortified settlements would indicate. After the Reconquista, the country was settled by Castilians who planted grain, vineyards and olives and drove their flocks of sheep across it. However, this arid zone does have enticing spots to visit. **Morella,** on the land side of Vonarós, is the gateway to Valencia from Aragón. Since Roman times it has been a defensive stronghold. Impregnably and

suberbly situated at 1000 m (3280 ft) above sea-level, it is surrounded by two kilometers of fortifications with three gates. Through the San Mateo Gate one reaches the medieval core over a road with 303 steps. The Gothic church of Sta. María, which is fortified and at the wall, has a 15th century choir reached by yet another stair. The palace of Cardinal Ram is now, most appropriately, a hotel. In the nearby **Valltorta Gorge**, megalithic wall paintings have been found. The **Civil Caves**, discovered by a member of the Guardia Civil, and the **Cueva de los Caballos** with its Stone Age drawings of horses are particularly remarkable.

To the south, on the road between Sagunto and Teruel, is **Segorbe,** Roman *Segobriga*. It has a magnificent cathedral which has retained its original Gothic tower, cloister and chapter house. Among the treasures exhibited in the museum are works of El Greco and Donatello. The present town hall of the village is the Baroque palace of the Medinaceli. In the vicinity there are the remains of a Roman aqueduct and the **Santa Cueva**, a vernacular chapel in a cave. One has to descend 80 steps to get to it. From here there are splendid views of the Sierra del Espadán. A day's excursion to Segorbe can be rounded off by a visit to medieval **Jérica** and the fort of Amonacíd.

The Huerta

The *huertas* extend along nearly the entire 480 km (300 mi) of coastal plain at the foot of the mountains. The motorway and the old road run from north to south through lush, seemingly endless gardens and fields planted with oranges, rice and vegetables which yield up to three crops a year. It was Arabs from Syria who laid the groundwork of agrarian prosperity in the area by expanding the Roman irrigation system. It is somehow reassuring that parts of it are still operating. With them, the Arabs brought citrus and mulberry trees. The latter became the basis of one of the most important industries: silk weaving. When the last of the Moriscos had been expelled from the country in 1609 by Philip III, many crafts, including silk weaving, came to a halt.

Above: The Huerta near Valencia is an ideal place to grow pineapples. Right: Paella comes in different variants in Valencia.

The Valencian coast was conquered in 1245 by Jaime I of Aragón and Castile and resettled by Catalans. Today the region is bilingual. It is interesting to note that Valencian is considered a Catalan dialect. From the 15th century the region underwent an upswing which was interrupted first by the rising of the "Germanias" against Charles V in 1521, and then by the War of the Spanish Succession against Philip V in 1701. The 20th century brought intensive industrialisation, particularly to the south, which is still going on. In the 1960s tourism discovered the mild local climate with its mean annual temperature of 20° C (68° F) and 300 days of sun. Holiday resorts mushroomed, often leaving the beaches in deplorable condition. In recent years the regional administration, the Generalitat Valenciana, has done its best to bring ecological damage under control.

The coastal towns are largely agrarian in character. Unlike some other parts of the country they do not look back on a glorious past. Nevertheless, it is fascinat-

ing to keep in mind that many towns have names of Arabic derivation. The prefix "Beni", meaning "son of", preceded the names of the original owners of the farms. Unlike most other Spanish ethnic groups, the Valencians have little or no tradition of folk dancing and songs. This is allegedly due to their boundless enthusiasm for gunpowder which was introduced to Europe by the Arabs, who were the first to deploy it strategically. It seems to have been "burnt into" *huerta* customs to such an extent that *fiestas* invariably turn into bursts of gunfire and firework displays: the *Fallas* of Valencia, the *Hogueras* of San Juan in Alicante and the *Moros y Christianos* of Alcoy. But tradition has survived in the regional costumes. Many a Valenciana thinks nothing of spending several million pesetas on her *fallera*. Tradition lives on in the bands, too, in the Habaneras Festival at Torrevieja, and particularly in the regional cuisine. Gastronomically speaking, this is rice country. Over 20,000 ha of it are cultivated. Rice dishes range

from the famous *paella* with all its variations – with white beans or turnips, if nothing else is available, but otherwise meat or shellfish – to "seafarer" rice dishes in the south and rice baked with pork. These are complicated dishes to prepare, yet plain good cooking rather than haute cuisine.

Costa del Azahar

"Azahar" means "citrus blossoms" – white with a pervasive fragrance among glossy green leaves. The saying goes that if one wanders into an orange grove at dawn, one may become intoxicated by the scent and not sober up until the next day. Orange blossoms are so important here that bridal bouquets are known as "azahar" bouquets. At orange blossom time, the scent pervades the countryside, and the trees, simultaneously bearing fruit, look like a fairytale.

The first place of note, **Peñiscola,** is a rocky promontory jutting up out of the sea with a walled town. The link with the

95

mainland is a popular beach. Its strategic position has always made the spot important. After being taken by the Moors, it was handed over to the Templars, who built the fort. The antipope at Avignon, Benidict XIII, Pedro de Luna, refused to bow to the might of Rome. In 1412 he fled here with his following and enlarged the fortifications. In the reign of Philip II they were strengthened again. They were thus well able to withstand various sieges in the War of the Spanish Succession and the French War.

Benicasim is the most important seaside resort in the area. Old villas, squeezed between hotels and blocks of flats, line the seafront boulevard.

Up in the steep coastal range is the "Palm Desert". There, amid lush vegetation, Carmelite nuns brew a liqueur just as they did in the 18th century. From the peak one can see as far as the **Colum-**

Above: The fortress of the Knights Templar at Peñiscola. Right: Papier-mâché scenes at the Fallas in Valencia.

bretes Islands, small volcanic islands 50 km (31 mi) off shore. They are named after the snakes which infested them until swine were set loose to destroy the reptiles. The islands are now a natural park.

Castellón, Vila Real and Burriana together form the conurbation about the port of El Grau and the Millars estuary. These are quiet *huerta* towns, moulded by both agriculture and industry, without distinctive historic cores. In them one can still find restaurants serving local cuisine without having to pay tourist prices.

The walls of **Sagunto** rise above endless orange groves. The town was by turns an Iberian, Roman and Arab fortified settlement. It gave rise to the Iberian heroic epic on the battle of the Romans and their allies against Carthaginian invaders in 219 BC. The townspeople preferred collective suicide to surrender. The historians Polibius and Livy immortalised the story. Rome rewarded the town's loyalty by making it one of the major centers of the Province of Hispania. The Roman theater held

8000 spectators; a view of the sea and the *huerta* served as a backdrop. By the river are the ruins of an amphitheater. Excavation finds can be viewed in the archaeological museum housed in the fort. The old town has a well preserved Jewish quarter with narrow alleys and traditional houses. The picturesque town is unfortunately in the grip of an industrial crisis. As a result, the blast furnaces, fed by the mines of the Ojos Negros, have nearly all shut down.

VALENCIA

Not far from Sagunto, the alluvial plain of the Turia broadens out into the *huerta* of Valencia. At its heart is Spain's third largest city. The river has been diverted into a sophisticated system of irrigation canals. The *huerta* is densely populated with numerous scattered fruit and vegetable farming towns. They are linked by good rail connections to the city, which are being extended into an underground rail network. The most important

spots to visit are the monastery at **Puig,** the stronghold of Valencian nationalism; **Monte Picayo,** with its casino in the midst of orange groves and guest cottages, and **Alboraya.** The last is known for its *chufa* crop. These are small tubers from which *horchata*, popular throughout Spain, is made. Horchata is a milky, refreshing drink rich in vitamins and with a distinctive, elusive taste.

To the east are **Manises** and **Paterna.** The pottery from these towns has been highly esteemed since the Middle Ages. To the south is **Sueca,** the rice-growing capital. The traditional local country dwellings, *barracas*, those simple wattle and daub structures which inspired the Blasco Ibañez' novel of that title, have virtually disappeared. Industrialisation in the past century has subjected the entire *huerta* to profound changes.

Valencia is the largest city in the Spanish Levante and the market center for the surrounding region. People come from all the nearby villages to spend the money they have earned from the orange

97

crop. The city is on the right bank of the Turia. The river has been diverted, leaving the riverbed to be landscaped into vast gardens and a park. The Catalan architect Bofill has been charged with this project. In recent decades the city has sprawled, gradually converging with the port of **El Grao**. The city's enormous growth has crowded out the old core. Little remains of its Roman, Arab or Renaissance past.

The city's center is its social center, as well. Everyone congregates here to drink coffee or *horchata* and to go shopping. They all seem to drop by several times a day. The city hall square is a magnet. No matter where one goes, this is where one ends up. The buildings framing the square are ornate. Their crenelation, sculptures and small temples make quite a cosmopolitan impression. The 18th century **city hall** houses the Tourist Information and the Historical Museum. In the latter, highly symbolic objects are displayed: the Senyera, the standards carried by Jaime I when he took the city from the Arabs in 1238; codices containing the *fueros*, privileges granted to the city; documents on the Consolat del Mar, a sort of maritime law commission; and the Taula de Cancis, the earliest document of Spanish dealings in foreign currency.

Where the old Roman road from Rome to Cádiz ran, San Vicente Street leads into the old city. The **cathedral** stands on the site of the Roman temple of Diana. A later mosque on the site was replaced by a Christian church after the first conquest by El Cid in 1095. Work on the present building began in 1262 and was finished in the 15th century. Every Thursday at 12 noon the Water Tribunal meets in front of the Gothic apostles' portal. One of the most venerable institutions of the *huerta*, this court still has jurisdiction over all issues and disputes connected with irrigation. Its seven officials, representatives of the estates irrigated by the seven canals of the Turia, decide what should be done

in each case after hearing the farmers' grievances. Their decisions cannot be appealed. On entering the cathedral through the Romanesque **Portal del Palau**, one stands in front of Ausias March's tomb. He was a great Valencian poet. The chapel of Santo Cáliz keeps the Holy Grail (one of the chalices) used at the Last Supper. The interior of the cathedral is mainly exuberant Baroque. The octagonal bell-tower, **Torre del Micalet**, is 14th century. It is 50.85 m (167 ft) in height as well as in circumference. One must climb 207 steps to reach the 12 bells spanning a full octave of seven tones and five semitones.

Next to the cathedral is the church of the **Virgen de los Desamperados,** Our Lady of the Defenceless, who is the patron saint of the city. On feast days Valencians bring abundant offerings of flowers. Many of the Valencian girls are christened *Amparo,* "Defence". The 14th century Gothic **Palace of the Regional Government** is on the same square. The Quart and Serranos towers housing the maritime museum are Gothic military structures.

Another meeting place is the market, Pl. del Mercado, a bustling agrarian plaza framed by three interesting buildings. The **Llotja**, once the Silk Exchange, was built in the 15th century by Valencia's oldest bank, the Taula. The old hall with its twisted columns houses the **Ninot Museum**. A tower forms the central section of the building, the Renaissance tract which houses the Consolat del Mar, the Maritime Commission. On the façade above the capital a figure being flogged serves as a warning to all too wily brokers. The **central market** is a 20th century Modernist building housing 1300 stalls on a floor space of 8000 square metres (9568 sq yd). The weather vane, a parrot, revolves above the dome. The third important building on the market place is the church of **Santos Juanes.** One of the oldest parish churches in the

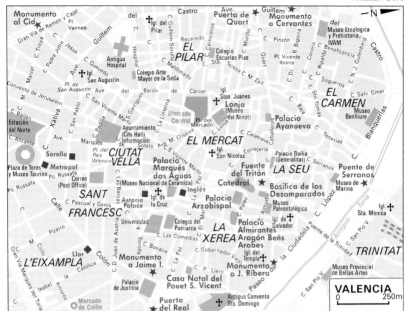

city, it was renovated in the Baroque style in the 17th century. This is where the patron saint of the *huerta*, San Vicente Ferrer, is said to have thrown a handkerchief into the air during a sermon. It came to earth again in a house in Tapinería Street. There a family was found to be dying of starvation and was saved through the saint's timely intervention. A tiled altar commemorates the miracle.

Between the market place and San Vicente Street is the round plaza known as **El Clot**. Laid out in 1831 to tidy up the chaotic street market, it has retained its traditional ambience of bars and haberdasher's shops. In fact, the whole city center is full of restaurants, bars and cafés where one can try chocolate with pumpkin profiteroles *(buñuelos de calabaza),* a *horchata* or, of course, *paella.*

Among Valencia's museums, the **Museo de Bellas Artes** is outstanding. Numerous works of Valencian Renaissance and Baroque artists are here: locals like Ribera, Ribalta, Masip and Juan de Juanes but also "foreigners" like El Greco, Goya, Velázquez, Van Dyck, Vicente López, Madrazo and Maella. There is also a collection of 16th and 17th century paintings in the **Colegio del Patriarca,** a venerable Renaissance palace. The **Museo Nacional de Cerámica** houses superb collections. In addition to regional and Spanish pottery, these include oriental and Saxon porcelain and one-of-a-kind signed pieces by celebrities like Picasso or Benlliure. The most admired room is, however, the reconstruction of a traditional Valencian kitchen. The **Palace of the Marqués de Dos Aguas,** one of the handsomest of 18th century Baroque buildings, houses the museum. Its architect, Ignacio Vergara, died insane. The mysterious figures on his superb portal are said to reflect his mental derangement.

Finally, on the far side of the river, the Valencian Institute of Modern Art (**IVAM),** is a must. In it, Spanish avantgarde works are exhibited, notably those of the Valencian Equipo Crónica, a milestone in Spanish Pop Art.

The Spanish comic strip tradition comes into its own in Valencia, particularly at the popular Feast of St Joseph, the *Fallas*. Streets and plazas in the city and outlying villages are transformed into gigantic cardboard comic strips. In Valencia alone over 3000 such monuments of cardboard art are displayed from 15 - 19 March. Most of them are caricatures. They are judged and awarded prizes before being ceremoniously burnt to put the immortality of art to the test. Only one is kept each year to be put into the **Museo del Ninot.** Considering how heavily built up the city center is, it is amazing that there are so few fires at these pyromaniac sprees. Music and garlands, but also continual bursts of gunfire and fireworks accompany the festivities. Vivacious *falleras*, the festival queens of the various associations putting on the *Fallas*, appear in regional costumes.

Harbors and Beaches

Valencians tend to use the beaches north and south of **El Grao** harbor. Despite the often rather uninviting water, these beaches are well worth a visit if only because of the vast array of restaurants serving the best *paella* in the Levante. Malvarrosa beach is frequented by the young. Here, restaurants tend to be bars and are open all night in the summer.

The **Albufera,** "lake" in Arabic, is one of Spain's major wetland bird sanctuaries. Swamps, ponds and the open lake are fed by the floodwaters of the Júcar and Turia. Their alluvial deposits are such that the wetlands area has been reduced to a tenth of what it was in Roman times. Draining and channelling the water for rice growing have accelerated the process, endangering the endemic flora and fauna. The large lagoon is linked to the sea by several canals. It has small ports

Right: The number of fishermen remains constant, but there are fewer fish.

where boats laden with rice can dock. The strip of land between the coast and the Albufera is known as **El Saler.** Here, shaded by thick pine woods, are the region's best beaches. Nazaret, Pinedo, Saler and La Dehesa are virtually deserted in the off season. To the south they are linked with beaches stretching for kilometers. The most popular towns are Cullera and Gandía. The small town of **Cullera,** overshadowed by a scenic rock topped by a fort and a pilgrims' chapel, is thronged with upwards of 100,000 visitors in summer. **Gandía** is the market town for the 30 villages in its *huerta*. This strip of land was once farmed by Moriscos. It was under the sway of the Aragonese family of Borja. They bought the title of Dukes of Gandía from Ferdinand the Catholic. Using money and influence, they also climbed high in the Church hierarchy, ultimately getting to Italy. The family became famous for its popes, saints like the Jesuit general San Francisco, and the many intrigues it involved itself in. Cesare and Lucrezia Borgia, as the name was written in Italian, were the illegitimate children of Pope Alexander VI. The fall of the family in Italy was engineered by their political adversaries, the Sforzas.

The ducal palace of the Borja at Gandía, a handsome Renaissance building, belongs to the Jesuits. Its magnificent halls house a museum. The collegiate chapel is pure Catalan Gothic. Its altar retable by Damian Forment is well worth a visit. **Játiva** in the interior also has links with the Borjas. It was the birthplace of the two popes. Palaces from the period when the Borjas made the town important still line **Calle Montcada**. In the church, known locally as "Seu" although it was never a cathedral, is the tomb of Archbishop Juan Borja. Like the altar by Ventura Rodríguez, it reveals elements of Renaissance elegance. In the War of the Spanish Succession, Philip V took Játiva, which had sided with the Habsburgs, by

force. He renamed it San Felipe, which it remained until 1811. In retaliation, the town museum has hung the portrait of Philip V upside down. The fort, Roman in origin, was a state prison for a long time. From it one has the best views over the town and the *huerta*.

COSTA BLANCA

The Sierra Aitana, the southernmost ridges of the Baetic Range traversing Andalusia, extends as far as **Cabo de la Nao** at the southern end of the Gulf of Valencia. Beyond Denia, the coast becomes more mountainous and the landscape more arid. Almond blossoms, chalky soil and white sand have given this section of the coast its name: the White Coast. **Denia,** at the foot of the Montgó Range, is called the gateway to the Costa Blanca. The core of the old town is picturesque. The fort above it houses the archaeological museum with Roman and Arab finds from the town's past. In the vicinity there are caves, such as the **Cova Tallada** ex-

tending 150 m (495 ft) under the sea, the **Cova de l'Aigua** or **Cova del Camell.**

Jávea is on Cabo de la Nao. The town's fortified Gothic church served as a refuge from pirate raids. Despite the inroads of tourism one still finds secluded coves and lovely walks through fir woods to the lighthouse or an old monastery. To the south at **Calpe,** the **Peñón de Ifach,** a massive monolith 328 m (1076 ft) high, is visible from a great distance. The regional government recently designated it a protected area to save it from being inundated with tourists.

Altea, reached by steep lanes and steps, has been almost absorbed by the moloch of Benidorm. Yet on its land side there are still some tranquil spots. Near it is a beautiful park with over 1500 species of cactus and subtropical plants. The road into the Sierra in the direction of **Alcoy,** which is famous for *Moros y Christianos* festivities, runs over numerous bridges. Here one often spots the devotees of a new sport for those with good heads for heights, *puenting*. This perhaps foolhardy

pursuit involves daring jumps from bridges into the depths. **Guadalest,** on a small reservoir, is well fortified and hidden by an outcropping of rock.

Alicante is not a city in which one does a lot of sightseeing. One strolls along the seafront, sits on a terrace with one's back to the high-rises, and enjoys the sweeping view over the sea which one hundred thousand Spanish old-age pensioners have in winter. The original Greek settlers named it *Akra Leuka* and the Romans *Castrum Album*. Both mean "White Fortress". To get the most out of the panoramic view from the fort of Santa Bárbara, one can be both lazy and venturesome and take the old-age pensioners' lift up Benacantil Mountain rising behind the town beach of **Postiguet**. From there, the towers of the Renaissance church of San Nicolás , and the Baroque Santa María can be picked out against the white town.

Above: When evening cools the air, women sit before their houses to do handiwork.

PROVINCE CASTELLÓN
(Telephone area code 964-)
Accommodation
CASTELLÓN: *LUXURY:* **Mindoro,** C/ Moyano 4, Tel: 222340. **Del Golf,** Playa del Pinar, Tel: 221950. *MODERATE:* **Amat,** C/ Temprado 15. Tel: 220600. **Doña Lola,.** C/ Lucena 3. Tel: 214011.
PEÑÍSCOLA: *LUXURY:* **Hostería del Mar,** Ave. Papa Luna 18, Tel:480600. **Papa Luna,** Ave. Papa Luna 6, Tel 480760.
MODERATE: **Playa,** C/ Primo de Rivera 32, Tel: 480760. *BUDGET:* **El Prado,** Ave. Papa Luna 3, Tel: 480289.
BENICASSIM: *LUXURY:* **Azor,** P. Marítimo, Tel. 300350. **Trinimar,** Ave. Ferrándiz Salvador, Tel:300850. *MODERATE:* **Tramontana,** P. Marítimo, Tel: 300300. *BUDGET:* **Benicasim,** C/ Bayer 50, Tel: 300558.
MORELLA: *MODERATE:* **Hostal Cardenal Ram,** Cuestra Suñer 2, Tel: 160000.
Museums / Sightseeing
PEÑÍSCOLA: Castillo: 10 a.m.–7 p.m.
CASTELLÓN: Museo de Bellas Artes und Museo Etnológico: 10 a.m.-2 p.m. and 4-6 p.m., Sat 10 a.m.-2 p.m., closed Sun. **Museo de Artesanía:** 10 a.m.-1 p.m. and 4-6 p.m., Sat 10 a.m.-1 p.m., closed Sun.
MORELLA: Museo Arciprestal: 11 a.m.-2 p.m. and 3–5 p.m.
SEGORBE: Museo Catredralicio: 11 a.m.-1 p.m.; additional opening Wed and Sun 4-7 p.m., closed Sun. **Museo Municipal:** Sat 4-6 p.m. and Sun 11 a.m.-1 p.m.
Restaurants
CASTELLÓN: Mesón Navarro, Pl. Tetuán 26. **Pairal,** C/ Dr. Fleming 24. **Nostra Casa,** C/ Isidro Villarroig 16. Tapa-bars in the streets Isaac Peral, Pl. Sta. Clara, Pl. de la Paz.
EL GRAO (harbor): **Nina y Angelo,** Paseo Buenavista.
Information / Oficina de Turismo
CASTELLÓN: Oficina de Turismo. C/ María Agustina 5, Tel: 227703

PROVINCE VALENCIA
(Telephone area code 96-)
Accommodation
VALENCIA: *LUXURY:* **Sidi Saler Palace-Sol,** Playa del Saler, Tel:1610411. **Parador Luis Vives,** Carretera del Saler, Tel:1611186. **Astoria Palace,** Pza. Rodrigo Botet 5, Tel:3526737.
MODERATE: **Inglés,** C/ Marqués de Dos Aguas 6, Tel: 3516426. **Oltra,** Pza. del Ayuntamiento 4, Tel: 3520612. *BUDGET:* **Bristol,** C/ San Martín 3. Tel: 3521176. **Hotel Continental,** C/

Correos 8, Tel: 3510926. **Alcázar**, Mosén Fernándes 11, Tel: 3529575.

ALZIRA: *MODERATE:* **Monasterio Aguas Vivas**, Ctra. Alzira – Tabernes at km 11, Tel: 2589011.

CULLERA: *MODERATE:* **Carabela II**, Av. País Valenciano 61, Tel: 1724070. *BUDGET:* Hostal El Cordobés, Ctra. del Estany, Tel: 1722323. **Hostal La Reina**, Av. País Valenciano 73, Tel: 1720563.

Museums / Sightseeing

VALENCIA: **Museo Bellas Artes**: 10 a.m.–2 p.m. and 4-6 p.m., Sundays and public holidays 10 a.m.-2 p.m., closed Mon. **Museo de la Catedral y Miguelete**: 10 a.m.-1 p.m. and 4–6 p.m. November - March: 10 a.m.-1 p.m. **Museo del Patriarca**: 11 a.m.-1.30 p.m. **Museo de Prehistoria y Etnológico**: 10 a.m.-2 p.m. and 4.30-6.30 p.m., Sundays and public holidays 10 a.m.-2 p.m., closed Mon. **IVAM** (Instituto Valenciano de Arte Moderno): 11 a.m.-8 p.m., closed Mon. **Casa-Museo José Benlliure**: 10 a.m.–1 p.m. and 4-6 p.m., Sat 10 a.m.-1 p.m., closed Sundays, Mondays and public holidays. **La Lonja**: 10 a.m.-2 p.m. and 4-6 p.m., Sundays 10 a.m.-1.30 p.m., closed Sun and Mon.

GANDÍA: **Palacio Ducal**: 10 a.m.-12 noon, 5-7 p.m. (in winter 11 a.m.-12 noon and 5-6 p.m.).

SAGUNTO: **Castillo** and **Teatro Romano**: 10 a.m.-8 p.m. (in winter: 10 a.m.–2 p.m. and 4-6 p.m.), Sun 10 a.m.-2 p.m., closed Mon.

Restaurants

VALENCIA: Rice specialities: **Larraz**, Ave Navarro Reverter 16. Rue de la Paix, C/ Paz 58. **Casa Vella**, C/ Roteros 25. (You'll find plenty of restaurants and eateries on Roteros Street). **La Forqueta D'Or**, C/ Rubén Vela 17. **Gure Etxea**, C/ Almirante Cadarso 6. **La Lluna** (vegetarian food) C/ San Ramón 23. **Gárgola**, C/ Caballeros 8. Restaurante **Palace Fesol**. C/Hernán Cortés 7. Restaurante **Játiva**, C/Játiva 14. Restaurante **la Taula**. C/ Pascual y Genís 3. Restaurante **Gula-Gula**. Na Jordana 3.

Information / Transportation

VALENCIA: Oficina Municipal de Turismo: Pza. del Ayuntamiento 1, Tel. 3510417, 8.30 a.m.-2.30 p.m. and 4-6.30 p.m., Sat 9 a.m.-1 p.m. C/ de la Paz 48, Tel: 3524000.

The airport is situated 8 km outside Valencia, Tel: 3709500. **Iberia Information**, Tel: 3519737. The port of Valencia (Grao) is 4 km from the city center. **Passenger Ship Information**, Tel: 3236512. Cía Transmediterránea, Tel: 3676512. **Train Information** Renfe, Tel: 3513612. **Ferrocarrils Generalitat Valenciana**, C/ Cronista Rivelles. Tel: 3472669. **Bus**

Terminal: Avda. Menéndez Pidal. Tel. 3497222. **Suburban Transportation**: Four train lines run from the villages of the *huerta* to the harbor. **SAGUNTO**: Oficina de Turismo: Pl. Cronista Chabret: weekdays 9.30 a.m.–2 p.m. and 4–6.30 p.m. (in summer until 8 p.m.); Sat 10 a.m.–2 p.m. and 5–8 p.m., Sun 10.30 a.m.–1 p.m.

PROVINCE ALICANTE

(Telephone area code 96-)

Accommodation

ALICANTE: *LUXURY:* **Gran Sol**, Ave. Méndez Núñez 3, Tel: 5203000. **Meliá Alicante**, Playa Postiguet, Tel. 5205000. *MODERATE:* **Cristal**, C/ López Torregrosa 9, Tel:5209600. *BUDGET:* Bahía, C/ Gravina 14, Tel: 206522.

BENIDORM: *LUXURY:* **Delfín**: Playa de Poniente – La Cala. Tel:5853400. **Avenida**, C/ Martínez Alejos 5, Tel: 5854100.

BUDGET: **Mar Blau**, C/ San Pedro 20, Tel: 5851646. **Iris**, C/ La Palma 47, Tel: 5853129.

Museums / Sightseeing

ALICANTE: **Castillo Sta. Barbara**: 10 a.m.-8 p.m., in winter 9 a.m.-7 p.m. **Museo de Arte – 20th century**.: 10.30 a.m.-1.30 p.m., 6-9 p.m., Oct–April: 10 a.m.-1 p.m., 5-8 p.m., closed Mon. **Cathedral**: 8 a.m.-12.30 p.m. and 6-8.30 p.m., Sun 9 a.m.-1.45 p.m. **Monasterio de Sta. Faz** (4 km in the direction of Valencia): 10 a.m.-1 p.m. and 4-8 p.m., closed on weekends.

ALCOY: **Museo de Moros y Cristianos** (in the Casal de San Jordi): Tue – Fri 11 a.m.-1 p.m. and 5.30-8 p.m.

Restaurants

ALICANTE: **Dársena**, Muelle del Puerto. **Regina**, Ave. Niza 19, Playa de San Juan. **La Tapeta**, Serrano 7. **Delfín**, Explanada de España 15. **Nou Manolín**, C/ Villegas 3.

BAHÍA: **Carretera de Alicante** s/n. Benidorm: **La Caserola**, Ave. Bruselas 7. **La Cocina**, Ave. Alcoy s/n.

CALPE: **Capri**, Ave. Gabriel Miró. **El Girasol**, Carretera de Moraira at km 1.

DENIA: **El Pegolí**, Playa les Rotes.

Information / Transportation

ALICANTE: Oficina de Turismo: Pl. de la Explanada 2, Tel: 5212285; Plaza del Ayuntamiento 1, Tel: 5205100 and 5200000.

Passenger Ships: Minicruceros: Marítima de Formentera, Tel: 5206129. Alicante – Ibiza, Transmediterránea, Tel: 5206011. Isla Tabarca, Tel: 5283736.

BENIDORM: Oficinas de Turismo: Ave. Martínez Alejo 16, Tel: 5853224 and Ave Marina Española, Tel: 5853075. **Post Office**: C/ Las Herrerías.

103

EAST ANDALUSIA

MURCIA
CARTAGENA
GRANADA
JAÉN
ALMERÍA
THE ALPUJARRAS
MÁLAGA
COSTA DEL SOL

The lush and verdant *huertas* of the Levante with their superabundance of glowing oranges stretch as far as the Segura Valley and the small autonomous region of Murcia. Beyond it rise the Sierras of the encircling Baetic Range. This is where the eight provinces of Andalusia begin. Representing a cross section of Spanish topography, they extend from the desert of Almería to Spain's mountains with the highest annual rainfall, the Sierra of Cádiz, from the Mediterranean to the Atlantic, and from the Sierra Nevada to the Guadalquivir Basin.

Elche and Murcia: Garden Landscapes

The inland route through a country of orchards and palm groves bears little resemblance to the arid coastal region. The palm groves are one of the most important sources of income for the city of **Elche,** where over 100,000 trees produce dates. They are also a part of Elche's charm. When walking through the park or the priest's garden, the **Huerto del Cura**, one cannot help getting the feeling of being in Africa. In August the unique *El Misteri* is performed anually in the

Left: A well-earned break from labor in the fields, a necessity in the midday heat.

church of Sta. María. The medieval mystery play on the miracle of the Ascension of the Virgin is staged under the dome of the church. The actors descend from the heavenly heights by means of ropes or mechanical devices – an overwhelming dramatic and musical experience.

Near Elche is **La Alcudia,** the site of the archaeological excavation where the beautiful Iberian sculpture of a woman's head, famous among art lovers as the *Dama de Elche*, came to light in 1897. The original was sold to the Louvre for 4000 pesetas, but it was later presented to the Prado.

The road goes on to the valley of the Segura, which often floods the entire plain. The lower parts of the houses here are colored brown with the mud washed up by the floodwaters, and applied like coats of dull paint. **Orihuela** was the birthplace of the poet Miguel Hernández. Its ambience, at once aristocratic and clerical, is not matched elsewhere in the region. Numerous churches testify to its affluent past: **Santiago** and the Gothic cathedral of **El Salvador** with its Romanesque cloister, Sta Justa and Sta. Rufina. The Renaissance buildings of the Colegio Sto. Domingo with its Baroque church once housed the **old university.** The cathedral museum boasts Velázquez' *Temptation of St Thomas* as well as works

105

of Morales and Juan de Juanes. From the 15th century **Seminar San Miguel** there is a sweeping view over the city, the palm groves, so reminiscent of Africa, and the floodplain.

MURCIA

Further up the Segura River lies **Murcia.** The city was founded in the early Moorish period, when it was the capital of the Kingdom of Murcia. Taken in 1266 by Jaime I of Aragón, Murcia was soon ceded to the Crown of Castile.

Its Moorish past lives on in the gardens of the surrounding, fertile floodplain. These wonders of hydraulic engineering were the work of ingenious Arab engineers, who laid out everything from reservoirs and a sophisticated system of canals, to irrigation ditches and shallow wells that enabled river water to reach each allotment. Some of these marvels of early medieval agriculture are still in use, such as the Ñora a few kilometers outside the city. The **Museum of the Huerta de Alcantarilla** offers a highly informative introduction to this gardening system which has only begun to be equalled in the latter half of the 20th century.

The Segura was always the source of the region's prosperity. It also bisects the city and is thus an important urban planning parameter. A walk along the **Malecon** takes one from the lush gardens of the floodplain, the *huerta*, up to the old city's tangle of alleys. Luxuriantly planted **La Glorieta Square** opening on to the river is part of the city center. It is framed by the city hall and the episcopal palace. Cardenal Belluga Square with the cathedral abuts on it to the rear.

Murcia's beauty, the consummate elegance of its urban planning, is in keeping with its luxuriant natural surroundings. Most of the city's historic buildings are Baroque. The most important of these is the 15th-century **cathedral**, which was, as was not infrequently the case, built on

the ruins of the principal mosque. Its Baroque exterior is dramatic and vibrant. The interplay of straight and curved lines with advancing and retreating surfaces contrasts sharply with the austerely Gothic interior. The structure of the edifice reflects Murcian relations with the Church. A plethora of side chapels belonged to the most prominent members of the community. The Velez chapel is particularly striking. Its exterior is decorated with chains of stone. The mind boggles at a huge likeness of San Cristobal, portrayed like Gulliver in the seas of Lilliput on the portal. Thrown in with numerous works of art in the cathedral and its museum is a treat for lovers of the morbid: the heart of Alfonso X the Wise

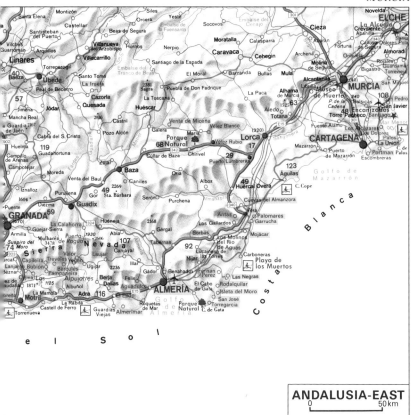

ANDALUSIA-EAST
0   50km

as well as the mortal remains of the four Martyrs of Cartagena are contained in urns on display here.

In a tangle of ancient alleys around the cathedral the streets of the rag (*Trapería*) and silver (*Platería*) dealers are the main thoroughfares. This is just the spot for strolling, shopping or nipping into a bar or two. In the mid 19th century the prosperous bourgeoisie had the **Casino,** actually a club, built in Modernist style. It is a peculiar blend of borrowed styles: Nasrid and Neoclassical *patios*, a ballroom à la Versailles and a ladies' cloakroom reminiscent of the celestial sphere with cherubs and clouds. Redolant of turn-of-the-century decadence, the Casino is still in use.

With its 300,000 inhabitants Murcia is a modern big city. Although it is bustling and noisy when the university is in session, it is tranquilly provincial in summer when the students are not there. Holy Week is the city's most festive time of the year. Then the lay brotherhoods (*cofradías*) of Jesus and the blacks, the *coloraos*, take part in the elaborate processions, carrying *pasos*, which are three dimensional scenes of the passion handing out sweets and hardboiled eggs decorated with verses intended to amuse the public, some of them erotic.

The woodcarver Salzillo was particularly adept at representing the customs and fashions of 18th century *huerta* life. The mysticism and elegance of his Holy

Week figures have not lost their appeal to Murcian religious feelings even in the era of Pop Art. The **Salzillo Museum** in the Church of Jesus exhibits eight procession scenes (*pasos*) and a great many crèche figures.

Costa Cálida and Mar Menor

Although the interior of this region is arid and deserted, the entire strip of coast is saturated with both new and old fishing villages, salt-works, high-rise apartment blocks, mostly tourist accommodation, and fine sandy beaches where sunbathers are frequently packed in like sardines.

The first town one reaches on this route after Alicante is the fishing village of **Sta. Pola.** It boasts a 16th-century fort that must have been a formidable defence against the onslaughts of Barbary pirates. The best thing to do in Sta. Pola is to eat:

Above: Some visitors spend their time angling. Right: A row of houses in a Cartagena street, obviously not fit for automobiles.

all types of rice dishes, shellfish and, a local speciality, pickled roe and tuna.

The **Island of Tabarca** can be reached by boat in half an hour. In the 18th century, 600 Genoese inhabited it. They had been held captive by pirates on the Tunisian island of Tabarca before managing to flee here. They named the island New Tabarca. It has lots of coves and conveys the feeling that the pirates have only just departed. Its 126 inhabitants are fishermen who are known for a superb rice dish: *arroz caldero*, which one can enjoy sitting outside.

The Segura estuary is to the south. Alluvial deposits brought down over 15 km, which have in the course of decades swollen at **Guardamar** to immense dunes, which are planted with pines. The charm of the port town of **Torrevieja,** encircled by white tips from the salt-works, is lessened by high-rise tourist accommodation. This should not be a discouraging factor. One can find less crowded beaches south of the town at **Dehesa de Campoamor** or **Punta del Gato.**

The Murcian coast, the Costa Cálida, starts at the **Mar Menor**, a salt lake covering 170 square kilometers and fed by the "Mar Mayor", i.e. the Mediterranean. It is almost completely cut off from the sea by a 22-km-long barrier island known as *La Manga* (the Sleeve). It has, unfortunately, been so built up that concrete makes both the sea and the salt lake visually and even physically inaccessible. The original charm of the scenery can only be glimpsed on the northern tip, at **Encañizadas de la Torre,** at **Ventorillo** and **Salinas**, where fish are driven to become entangled in the reed labyrinths where they are then caught by fishermen showing a great deal of tradition-conscious ingenuity.

The high air and water temperatures (18˚ C in the coldest month), the shallowness of the water and its salinity (50 %) give the waters of the Mar Menor strong therapeutic powers. Near **Vivero** or **Isla del Ciervo** one can take mudbaths. In fact the lake is more suited to wading than bathing.

Although about 500,000 visitors populate the Manga in summer, one can still find pleasant summer holiday spots on the land side of the Mar Menor, at **San Pedro del Pinatar, Santiago de la Rivera** or **Los Alcázares.** The villas there are awash in turn-of-the-century charm and landing stages ending in wooden bath houses jut into the salt lake. At the southern tip of the cape is the small fishing village of **Cabo de Palos,** which boasts a lighthouse nearly 100 m high and lots of good restaurants. A stretch of steep coastline begins here. Then there are bays, dunes and beaches in a protected area where there are still lonely spots for bathing.

The mining town of **La Unión** had its heyday at the close of the 19th century. From that period some noteworthy Modernist buildings have survived: the Market and the Casa del Piñón. In the former the miners' songfestival takes

place each August. This is a good opportunity to get acquainted with the local Flamenco styles: *Tarantas, Mineras* and *Cartagenas.* **Portman,** in the coastal range, where things seem to be topsy-turvy, is just an excursion away. The oldest houses were actually copied from miniature tin and lead models. The blended earth colors – yellow, purple and grey – form a colorful yet restful composition. *Portus Magnus,* the Roman port, is in a bay filled in with mining tips. Nevertheless, despite considerable environmental pollution this section of the coast has a charm all its own.

CARTAGENA

Just outside Cartagena is *Carthago Nova,* founded by Hasdrubal, the Carthaginian conqueror in the 3rd century BC. Modern **Cartagena** is a dynamic big city with major industries (docks, oil refineries, metalworking), an important trading port and a large military base. Nonetheless, it thrives on the nostalgic recollection of past glories. Its historical significance rested on its strategic position as a port for the nearby mines. One can survey the city from the park on Esculapio Hill with its fort rebuilt of Roman and medieval material after the Reconquista. Cartagena was built on a Roman settlement which is being excavated. At 28 Calle Duque and on Tres Reyes Square, the remains of Roman walls, streets, houses and water conduits have been laid bare.

In the 19th century, the city was one of the few enclaves to free itself from Napoleonic occupation. As a result there was large-scale immigration into the area leading to intensified exploitation of the local mines. Here too, prosperity financed Modernist buildings such as the city hall, the Casino, the old Café España in Calle Mayor and the Casa Maestre. The Archaeological Museum and the National Center for Underwater Archaeology on the harbor are highly instructive on the city's uninterrupted record of historical significance.

Outside **Aguilas** there is a series of deserted beaches. The town is situated on two bays separated by a rocky promontory crowned by the ruins of a 16th century fort. It is pleasant to stroll through the streets of this city, which are laid out in the 18th century according to rational Enlightenment tenets, and enjoyable to eat in any of the city's many good seafood restaurants.

From Murcia into the Mountains

With Murcia the fertile plain is left behind and the arid foothills of the Sierra de Espuña begin. Nestled at the bottom, about the 16th century church of Santiago, is the farming village of **Totana,** in which pottery-making is still a major

craft. The road past the 13th-century church of Santa Eulalia leads to **Aledo,** which has retained its medieval charm. The fortified tower of Calahorra and the church of Sta. María loom over it on a hill. In the 11th and 12th centuries the village belonged to the domains of the Order of Knights of Santiago. One is not at all surprised to learn that El Cid himself stopped here.

One gets the feeling of the transition from the Levante to southern Spain in the district of Campo de Lorca. Its principle town, **Lorca,** is historically important. Founded by the Iberians, it became the colony of *Heliocroca* under the Romans, which means "the city of the sun". In Moorish times it was an independent *taifa* until it and its lands were conquered by the Christians. From the 16th to the 18th centuries it was a major cultural and administrative center with its own university. Crowned by the Arab fort in which Alfonso X later lived, the city extends across the southern slopes of Caño Mountain and down into the plain. Most of the fortifications as well as the Alfonsina and El Espolón towers have been preserved. Coming down from the town, one first passes through a modest residential area with Moorish houses. Below it is the Plaza de España with the collegiate church (16th – 18th centuries) and the city hall. In the lower city there are more recent churches, and Renaissance and Baroque façades often encrusted with the coats of arms of noble families, indicating the grandeur and ubiquitous power of the land owning oligarchy. During Holy Week festivities, Lorca has split from time immemorial into two rival factions, the Blues and the Whites. Magnificently costumed as ancient and biblical personages, they mingle with penitents and the general public.

At **Puerto Lumbreras,** a town consisting almost entirely of pottery shops, the road forks in the directions of either Granada or Almería. The road to Granada

Right: Every region in Spain has its own earthenwares, here pottery near Lorca.

passes through rugged country thickly overgrown with maquis and olive trees to reach **Velez Rubio** with its turreted and domed Baroque church of the Encarnación. The town is a play of contrasts between the austere white of the modest dwellings and the opulent magnificence of the monastery of **San Francisco** and several aristocratic residences like that of the Serna family.

Velez Blanco, on the other hand, nestled at the foot of Maimón Grande, is dominated by a formidable fort. The building can be visited, but one would have to go to New York to admire the white marble Renaissance inner courtyard, which has been on exhibit since 1964 in the Metropolitan Museum. From the fort, one has a view over the village, the church of Santiago and the Monastery of St Luis. Both of the latter are 16th century with Mudéjar elements. Vocal and instrumental groups, *cuadrillas de ánimas*, stroll through the village. Probably without really being aware of it, they are keeping up a lively folk custom.

Not far from Velez Blanco, the **Sierra de María National Reserve** begins – an oasis of green in a semi-arid landscape. The town of **María** is set in pine woods over 1000 m above sea level. The park includes up-to-date recreation facilities and restaurants: Los Alaminos and La Piza are popular excursion destinations. The park's abundant flora includes several endemic species in the pine woods covering the central and lower slopes as well as among the holm oaks of the upper regions. It has become a sanctuary for many bird species such as the golden eagle and other eagles, hawks and sparrow hawks.

The region was already inhabited in prehistoric times. Major finds have been made in caves like Cueva de Ambrosio or the cave of Cerro de las Canteras. In others, such as the Cuevas de los Letreros, stylized wall paintings have been found. This is where the representation of the *Indalo figure*, now the symbol of Almería, first came to light. To the west, at Orce near **Venta de Micena,** part of

111

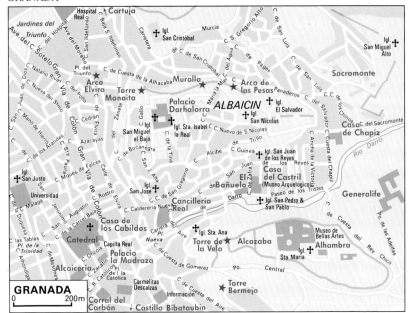

what is known as "Orce Man" was found in 1982. If this fragment really was of hominid provenance, it would have belonged to the earliest ancestors of all Europeans, dating back 1,400,000 years.

In **Baza,** *Basti* to the ancient Iberians, is the necropolis on Cerro del Santuriano where the sculpture in the Madrid Ar–chaeological Museum known as the *Dama de Baza* was found. In Baza one can visit the collegiate church, the fountain with its proud golden cocks and the palace of the Dukes of Obrantes.

From here it is not far to **Guadix.** The strategic position of this town at the crossroads of coast and interior, eastern and western Andalusia caused Augustus Caesar to found the Roman military colony of *Julia G. Acci* here. San Tor-quato and the seven missionaries are said to have brought Christianity to the settle-ment. If the legend has a kernel of truth in

it, Guadix is the earliest Christian com-munity on Spanish soil. The cathedral, however, is both Renaissance and Ba-roque. Diego de Siloe was its first archi-tect. Near it is the 16th-century church of Santiago. The **Alcazaba,** towering over the Moorish *medina,* has, unfortunately, recently been subjected to extremely un-convincing restoration. It overlooks the region of the caves, which seems almost unreal by contrast.

Whitewashed chimneys look as if they have grown out of the ground. Terraces are the roofs of neighbouring houses. The clay topsoil covering the entire Guadix Basin region creates ideal conditions for insulating and roofing dwellings since it is permeable and provides superb insula-tion against extremes of temperature. Some of the caves, buried in innumerable mounds, are the homes of potters who make the traditional Guadix pottery of red unglazed clay.

On 9 September, the annual *Cas-camorras Festival* takes place. Tradition has it that in 1490 the Virgin appeared in

Right: The Generalife, the Alhambra and the snow-capped mountains of the Sierra Nevada are all the hallmarks of Granada.

Baza to a laborer from Guadix. He wanted to keep the miraculous statue of the Virgin but was prevented from doing so by the *Bastetanos* (Baza towns–people). Every year the *Accitanos* of Guadix attempt to recapture the statue, which has been spotted by their fellow townspeople. For this purpose they send the *cascamorras,* a colorfully disguised figure, carrying a big club.

Visitors to Guadix should try local delicacies like the lamb basted in sherry (*cordero al jerez*), or braised partridge, or, as a dessert, the rich dish known as "heavenly bacon" (*tocinos de cielo*), all of which belong to a thousand-year-old local tradition.

GRANADA

Granada, the famous city in a fertile valley, sprawled across gentle hills below the lofty white-crested peaks of the Sierra Nevada. Upon arrival, one is met by a modern concrete section congested with traffic. The tradition-conscious towns-people of Granada have taken great pains to keep traffic as chaotic as their Moorish forefathers did. Beyond, barely visible through the high-rise jungle, stretches the incredible cityscape of hills on which the Arabs built their palaces and dwellings. Up there, once one has left humming modern Granada behind, one of the world's most timelessly beautiful cities awaits the visitor.

The **Alhambra** stands on Sabica Hill. Alhambra means "red" in Arabic. This does not refer to the color of the structure, which was painted white at the time it was built, but to the raw red earth surrounding the building that did not offer even the shadowy benefit of trees. It was the royal seat of the Nasrid dynasty. In the 14th and 15th centuries seven palaces were built in the compound. Surrounded by strong walls with fortified towers, it also enclosed the military precinct of the Alcazaba, which predated the Nasrid palaces. The foundation walls of the warriors' quarters, the baths, the dungeon and the stalls can still be seen. From the

Torre de la Vela one can view the entire city and see how its history unfolded. Across from Sabica Hill is the **Albaicín** enclosed in walls. In Moorish times a quarter densely populated with craftsmen, it has retained its Arab character. In it is the **Old Alcazaba,** the royal residence of the pre-Nasrid dynasty. Below the Albaicín was the *medina*, the walled-in commercial quarter surrounding the principal mosque. Beyond are yet other walled-in quarters, such as the Jewish quarter. After the conquest, the Christian rulers extended the city into the floodplain and built the cathedral on the site of the mosque. Much later, Charles V built a a splendid Renaissance palace in the Alhambra, which today houses a museum of Moorish art as well as a general art museum.

The best preserved historic residences in the Alhambra are the **Comares Palace** of Yussuf I (1333-54) and the **Lion Palace** of his son, Mohammed V (1354-91). After they had been incorporated in the Alhambra complex, the former was used for representational purposes. In it was the throne under the dome of the Comares Tower, representing the Seven Heavenly Kingdoms. There the king received ambassadors who had entered through the Arrayanes Courtyard, awed and dazzled – as was intended by both the architects and their royal masters – at the sight of such overwhelming riches.

The private quarters were around the **Court of the Lions** with its fountain supported by 12 lions and what seems like a veritable forest of symmetrical corbel arches on delicate columns producing an enchanting play of light on the whitewashed walls. On either side are halls with overwhelming Mocárabe ceilings. One is the Abencerraje, in which members of that aristocratic house are said to

Right: A veritable forest of columns in the Patio de los Leones, the Lions' Court, in the Alhambra in Granada.

have been beheaded by the king. Then there is the Hall of the Two Sisters (**Sala de los dos Hermanas**), named after the twin marble slabs in the floor. The **Mirador de Daraxa** leading to the harem is now a Renaissance court. The adjacent baths have been unconvincingly restored. The throne room of Mohammed III opens on to the Portal Gardens and is more reminiscent of Versailles than of Arab architecture. Above it remain only the foundations of the palaces of Mohammed II and Yussuf III. If one is still not tired, one can proceed through the gardens past the tower residences Torre de las Infantas and Torre de la Cautiva to the **Generalife,** the summer residence of the Arab rulers. Its lavish gardens and playful fountains seem to the modern observer more Romantic than Arabic.

The way to the **Albaicín** leads through a mysterious tangle of streets which date from times untouched by technology. Tortuous alleys, cisterns, houses and walls are Arab in character. One reaches this quarter via Plaza Nueva, built over the Darro River. The **Chancillería Real** looms almost menacingly over the square. It was the high court of the Catholic Kings and its façade incorporates Baroque elements, a style which was just coming into its own then. Behind the Mudéjar church of Sta. Ana, the Darro emerges to flow past the **Casa de Castril** housing the Archaeological Museum and Paseo de los Tristes in the shadow of the Alhambra. One can spend hot summer evenings pleasantly sitting outside there.

Crossing the Cuesta del Chapiz one reaches the **Sacramonte,** a gypsy quarter with cave dwellings. Here the tradition of flamenco singing and dancing is alive, with a great many performances for tourists. Higher up is the **Plaza de Aliatar**, a rendezvous for gourmets, and particularly lovers of snails and wines from the coast. The church of San Salvador is to the left. Its inner courtyard formed part of

a mosque. From here Calle Panaderos leads to **Plaza Larga**, which has, since Moorish times, been a stronghold of tradesmen and artisans. On it stands the Arco de las Pesas, an arch from which the weights used by fraudulent tradesmen were hung.

Aljibe de la Gitana and Callejón de las Monjas lead to the only Arab residence preserved in the Albaicín: the 15th century **Darhalorra Palace** which belonged to the royal family. The original painted ceilings and archways are of special interest. **Callejón del Gallo** is an alley leading to the church of San Miguel Bajo and the plaza of the same name with its cafés and bars. Not far off is a church built by the Catholic Kings, together with the monastery of Sta. Isabel la Real. From the square in front of the Mudéjar church of San Nicolás, the view of the Alhambra, the Sierra and the lower city is, without exaggeration, breathtaking.

The lower city was built by the Christian conquerors. The Catholic Kings began work on the **cathedral,** which took, in the usual manner of cathedrals, 181 years to complete. Consequently, although the plan is Gothic, the front with Alonso Cano's intriguing handling of space, is Baroque.

Since the Catholic Kings wanted to be buried on the site of their signal victory, they had the royal chapel built on to the cathedral. It is in the Isabelline style. Here is the tomb of Ferdinand and Isabella, designed by Fancelli, and also the tomb of Juana the Mad and Philip the Fair, the work of Ordóñez. The chapel is a masterpiece, culminating in the altar retable by Bigarny.

In Arab cities the *Zoco* is adjacent to the mosque. At Granada only badly restored remnants of the silk market, the **Alcaiceria,** have been preserved. Now the wares of local craftsmen are sold in it. Across Reyes Catolicos Street, above the riverbed which was until recently uncovered, is the **Corral de Carbón,** an inn dating from Moorish times which must be one of the oldest restaurants known. Tournaments were once held on Pl. de

115

Bibarrambla. Nowadays, one can sit among the flower stalls and enjoy hot chocolate and delicate *churros* (deep-fried pastries) at a café.

Outside the city walls, the Catholic Kings commissioned a charity hospital, the **Hospital Real,** with a ground plan in the form of a Greek cross. Patients were lodged in the aisles. The altar, which was visible from all points and thus was a symbol of hope, stood in the intersection. In Ainada Mar (Fountain of Tears), the section in which the Arabs had their summer residences and now a rather run-down residential area, the Carthusian order took over 300 years, which encompassed the transition from Gothic to Baroque, to complete the monastery of **La Cartuja.**

In addition to various music and theater festivals, the most important annual religious celebration is Corpus Christi Day. The most unusual event is undoubtedly the Sacred Cross Festival on 3 May, when the city celebrates amidst a throng of decorated crosses crowding the streets.

It is only half an hour's drive from Granada up into the **Sierra Nevada.** The range boasts the Iberian Peninsula's highest peaks, Mulhacén and Veleta, both about 3500 m.

Snow lies here until late spring. Consequently, Europe's southernmost ski resort, which can nevertheless be proud of about 50 kilometers of runs, is extremely popular. It is optimistically preparing for the 1995 World Skiing Championship.

JAÉN

The Jaén region is a transition zone between Castile and Andalusia. "Geén" means "caravan stop" in Arabic. The armies halted here on their way to the Battle of Navas de Tolosa in 1212, at which Alfonso VIII won a large part of Andalusia back from the Muslim Almohads. In 1808 they rested here on the way

Above: The view on Jaén, with an endless stretch of olive groves in the background.

to Bailén, where Napoleon suffered his first defeat in Spain.

The city of **Jaén** is dominated by the Fort of Sta. Catalina looming over the city. Fully restored, it is now a *parador.* In the Barrio de la Magdalena, at the foot of the citadel, the narrow tortuous pattern of alleys dates back to the Moors. Here are the underground baths of the Moorish King Alí. Due to their excellent state of preservation and their size (470 square meters) they are among Spain's most interesting Arab baths. Above them is the Palace of Villadonpardo. The monastery of Sto. Domingo, once a university, with its lovely Renaissance inner courtyard, is in the same quarter. Here too is the 13th-century Sta. Clara, in which the "Bamboo Christ" – a figure symbolic of conquest in more ways than one and brought back from the colonies, is kept. The Renaissance cathedral with its Baroque façade was built by the architect Vandelvira. Its greatest treasure is the shrine with the sudarium of St Veronica. On his way to Calvary, Christ is said to have left the imprint of his face on it.

Jaén is a city still marked by the Franco era, when it was a provincial administrative center. The provincial museum exhibits archaeological finds and also many works by the painter Alonso Cano.

It is well worth one's while to take a day's trip to the northeast from here through sheer endless olive groves to the rival towns of Baeza and Ubeda. **Baeza** is one of those places whose ravishing beauty leaves one at a loss for words. Plaza del Pópulo, with its lion fountain and realistic statue of Imilce, Hannibal's wife, makes a striking impression right at the outset. In the 16th-century, Renaissance buildings went up around it at the edge of town: the abattoir and the Court of Appeals, known as the Casa del Pópulo. The Puerta de Jaén and Arco de Villarlar arches were erected in honor of Charles V. The former commemorates his stay here after his betrothal at Sevilla in 1526, the latter his victory over the rebellious Comuneros.

Strolling down the Paseo de Las Murallas above the Guadalquivir Valley inspired the melancholy poetry of Antonio Machado, who taught here from 1912-19. Baeza is a farming town. The story goes that when Machado arrived and asked for the headmaster, he was told that the latter was "in agony". "Good Lord!", he is said to have expostulated but was relieved to hear that this was the name of the farmhands' pub. Such pubs still give locals a cosy place to complain about the weather and bad harvests. Many such farmhands are the descendants of landed gentry, *hidalgos*. Although they own vast olive groves, they prefer to keep quiet about their lineage, considering what some of them have come down to. They work with day laborers in the coldest months of the year at the bone-wrenching task of harvesting the olives. Emigration, understandibly, is depleting the country and as yet does not show signs of stopping.

Plaza Sta. María recalls the grandeur of 16th-century Baeza. A great stair leads up to the enormous Renaissance **cathedral.** The side portal is Gothic in the Mudéjar style. The interior boasts an impressive Baroque monstrance. Across from the cathedral the **Seminario de San Felipe Neri** not only has a magnificent Isabelline façade, but flaunts the very bone of contention documenting the old rivalry between Baeza and Ubeda, an early example of subversive graffiti: on the façade is a 17th century drawing of the Bishop of Ubeda irreverently sitting on a chamber pot.

A small square lower down displays a veritable cross section of Spanish architecture: the Romanesque church of Sta. Cruz with its twin pointed portals; the Isabelline Jabalquinto Palace with its lavishly eccentric façade, a Renaissance inner courtyard and a Baroque stair; and the old university, now a school and

venue of summer courses, bearing a Mannerist façade. The **city hall** too is noteworthy. It was built as a prison, though this lowly status certainly belies its magnificent exterior. Strolling through Baeza, one comes across buildings recalling past grandeur at virtually every turn of the street. The same holds true for **Ubeda,** within sights across the river. A hymn to the Renaissance in stone, it is as hot as an oven in summer, and bleak and cold in the winter. Each of its buildings is unique. Vandelvira's work moulded the entire city. At the edge of town is a large Mannerist building with high towers, the **Hospital of Santiago** including its church and two-storeyed arcaded court. The Plaza de Sta. María is nothing if not a tribute to the affluence of the de los Cobos family. The church of **San Salvador** was built by Vandelvira and Diego de Siloe as a mausoleum for Don Fran-

cisco de los Cobos, Secretary to Charles V. The adjacent palace, now a *parador*, belonged to the chaplain. At the other end of the square is the city hall with its ordered Neoclassical façade revealing a strong Italian influence. Across from it, the church of **Sta. María** was built on the foundations of the mosque and its Gothic cloister was a forecourt. The market place is higher up. At one end is the Gothic church of San Pablo, at the other the old city hall. Nearby are the Casa Mudéjar, the Archaeological Museum, the Casa de los Salvajes (savages), named after the figures in relief on the façade, and the Carmelite monastery in which San Juan de la Cruz died. Then come the Casa de las Torres with its two massive towers and ordered but elaborate Plateresque façade, and the Moorish wall. By going through the Puerta del Losal and down into the San Millán quarter, one can find the town's potters' workshops in Calle Valencia. Inherently worth seeing, these represent the remains of what was once an influential guild here.

Above: Donkeys are still the most reliable way of covering certain distances. Right: The many layers of the town of Mojácar.

From Ubeda, one can trace the headwaters of the Gualdalquivir and the Segura. At the foot of the Cazorla and Segur Ranges is the town of **Cazorla,** guarded by two forts, a Moorish one and the fort of Yedra. Zabaleta painted the *Sierra* here and Vandelvira came this far to build the church of Sta. María.

La Iruela is adjacent to it; its fort is an extension of a sharp crag. This is the gateway to the Sierra Natural Reserve. Vast woods of holm oak and fir grow as far up as 2000 m. Squirrels leap across one's path. A mountain goat on a rock may be silhouetted against the sky. Other species may be more difficult to spot: wild boar, moufflon, eagles, falcons, deer and particularly golden vultures, which are faced with extinction. They have a wingspan of up to three meters. At 1400 m there is a *parador*, a marvellous place from which to explore the area. The road climbs as far as the **Vadillo saw mill**. From there the **Devil's Falls** can be reached on foot. The road continues to the de las Herrerías Bridge, said to have been built overnight to speed Isabella the Catholic on her way to the conquest of Granada. Higher still is a footpath to **Cañada de las Fuentes**, officially the original source of the Guadalquivir. Lower down, at the Vinegar Tower, Torre de Vinagre, and the fish hatchery, one can walk along the Río Borosa to the game reserve at **Elías** or to the quiet of the wildlife sanctuary.

The northern exit is at **Tranco**. The road passes by the Tranco Reservoir. Its waters have engulfed the village of **Bujaraiza**, leaving only the Arab fort showing. Towards evening one sometimes sees a herd of deer coming out of the woods to drink in the lake. September is rutting season. The sound of combative antlers locking horns can be heard far off.

ALMERÍA

Beyond Aguilas begins the part of Andalusia which has been one of the least developed regions of Spain, Almería. Like the rest of eastern Andalusia, it is primanily rugged and mountainous. The mountain ranges extend to the coast. Roads have only recently been built, making the towns less isolated. This is where the typical Andalusian villages with their whitewashed houses begin. In addition, there are many bizarre, or at the very least picturesque, cave dwellings in Almería that have been dug out of impermeable layers of clay. The town of **Cuevas de Almanzora** is named after them. It is situated in the delta of the Almanzora, whose bed, like that of all local rivers, is a *rambla*, dry for most of the year but a floodplain after heavy rains.

At **Antas,** near Vera, are the finds from Spain's most important prehistoric settlement, Argar, after which the Bronze Age Argar Culture which existed here about 3700 years ago was named.

The beaches in this area are wide and not very crowded, at least as far as Cabo de Gata. This is where the beach at **Palomares** is. In 1966 Franco's Minister of Tourism, Manuel Fraga, now President of Galicia, went for his well-publizised swim here to demonstrate that the three atomic bombs, which had inadvertently been lost by a US military aircraft, had not contaminated the water. Nowadays the Minister would have to swim in the nude: The area has meanwhile been developed as a nudist colony.

The towns of this region, **Garrucha** and **Mojácar,** are fishing villages which serve as family seaside resorts rather than meccas of mass tourism. New building has been confined to the beaches, leaving the old town cores untouched. Mojácar has narrow alleys laid out by the Moors. Most restaurants are cosmopolitan, but ancient Mediterranean culture has still maintained strong roots in the area. Until recently local women even wore veils in the Arab manner.

Right: Fishing boats going through the daily routine of preparing for another work stint on the high seas.

Cabo de Gata Nature Reserve

The coastal road is deserted and highly scenic, and in many places is even guarded by forts. 30 km south of Mojácar is **Playa de los Muertos,** a beach of fine sand that can be reached by footpaths from Barranco del Horno, the gateway to Cabo de Gata Nature Reserve famous for its volcanic rock formations. The road to the cape does not follow the coast. One has to drive inland from Carboneras to Nijar. From there small roads go into the protected area.

Between the Cabo de Gata and the Sierra de Alhamilla Ranges stretches the arid plain of **Campos de Nijar**. Modern plastic tunnels for forcing early vegetables cover the countryside. Yet as recently as 1960, Goytisolo published a book on the natural way of life characteristic of this remote region.

The town of **Nijar,** clinging to the slopes of the Sierra de Alhamilla and dominated by a watchtower, is famous for its tradition of craftsmanship: blue-green pottery and patchwork rugs (*har–apos*). Moreover, the local women cut and shape colorful rags by hand to be woven into rugs in weaving mills that one can easily visit.

Cabo de Gata Nature Reserve covers an area of over 26,000 hectares. There, water and light have moulded strange forms from the volcanic rock. Tiny white villages in the stark anthracite rock intensify the merciless light. The interior of the park is a sparse scorched landscape in which only a few endemic plants have survived: dwarf palms, cork oaks, wild olives, buckthorn (mastica) and agave. In the valleys, few and far between, there are occasional palm groves like oases. Man fought for millenia to adapt to this environment but has obviously given up. Abandoned farmsteads, *cortijos*, indicate that the area was once populous. In one of them the events took place which inspired García Lorca's tragedy, *Blood*

Wedding. The harsh story is highly revealing of the earthy life of people here about 1933. The bride is kidnapped by an earlier, unsuccessful suitor who dies in mortal combat with the groom.

Windmills, cisterns, wells and water wheels are signs that grain was once cultivated here. What grows now is no longer sufficient even for sustenance farming. From **Fernán Pérez** via the abandoned village of Higo Seco and the old goldmine of Rodalquilar, one reaches a magnificent beach of fine sand, the **Playazo of Rodalquilar.** The coast is more densely populated than the interior. Despite stony beaches, which some bathers prefer to clinging sand, some tourist amenities exist at **Las Negras** and **San José.** This coast is breathtaking when seen from a ship. Many coves can only be reached by sea.

Isleta del Moro is a typical fishing village with white houses, beached fishing boats and the communal wash-house on the main square. At the far end of the bay is the Playa de los Escullos with steep cliffs of white porous rock. From there one can see the two rocks of Isleta, which are often compared by the locals to a whale and its offspring. After most of the forests in the Sierra de Cabrera had been cut down to build them, the ships of Philip II departed from these beaches to fight the Turks in the 16th century.

The most beautiful of beaches and steep rocky coasts stretch between San José and the actual cape. A wretched little road goes via Playa de Monsul to the beach where the Genoese lay at anchor. There they laded their ships with silk which they had bought from the Moors and brought by caravan from Granada through the Alpujarras. The deserted coves beyond can only be reached by footpaths. This is where the incredibly bizarre rock formations of the **Arrecife de las Sirenas** begin.

Beyond, only accessible from the other side by small roads, are the salt-works and beaches of **Torregarcía.** In 1502, a statue of the Virgen del Mar is said to have been washed ashore here. In nearly

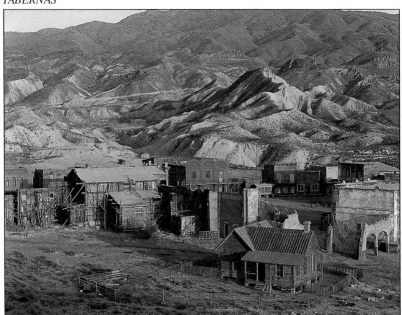

all local villages processions take to the sea to honor the Virgin on August 15th or 16th. Adjacent to the chapel at Torregarcía, a Roman factory has been excavated in which fish was salted and pickled.

Through the Desert

The most scenic way to reach Almería from Vera is to drive inland through the desert. Mountain ranges cut this region off on all sides from coastal rainfall. Although the landscape becomes increasingly arid the farther one goes, rushing waters startle travellers at **Los Molinos del Río de Aguas,** 5 km from Sorbas. A short footpath leads to streams flowing round glistening rocks where aquatic tortoises sun themselves and the vegetation is luxuriant.

Sorbas is picturesquely situated on a flat-topped mountain. White houses seem

Above: Ghost towns remaining from the Westerns filmed in the sixties. Right: View of Almería from its fortress.

to lean out over the edge, and the doors of cliff dwellings have been hacked into its steep sides. The local cottage industry is red clay pottery. This entire area is marked by such phenomena as limestone caves, funnel-shaped sinkholes and utterly breathtaking subterranean lakes. Since they have not been developed for tourism, one is on one's own and must be suitably equipped if intending to explore them.

The Alcazaba of **Tabernas** was one of the last Arab strongholds to withstand the Reconquista. In the vicinity is one of the largest European experimental stations for solar energy. Situated as it is, it exploits Europe's largest annual number of hours of sun. West of Tabernas the desert begins in earnest. Its core is a moonscape covering about 2200 square kilometers; it is cleft by deep ravines that turn into churning torrents when a cloudburst does occur. Although it might seem that nothing could thrive here, the area is nonetheless a unique reserve of African flora and fauna, harboring over 2500 species en-

demic to arid zones. Some of the plants burst into magnificent bloom in spring. This is a paradise for reptiles like the agile red-tailed lizards, poisonous vipers and aggressive scorpions, and for bird species such as kestrels, little Athene noctua owls, barn owls, partridges, warblers and linnets.

Where the road forks off to Granada a small road leads southeast to the **Colativí** at 1369m. From there one has a panoramic view over the desert, the Campo de Nijar and the coast.

Terrain and light conditions here are so reminiscent of the Arizona desert that in the 1960s and '70s the area became a second "Wild West". World-famous cinema productions and quite a few so-called spaghetti westerns were filmed here. The film scenery, long since abandoned by the film companies, serves as backdrops for performances of stunts which are put on for tourists passing through this odd place. But if one is interested in things prehistoric, one is advised to turn off further south to Sta. Fé de Mondújar.

Near there, at **Los Millares**, a civilization has been unearthed that existed about 4700 years ago in the transitional period between the Neolithic and the Bronze Age in Andalusia and the Levante. Where the desert of Tabernas now stretches must at that time have been the most densely populated of regions. One can recognize the traces of a walled settlement as well as the foundations of round houses, towers and wells. Over one hundred fascinating megalithic burial spots have been found in the adjacent necropolis.

The City of Almería

Always isolated from the rest of Spain due to its location, **Almería** subsisted solely from its ports. *Al-mariya* means "reflection on the sea" in Arabic. The harbor is framed by a palm park with a North African colonial air stretching from the fishermen's quarter to the city center. In the reign of Abderramán III (10th century), it was the most important architectural port and arsenal in the Caliphate of

123

Córdoba. Then it was an independent *taifa* for 100 years. The most important legacy of Moorish Almería is the **Alcazaba**, the fortifications built by Abderramán III on a hill above the city. The towers Torre del Homenaje, Torre de la Justicia and Torre de los Espejos, the bastion of Espolón, as well as remnants of three ring walls are all that is left of what was once a larger walled precinct. The church of **San Juan** was the principal mosque. Its prayer niche has been preserved. The church is in the fascinating Almedina quarter where there is an Arab tangle of alleys between the Alcazaba and the harbor.

The peculiar contours of the **cathedral**, half Gothic church, half fort, are an indication of what was once needed to withstand the continual raids of Barbary pirates on the city. A stroll through the cathedral quarter takes one to attractive Bendicho Square with its intimate atmosphere or to the old plaza, Pl. de la Constitución, framed by arcades. The city hall is located on the latter.

Most of the city's daily life goes on near the Puerta de Purchena, on Paseo de Almería and Calle des las Tiendas. If one leaves the city center going west through the Puerta de Purchena, one arrives at a quarter noted for its distinctive vernacular architecture of one-storeyed, pastel-tinted houses. Almería's ambience is pleasantly peaceful, in tune with the mild climate throughout the year. In the summer, music, flamenco and jazz performances are popular. The cuisine is abundant and hearty and there are lots of bars and restaurants serving fish, shellfish and traditional local dishes.

Costa de Almería and Costa Tropical

The foothills of the Sierra de Gador run down to the sea, making it difficult to

Right: The earth-covered roofs of Alpujarras serve as convenient terraces.

leave Almería from the west. **Aguadulce,** 13 km away, is called the city's summer extension. The youth of the province spend the summer evenings in the bars and discos on the marina. The coast is lined with more or less attractive holiday housing, *urbanizaciones.*

Beyond Aguadulce, the stark mountains recede. In front of them stretches the **Campo de Dalías**, until only recently populated by small herds of goats in the maquis. Here too the plastic vaulting of early vegetable plantations is ubiquitous, making the region the prosperous purveyor of fruit and vegetables to all of Europe. The sparsely settled region's inhabitants have retained the vernacular architecture of the Alpujarras, where they originally came from.

The center of the region is **El Ejido,** a town which has mushroomed wildly with the runaway economic upswing. To the south is the resort of **Almerimar,** which offers tourists more comfortable amenities, such as hotels, beaches, a marina and a golf course.

From here one follows the coast, which is often steep, only opening out into small coves. There are larger beaches again at Castell de Ferro and Carchuna. From La Rábita one can turn off into the mountains to visit **Albuñol,** where a mild coastal wine is produced and served.

Motril, the most important town on the Costa del Sol near Granada, lies in the valley of the Río Guadalfeo where sugar cane, which was introduced by the Arabs, used to be cultivated. Centuries later, it was exported from here to the Caribbean, a fact of which few are aware. Sugar cane went from east to west. One can still see abandoned cane mills and rum distilleries. The climate here is tropical. Recently avocados and cherimoyas have successfully been introduced. This section of the coast is, not inaccurately, often advertised as the "Costa Tropical".

Salobreña is right on the coast on a steep cliff which drops sheer to the beach.

It is nevertheless well worth one's while to clamber up the narrow alleys lined with gleaming white houses to the – for once – skilfully restored Arab fort. From it one has a view over the entire coast.

At **Almuñecar** too the mountains run down to the coast. The beaches here are lovely but crowded. The old town is on a hill. 2800 years ago, the Phenicians founded the settlement of Sexi here. Archaeological sites include two Phenician necropolises and an enormous Roman fish-pickling factory where one can see an array of vats in which fish had to soak in brine for 21 days. The archeological museum is well provided with Phenician and Roman finds from the sites. At the edge of town, almost hidden by tropical trees, is a 7 km-long (4 mi) Roman aqueduct which is still in use.

THE ALPUJARRAS

Along the imposing Sierra Nevada Range, and parallel to the coast, stretch vast wide plateaus. In Almería Province they were formed by the Río Andarax, and in Granada by the Guadalfeo and Yator Rivers. This is the region known as the **Alpujarras,** where the last of the Arabs, the Moriscos, lived despite frequent revolts against their repressive conquerors until they were expelled in 1570. The local houses and villages reveal their Arab lineage. Until recently the area was isolated and poor. Tradition is very much alive among the locals. Here one may see farmers riding home in the evening on their donkeys, women dressed in black, their heads covered, practitioners of natural medicine and faith healers and an array of ancient customs that have died out in other regions.

From the coast the road ascends into the Sierra de Gador, leaving a sea of plastic behind. **Berja** is in the midst of lovely country. From bare hills white villages overlook a green valley. Wine is grown everywhere. In autumn the vine leaves turn the valley gold. Delicious mountain ham is served with the local wine and, as everywhere in the Alpujarras, *migas* (roasted chunks of bread). North of Berja the road narrows, winding tortuously through blue hills of magnesium-rich clay. This water impervious material is used in the Alpujarras to cover flat roofs and is utterly effective and even insulating. Finally one reaches the high plateau where to the west the scenic Alpujarra Granadina begins at Ugíjar.

To the east is the Alpujarra Almeriense. **Laujar** is a typical Moriscan village with perfectly white, clay-roofed houses. From here a road leads across the Sierra Nevada via Paterna and Bayarcal, continuing north towards Guadix and Gra–nada. At 1995 m one crosses **Puerto de la Ragua** Pass, where a fresh spring bubbles up, to descend on the north side into the Margravate of Zeneta, which is cut up into grain fields like a jigsaw puzzle.

The castle of the Margrave, **La Calahorra,** soon comes into view on a hill. The Marqués Rodrigo de Mendoza was banished here at the beginning of the 16th century for inciting revolt. "Not of my own free will", he had inscribed at the entrance to the castle, which he had had built in the record time of seven years by 1510. The military austerity of its exterior belies its palatial interior.

Carrara marble and decorations consisting of mythological themes and floral motifs were then a new departure. This was Spain's first Renaissance castle. The plain was then verdant with ingeniously laid out plantations and trees. After the Moriscos had been expelled, the Christian settlers felled the trees and introduced the crops which are still under cultivation today.

The Alpujarra Granadina

Over 30 villages on the plateau encircled by the southern slopes of the

Right: Dry mountain air cures the hams of Trevélez. Far right: Sorting beans.

Sierra Nevada and the coastal range belong to the Alpujarra of Granada. The Alpujarra Alta on the slopes of the Sierra Nevada is the more lush and sunny part; the Alpujarra Baja, which is more arid and rugged, is across from it on the Contraviesa. Seen from below, the villages are white. Yet looking down on the flat roofs and paraphrasing one's impression with Gerald Brenan, one sees "an agglomeration of grey rectangles resembling a Cubist painting by Braque".

The Berbers who settled here turned the valley into a productive region. The terraces of their fields are still there, but the mulberry trees, which fed the silkworms have gone. The fields lie fallow, except in a few places where they are still cultivated in the traditional manner. The young are moving to the cities. About 40,000 people still live in the valley, but most of them are old. The saying goes that if one wants to watch a traditional way of life vanish, all one has to do is go to the Alpujarras.

Ugíjar was an important link between Almería and Granada and an independent Moorish province (*taha*). **Valor** made history with its Moriscan uprisings against Philip II. After the conquest of Granada, the Moors were oppressed, yet they were allowed to retain their religion and customs. Not until the reign of Philip II did repression become intolerable. The use of the baths was forbidden, the doors of houses had to be open at all times and women were forbidden to wear the veil. Ferdinand de Valor, a rich Christian who was at odds with the authorities, crowned himself king as Aben-Humeya of the Moriscos.

Philip II sent Don John of Austria to overthrow him. The death of de Valor, betrayed by an *inamorata*, put an end to the uprising. The Moriscos were expelled from Granada and the land was resettled by Christians from other regions. This had a damaging effect on the economy. A festival celebrated on different days in

many towns of the Levante and eastern Andalusia commemorates those events, and it is called the festival of *Moros y Christianos*. At Valor it is celebrated on 15 September. All day the armies of the Moriscos and Christians, splendidly costumed, on foot or mounted and armed with powder or simply resorting to explosively expressive tirades, fight to take the fort.

The English writer Gerald Brenan lived in the neighbouring village of **Yegen.** In the 1950s he wrote an interesting and highly readable account of the area, *South from Granada*. He describes the inhabitants of the Alpujarras as friendly and endearing. And so they have remained. The farmers wear felt hats, jackets and spotless white shirts for all the world like city dwellers. And they have every reason to show pride of ownership, for as small as they may be, the parcels of land they cultivate belong to them. The women, who seem to be in perpetual mourning, are tradition-min–ded. However, the communal wash-

houses, once what could he termed in modern parlance "village communication hubs", are not much in use now. In this area, there are still many practitioners of natural cures who wrench one's bones and hawk herbal panaceas. Some of them know apotropaic rituals to ward off the "evil eye". The young have begun to laugh at them but the elderly accord them cautious respect.

Los Bérchules is in a lush green area. People used to come here from all over the Alpujarras to drink the notably healthful water, which contains iron. Herds of sheep and goats come to graze here in summer to get the most out of every bit of local vegetation.

Trevélez has the honor of being Spain's highest village. Its crisp, dry climate is admirably suited to maturing mountain hams, which, after a stage of pickling in brine, are air-cured for over a year. These hams are the chief delicacy of a region known for hearty food. Most dishes are based on pork. Almost the entire animal is utilized. Pigs are fattened

127

all year long to be slaughtered at Christmas. The entire family participates in the ceremony.

The most beautiful but also the most frequented area is the **Barranco del Poqueira**. There, below the highest peaks of the Sierra Nevada, small white villages are dotted about the stream among islands of green: Capileira, Pampaneira and Bubión.

One should allow oneself plenty of time to wander through these quiet villages. The houses built one on top of the other and a labyrinth of steep alleys continually open up new vistas. While one is standing in front of the white façade of one house one may be on the roofs of another.

Laundry is hung out on the roofs to dry. Peppers, figs, tomatoes and anchovies are laid out to dry as well. Balconies are ablaze with carefully tended pots of flowers. At ground level one spots rabbits and chickens behind wire.

At **Capileira** is a small Alpujarras ethnological museum. A Tibetan Buddhist meditation community has settled at **Bubión.** The next Dalai Lama was born here a few years ago. **Pampaneira** boasts a pretty church and an array of shops selling handmade patchwork rugs, pottery and woollen blankets.

Orgiva and **Lanjarón** are the largest villages in the region. Lanjarón is renowned for its mineral water and esteemed as a spa for all sorts of diseases. The summer solstice on 23/24 June is a major festival here. Residents pour water from their balconies in a playful spirit onto passers-by but are generous with free rounds of wine and ham.

MÁLAGA

When one enters Málaga Province, one is at the heart of the Costa del Sol. **Nerja** is the best known seaside resort on this coast. Just outside town the Cuevas de Nerja are not far from the road. They are extraordinary limestone caves in which a bizarre subterranean landscape has formed of water and limestone deposits. The 400 metres open to the public make up only one fifth of these extensive caverns. The drawings and remains found here suggest that the caves were inhabited even in Palaeolithic times. The old town core of Nerja resembles West Andalusian villages. A broad promenade ends at a look-out above the sea known as the Balcón de Europa. Here one's gaze can wander over the coast and the Sierra de Almijara, which juts far out into the sea. The Sierra, which is a nature reserve, can only be approached from the coast by small twisting roads.

Frigiliana, one of the Sierra villages, is divided by the lay of the land into three sections, of which the highest, the Barrio Alto, is the most picturesque. It is surrounded by olive groves and vineyards producing the famous dry and sweet wines of Axarquia.

Torrox is in a valley which opens out towards the coast, ending in wide beaches. Here, too, a Roman necropolis and a fish-pickling factory have been excavated. The next town is **Torre del Mar,** the heart of the Axarquia, an up-to-date seaside resort with good bathing.

Vélez-Málaga further inland has an Alcázar and some noteworthy churches. In San Juan Bautista one can see marvellous figures, *pasos*, which are carried in processions and were made by Pedro de Mena. Na. Señora de la Encarnación is an early Christian church which was a mosque for a time.

Málaga, a modern big city, was founded by the Phoenicians as *Malaka*. On the eastern edge of town is the fishermen's quarter of **El Palo** with its low houses and artificially built up beaches. There one finds *merenderos* (snack bars) serving superb fish (*pescaito*). In the 19th century, Málaga, became a resort where English and Spanish upper-class families spent the winter. There is even an English

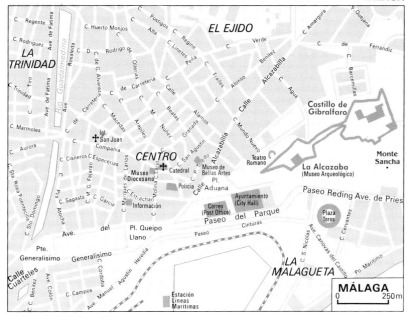

graveyard situated rather inappropriately across from the bullfighting arena. Near it is a turn-of-the-century residential section, **Limonal**, with attractive Modernist houses and superb gardens behind fences covered with jasmine and bougainvillea. A long park with palms, and traversed by leisurely horse-drawn carriages, stretches from the fort with the Alcazaba to the city centre and harbor.

Built by the Moors, the Alcazaba was added to by the Nasrids. Its entrance is a typical *coraza*, which means that it is shaped like an elbow to make it inaccessible to invaders. The building has been restored and is surrounded by lovely gardens. It houses the local archaeological museum. Above it is the **Castillo de Gibralfaro**, a Nasrid fort. Inside its walls are a lighthouse and a mosque. Next to it is a national *parador*.

The old city is relatively small yet at its centre stands a Renaissance cathedral. The choir was carved by Pedro de Mena, who is known for his *pasos*. The kneeling figures of the Catholic Kings in an apsid-

iole are also his work (17th century). Behind the choir is a *Pietá* by Alonso Cano. The church of Na. Señora de la Victoria was built by the Catholic Kings on the site of their encampment after the city had been taken. The Provincial Museum in the **Palacio de Buenavista** has a good many important paintings by Luca Giordano, Alonso Cano and even Pablo Picasso, who was born in the city.

From Granada to Marbella

From Granada, the quickest route to the Costa del Sol is south via Motril. A more interesting route goes west through the broad valley beyond the coastal range. **Santa Fé,** in poplar groves and with tobacconists' stalls, is a farming town in the Vega of Granada. Its grid pattern streets date from the encampment of the Catholic Kings. The town was actually founded as a base for laying siege to Granada, the seat of the Nasrids. Annual festivities commemorate the contract in 1492 between Columbus and the Ca-

129

tholic Kings, which was known to history as the "Capitulations of Santa Fé".

The next town is **Fuente Vaqueros,** where Federico García Lorca was born. "In that village I dreamed my earliest dreams of distant lands. In that village I shall become earth and flowers...". The house in which he was born has been made into a small museum where personal effects, manuscripts and photos of the writer are exhibited.

In the deep Genil Valley is **Loja,** which boasts a handsome Arab fort. Near the village the Genil undergoes a transformation and drops to become **Cola de Caballo** ("Horsetail") and **Los Infiernos Falls**. At the edge of town the Ríofrio hatchery adjacent to the Arab bridge from the time of the Caliphate of Córdoba serves excellent trout.

In order to see **Archidona,** the next town, one is advised to climb its steep streets to the **Santuario de la Virgen de Gracia**, where one has a panoramic view of the village and surrounding mountains. Two walled Arab precincts are embedded in the natural barrier of the Sierra de Gracia.

One of them contains a mosque which was converted into a church after the conquest in 1462. The other holds an Arab fort. The tiny sleepy village boasts an intriguing 18th century town square, Plaza Ochavada, which is a blend of Baroque and Mudéjar elements.

From Archidona, the road goes past Peña de los Enamorados. Local legend has it that an ill-starred pair of lovers jumped to their death from this rock. The fertile valley of **Antequera** follows. At the far end is the city of the same name, situated in the foothills of the Sierra de Chimenea. The city's great age is documented by the megalithic buildings on its outskirts, locally called caves: **Cuevas del Romeral, de Viera** and **de la Menga.**

Right: The Costa del Sol also offers dramatic coastline and seascapes.

They are not caves at all but actually dolmens, collective tombs of a Bronze Age people which had ventured from Almería across the Iberian Peninsula as far as the British Isles in search of mineral wealth. The largest dolmen is 25 m long, consisting of stones weighing up to 180 tons each. This large and relatively complex structure suggests that a highly developed urban culture must have lived here about 4300 years ago.

Antequera is an unusual city in which Baroque forms and Mudéjar techniques blend to form a distinctive style. The best example of this is the tower of San Sebastian (1701), surmounted by an angel, *El Angelonte*. A handsome architectural vista opens up from Plaza del Coso Viejo, where the 18th-century Palacio de Nájera faces the convent of Santa Catalina de Siena. There are 12 monasteries in the area. In some of them baked goods are sold over the turnstiles to make ends meet, but all of them only open their doors for divine service.

Climbing up to the Alcazaba, one passes the **Arco de los Gigantes**, a Mannerist arch of triumph dating from the reign of Philip II. Roman heads and other finds are built into it. Beyond it, is the collegiate church of Sta María and the fort with remnants of the Moorish fortifications. From here one overlooks a sea of white houses dotted with the red of monasteries and churches.

On the other side the scenic grandeur of **Torcal Nature Reserve** enfolds, where well-marked footpaths (3 and 6 km) wind through steep escarpments and bizarre formations of red marble and limestone. In the crisp mountain air here aromatic flowers and herbs thrive.

To the west are the artificial lakes created by damming the Guadalhorce River, which flows south in the narrow gorge of **Garganta del Chorro.** It is a spectacular natural course for the railway. From El Chorro one reaches the narrow footpath of Camino del Rey, which also

twists through the gorge. A tortuous mountain road leads to **Alora** on the same river, squeezed in between two mountains and under a rocky cliff. The stretch from here to the Mediterranean is bounded on the east by the white mountain villages of the Sierra de Ronda. Although **Coín** is a modern town, the villages on the road to Marbella through vast pine woods are whitewashed and extraordinarily charming.

COSTA DEL SOL

The western section of the Costa del Sol is a conurbation sprawling from Málaga along more than 100 km (62 mi) of coast to Estepona. The population is a hodgepodge and a rather uneasy one at that. Members of the Spanish and foreign upper classes rub shoulders here with the better criminal classes, who feel safe to launder their money here. Tourists crowd into the area in droves, service-sector workers from all over Spain earn a years' wages in a summer here and, finally,

there are the natives of the region in the old fishing and farming villages.

The area about **Torremolinos** and **Benalmádena Costa** is the most densely populated. High-rise hotels, *urbanizaciónes*, marinas and amusement parks, shops and restaurants jostle each other.

Beyond this area, with the exception of the congested high-rise city of **Fuengirola,** urban and tourist development has been more carefully adapted to the environment.

Stands of fir stretch from mountain slopes to the coast. Hotels and holiday cottage colonies are set in manicured groves and building is more in harmony with local architecture. However, it is an inescapable fact that golf courses and marinas have moulded the landscape. Not far inland there are still towns like **Mijas,** which despite mass tourism have preserved their traditional architecture. The stalls in front of shops, terraces in front of bars, donkey rides and parking problems are the inevitable phenomena of modern mass tourism.

131

In a grotto is the shrine of the Virgen de la Peña, who is said to have appeared to shepherds. Votive pictures, little oil lamps, candles, any number of devotional articles can be seen here. Here, venerable customs are still observed as if they had been staged just for tourist cameras. Higher up on a hill is the rectangular bullfighting arena and several look-out spots offering views over the coast.

The views are also spectacular on the road from Mijar to Benalmádena. In the town of **Benalmádena** there is an interesting archaeological museum emphasizing South American civilisations. It houses spectacular finds from various Pre-Columbian periods in Mexico, Peru, Nicaragua and Ecuador.

The main town of this section of the Costa del Sol is **Marbella.** The old core of what was a fishing village until tourism invaded it in the 1950s is still intact,

Above: New thrills for passing the time on the beach. Right: The Straits of Gibraltar, nothing too dire for this lonely surfer.

with white houses flaunting flower pots from balconies and façades, Pl. de los Naranjos, the handsome façade of the town hall, the **Palacio del Corregidor,** the white church of the Encarnación and the Arab fortress.

To the east, the Roman city at **Río Verde** has been excavated and perfect mosaics have come to light. From **Torre la Sal,** an excursion to the pretty town of **Casares** is worth one's while. It is situated on a hill below an Arab fort. Blas Infante, the most important 20th-century advocate of Andalusian separatism, was born here in 1885. He was shot in 1936 by Franco's minions.

Where Europe and North Africa Blend

Close to the Atlantic, the temperature is cooler, the vegetation is more luxuriant and the beaches are lavishly wider. The first town in the Campo de Gibraltar is **San Roque**. It sprang up in 1704 as stopgap quarters for the inhabitants of the

nearby village of Gibraltar where they could sit out the British occupation and there it has remained, a demographical fixture. Cannon Square and the Governor's Palace are places of interest. The latter houses the Gibraltar historical museum. **Sotogrande,** right on the Guadiaro River, is a posh residential area.

Algeciras, Roman *Portus Albus Romanus,* is on the east side of the bay of the same name. There, in 711, the Moors under Muza and Tarik first landed on the Iberian Peninsula. This large-scale invasion marked the beginning of an era of Spanish history which lasted nearly nine centuries.

The area is also full of reminders of the Roman era. The most interesting are the ruins at **Carteya,** the Roman colony which guarded the Straits of Gibraltar. To get there one turns off in the direction of Guadarranque 11 km outside Algeciras. The name of the city derives from the Arabic word for "green island".

Algeciras, the westernmost port of all on the Mediterranean, is the jumping-off place for Africa. Its ferries carry nearly four million passengers a year. They cross over to the Spanish possession of **Ceuta,** a free port encompassing an Arab market town, a bazaar for all oriental and Western wares imaginable.

The **Rock of Gibraltar** is visible from virtually all directions. The crouching hulk of its 400 meters of solid rock looms over the bay.

From La Linea one can take day trips to the English colony. The peninsula is a mass of contradictions. For three centuries, British institutions and the British way of life have commingled with the broad Andalusian dialect. The inhabitants of this off-shore rock guarding the entrance to the Mediterranean are known as *llanitos.*

On Gibraltar, lush vegetation and unusual fauna such as Magot monkeys have had to make room for atomic warheads and military institutions. On the southernmost tip of Europe, the **Punta de Europa**, the civilizations of the North, the South and Africa blend.

133

PROVINCE ALICANTE
(Telephone area code: 96-)
Accommodation
STA. POLA: *MODERATE:* **Rocas Blancas,** Ctra. Alicante – Cartagena at km 17, Tel: 411312. **TORREVIEJA:** *LUXURY:* **Masa Intern.,** C/ Alfredo Nobel 150, Tel: 5711537. *MODERATE:* **Edén Roc,** C/ Alfredo Nobel, Tel: 5716237.
Museums / Sightseeing
ELCHE: Museo Arqueologico Municipal: 11 a.m.–1 p.m., 4–7 p.m. **Huerto del Cura:** 9 a.m.– 6 p.m., in summer 9 a.m.–8 p.m. **ORIHUELA: Colegio de Sto. Domingo:** weekdays 9 a.m.–1 p.m. and 4–6 p.m. **Museo Catedralicio:** 10.30 a.m.–12.30 p.m., closed Sundays.
Information / Oficina de Turismo
ELCHE: Parque Municipal, Tel: 452747. **TORREVIEJA:** Av. de la Libertad 5, Tel: 710722

PROVINCE MURCIA
(Telephone area code: 968-)
Accommodation
MURCIA: *LUXURY:* **Rincón de Pepe,** C/ Apóstoles 34, Tel: 212239. *MODERATE:* **Pacoche,** C/ Cartagena 30, Tel: 213385. *BUDGET:* **Hostal Pacoche,** C/ Cartagena 23, Tel: 217605. **PUERTO LUMBRERAS:** *LUXURY:* **Parador Nacional,** Tel: 402025. **CARTAGENA:** *MODERATE:* **Alfonso XIII.,** Paseo Alfonso XIII, Tel: 520000. **MANGA DEL MAR MENOR:** *MODERATE:* **Entremares,** Gran Vía de la Manga, Tel: 563100. **PUERTO DE MAZARRÓN:** *MODERATE:* **Bahía,** Playa de la Reya, Tel: 594000. **CABO DE PALOS:** **El Cortijo I, II,** Ctra. Subida als Faro (road to the lighthouse), Tel: 563015.
Museums / Sightseeing
MURCIA: Museo Salzillo: 9.30 a.m.-1 p.m., 4-7 p.m., in winter 3-6 p.m. **Museo de la Muralla Hispano–Arabe,** Pl. Sta. **Eulalia** and **Museo de Murcia,** C/ Alfonso X. 5: 10 a.m.-2 p.m. and 6-7.30 p.m., Sun 10 a.m.-2 p.m., closed Mon. **Cathedral** and **Museum:** 10 a.m.-1 p.m. and 5-8 p.m. **Museo Taurino** (Bullfighting Museum): 10 a.m.–1 p.m. **ALCANTARILLA: Museo Etnológico de la Huerta Murciana:** 9 a.m.-1 p.m., closed Mon. **CARTAGENA: Museo Arqueologico:** C/ Ramón y Cajal 45, 10 a.m.-1 p.m. and 4-6 p.m., Sun 10 a.m.-1 p.m., closed Mon. **Museo y Centro Nacional de Investigaciones Submarines,** Harbor, Dique de Navidad: 10 a.m.-2 p.m., 5-7 p.m., Sun 10 a.m.-2 p.m., closed Mon. **Casino Mar Menor,** Gran Vía de la Manga: 9 a.m.-3 a.m., Fri and Sat 9 p.m.-4 a.m., closed Wed.

Information / Oficina de Turismo
MURCIA: C/ Alejandro Seiquer 4, Tel: 213716. **LORCA:** C/ Lopez Gisbert, Tel: 466157. **MAR MENOR – LOS ALCÁZARES,** Av. de la Libertad 50. **LA MANGA:** Gran Vía. **CARTAGENA:** city hall, Pl. del Ayuntamiento.

PROVINCE ALMERÍA
(Telephone area code: 951-)
Accommodation
ALMERÍA: *LUXURY:* **Guitart Club Alborán,** Alquián Retamar (beach colony), Tel: 225800. *MODERATE:* **La Perla,** Pl. del Carmen 7, Tel: 238877. **VERA:** *MODERATE:* **Vera Playa Club,** Ctra. de Garrucha, Tel: 456575. **GARRUCHA:** *BUDGET:* **Hostal Cervantes,** C/ Colon 2, Tel: 460252. **MOJÁCAR:** *LUXURY:* **Parador Reyes Católicos,** Playa, Tel: 478250. *BUDGET:* El Puntazo, C/ El Catalan, Tel: 478229. **SAN JOSÉ:** *MODERATE:* San José, Barriada S. José, Tel: 366974.
Museums / Sightseeing
ALMERÍA: Alcazaba: 10 a.m.-2 p.m., 4-8 p.m., in winter: 9 a.m.-2 p.m., 3-7 p.m. **Estación Experimental de Energía Solar:** Weekdays 9 a.m.-12 noon, Visits by prior appointment, Tel: 365189. **Cooperativa Artesana de la Aguja** (Ceramics-Cooperative), C/ Lope de Vega 7.
Information / Oficina de Turismo
Almería: C/ Hermanos Machado 4, Tel: 230858.

PROVINCE GRANADA
(Telephone area code: 958-)
Accommodation
GUADIX: *BUDGET:* **Comercio,** Mira de Amezcua 3, Tel: 660500. **GRANADA:** *LUXURY:* **Alhambra Palace,** Peña Partida 2, Tel: 221468. *MODERATE:* **Montecarlo,** Acera de Darro 44, Tel: 257900. **Hostal Carlos V,** Pl. de los Campos 4, Tel: 221587. *BUDGET:* **Los Jerónimos,** C/ Grán Capitán 1, Tel: 294461. **Youth Hostel:** Camino de Ronda 171, Tel: 272638. **SIERRA NEVADA:** *MODERATE:* **Parador Nacional,** Ctra. at km 35, Tel: 480200. **GUADIX:** *MODERATE:* **Mulhacén,** Ctra. de Murcia, 43, Tel: 660750. **ALPUJARRAS:** *MODERATE:* **Andalucía,** Av. Andalucía 15-17, Tel: 770136. *BUDGET:* **Lanjarón,** C/ Pérez Chaves 7, Tel: 770094. **TREVÉLEZ:** *BUDGET:* **Pension Regina,** Pl. Francisco Abellán, Tel: 765064. **BUBIÓN:** *MODERATE:* **Villa Turística de Poqueira,** Barrio Alto, Tel: 763111.
Museums / Sightseeing
GUADIX: Cathedral: 10.30 a.m.-1 p.m., 5-7 p.m., Sun 10.30 a.m.–2 p.m. **GRANADA:**

Alhambra and **Generalife**: 9 a.m.-8 p.m. Cathedral, Capilla Real, Cartuja, Iglesia de San Jerónimo: 10.30 a.m.-1 p.m., 4-7 p.m. **Carmen de los Martires**: 11 a.m.-2 p.m., 4-7 p.m. **Museo Arqueologico**: Tue–Sat 10 a.m.–2 p.m. **Museo de Bellas Artes** (Pal. Carlos V, Alhambra): Mon - Fri 10 a.m. - 2 p.m. **LA CALAHORRA**: **Castillo**: Wed 10 a.m.-1 p.m., 4-6 p.m.

Information / Oficina de Turismo
GRANADA: C/ Libreros 2, Tel: 225990, 10 a.m.-1 p.m. and 4-7 p.m.

PROVINCE JAÉN
(Telephone area code: 953-)
Accommodation
JAÉN: *LUXURY:* **Parador Castillo de Sta. Catalina**. Tel: 264411. *MODERATE:* **Rey Fernando**, Pl. de Coca de la Piñera 7, Tel: 251840. **UBEDA**: *LUXURY:* **Parador Condestable Dávalos**, Pl. Vazquez de Molina 1, Tel: 750345. *MODERATE:* **Consuelo**, C/ Ramón y Cajál 12, Tel: 750840.
CAZORLA: *LUXURY:* **Parador El Adelantado**, Tel: 721075. *MODERATE:* **Cazorla**, Pl. del Generalissimo 4, Tel: 720203. **Sierra de Cazorla**, Ctra. de la Sierra (2 km outside of town), Tel: 720015.

Museums / Sightseeing
JAEN: **Cathedral**: 8.30 a.m.-1 p.m. and 4.30-7 p.m., Museum open on weekends only, 11 a.m.-1 p.m. **Arab Baths**: 10 a.m.-2 p.m. and 5-8 p.m., Sun 10 a.m.-2 p.m., closed Mon. **San Ildefonso**: 8 a.m.-12 noon and 6-9 p.m.
JAÉN: Av. de Madrid 10, Tel: 222737.
UBEDA: Pl. del Ayuntamiento. **Nature Reserve Sierra de Cazorla**: Information bureaus at the park entrances in Cazorla, C/ Martínez Falero 11, Tel: 720125 (La Iruela), Tronca and Siles (at the fringe of the Sierra de Segura).

PROVINCE MALAGA
(Telephone area code: 952-)
Accommodation
ANTEQUERA: *LUXURY:* **Parador**, C/ García del Olmo, Tel: 840061. *BUDGET:* **La Yedra**, Ctra. Córdoba–Malaga at km 540, Tel: 842287. **NERJA**: *LUXURY:* **Parador de Nerja**, El Tablazo, Tel: 520050. *MODERATE:* **Portofino**, Puerta del Mar 2, Tel: 520150.
MALAGA: *LUXURY:* **Malaga Palacio**, Cortina del Muelle 1, Tel: 215185. **Parador Gibralfaro**, on top of the castle hill, Tel: 221902. *MODERATE:* **California**, Paseo de Sancha 19, Tel: 215165.
BENAJARAFE: *BUDGET:* **Esperanza**, Urb. La Esperanza, Tel: 513123.

MARBELLA: *LUXURY:* **Marbella-Dinamar Club 24**, Ctra. de Cádiz km 175, Tel: 810500. *MODERATE:* **Club Pinomar I** and **II**, Ctra. de Cádiz at km 189, Tel: 831345/ 831306.
TORREMOLINOS: *LUXURY:* **Cervantes**, C/ Las Mercedes, Tel: 384033. *MODERATE:* **Montemar**, Av. Carlota Alessandry, Tel: 381577.
MIJAS: *LUXURY:* **Mijas**, Urb. Tamisa, Tel: 485800. *BUDGET:* **El Mirlo Blanco**, Pl. de la Constitución 13, Tel: 485700.

Museums / Sightseeing
CUEVAS DE NERJA: 9 a.m.-9 p.m.; Sept 16–April 30: 10 a.m.-2 p.m., 4-7 p.m.
MALAGA: **Cathedral**: 10 a.m.-1 p.m., 4-5.50 p.m. **Museo de Artes Populares**, Pasillo de Sta. Isabel 10: 10 a.m.-1 p.m., 4-7 p.m., closed Mon. **Museo de Bellas Artes**, C/ San Agustín 6: 10 a.m.-1.30 p.m., 5-8 p.m., Sat and Sun 10 a.m.-1 p.m., closed Mon. **Museo de Cofradías**, in the Iglesia y Hospital de San Julián. **Alcazaba**, **Museo Arqueologico** and **Ceramics Museum**: 11 a.m.-2 p.m., 5-8 p.m. (in winter 10 a.m.-1 p.m., 4-7 p.m.), Sat 10 a.m.-2 p.m.
ARCHIDONA: **Santuario de la Virgen de Gracia**: 9 a.m.-2 p.m., 4-8 p.m.
ANTEQUERA: **Cuevas de Menga y Viera** and **del Romeral** (Dolmen): 9.30 a.m.-13.30 p.m., 3-6 p.m., Sun 10 a.m.-2 p.m. **FUENTE VAQUEROS**: **Casa Museo de García Lorca**: 10 a.m.-2 p.m., 6-9 p.m.(in winter 4-6 p.m.).
BENALMÁDENA: **Museo Arqueologico** (Precolumbian cultures) 10 a.m.-2 p.m., 5-7 p.m., Sat 10 a.m.-2 p.m., Sun 5-7 p.m.

Information / Oficina de Turismo
NERJA: Puerta del Mar 4, Tel: 521531. **MALAGA**: C/ Marqués de Larios 5, Tel: 213445. Paseo del Parque, C/ Cister 11.
ANTEQUERA: Palacio de Nájera, Coso Viejo, Tel: 842180.
MARBELLA: C/ Miguel Cano 1, Tel:771442.

PROVINCE CÁDIZ
(Telephone area code: 956-)
Accommodation
CASTELLAR DE LA FRONTERA: *LUXURY:* **La Almoraima** (former monastery), Tel: 693004-51. **ALGECIRAS**: *MODERATE:* **Alarde**, C/ Alfonso XI. 4, Tel: 660408.

Information / Oficina de Turismo
GIBRALTAR: Four Corner's Frontier, Tel: 76400.
ALGECIRAS: C/ Juan de la Cierva, Tel: 660911.

Museums / Sightseeing
SAN ROQUE: **Museo Historico del Campo de Gibraltar.**

135

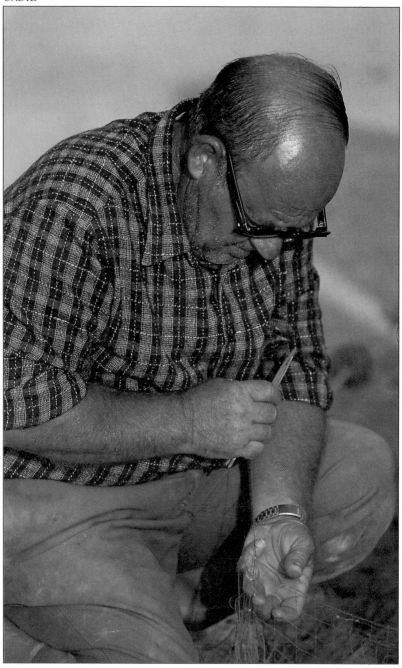

ATLANTIC ANDALUSIA

CÁDIZ
SHERRY TRIANGLE
WHITE TOWNS OF
THE SIERRA
SEVILLA
HUELVA

From the mouth of the Guadiana all the way to the Straits of Gibraltar stretch the fine sandy beaches known as "The Coast of Light". Embraced by stands of fir and salt flats, they are punctuated by rivers which pour out of confining valleys into wide deltas. The name is due to the inimitable light conditions prevailing here almost the year round, white and blinding from sun, salt and reflections off the water.

Since the 16th century the towns here have maintained close ties to the Spanish-speaking nations overseas. In fact, accent, physiognomy, way of life and urban configuration are so astonishingly similar in both parts of the Spanish world that it seems incredible that 10,000 km (6210 mi) separate them. On the entire Coast of Light, the wine is good and the fish is invariably fresh. Each village has its own festival and *bodegas*, large wine and sherry cellars, are ubiquitous. The climate is temperate all year, with mild winters and summers that are not as hot as in the interior. What is more important and at first sight inexplicable, until recently the region was spared the on-

slaught of mass tourism. The only explanation, in fact, which comes to mind is that the wind may have been a deterrent, the dry Levante from Africa which scorches the earth and cools the water, an unpleasant wind which gets on one's nerves and sweeps clouds of sand through village streets. When it does blow, it usually blows for three days, sometimes longer, and has been known to ruin bathing holidays. When it is blowing, the best thing to do is to go on an excursion to the mountains and get as far away from the coast as possible. Yet this wind has enticed a different sort of tourist and has, after all, made the region famous. Windsurfers from all over Europe gather here, boards lashed to the roofs of their cars or even as airline luggage, to revel in the magnificent surfing conditions here and on the Portuguese Algarve. With them came the Jet Set. Golf courses, polo fields and first-class hotels have mushroomed. Still, the wide beaches are so vast that congestion is impossible.

Coastal towns here have always been fishing villages with large ocean-going fleets. The coast is full of *almadrabas*, ingeniously complex yet traditionally constructed facilities for catching tuna. The entire bay of Cádiz was once one vast and complex trap of this sort despite the ship-

Preceding pages: Picturesque Mojácar consists of a jumble of houses clutching to a hill. Left: After every bout of fishing a bout of net fixing.

139

ping going in and out of it. Tuna came into it and were trapped. Sometimes dolphins stray here and then, as a matter of course, it takes them days to find the natural exits to the sea. Oysters, various kinds of prawns and shrimp, mussels, mild river mussels, varieties of monkfish, small squid, sea bream and wrasse, sea trout and ray are just a few of the delightfully fresh and deliciously prepared regional seafood specialties. Invariably there are *tapas* at bars and in restaurants, accompanied by good local wine.

The Cádiz Coast

Tarifa is the magic word for devotees of that fast water sport. Long rollers and a steady stiff breeze guarantee conditions to put a windsurfer's skills to the test. The old town of **Tarifa** was built in 711 on the site of a Roman settlement when the Moors came. It has an Arab fort. The **Guzmán el Bueno Tower** recalls the battles of the Reconquista when the Moors wanted to recapture the fort from the Christians. To force the Christians to surrender they took Guzmán's son hostage, threatening to cut his throat. The heroic father threw his knife down to them from the tower.

From the harbor one can look across the 15 kilometers (9 mi) of water separating Africa from Europe. The Straits of Gibraltar are always choppy and stirred up because of the many ships plying to and from mare nostrum.

Far from Tarifa, across the Bay of **Bolonia,** is the excavated Roman city of *Baelo Claudia.* Columns from Jupiter, Juno and Minerva temples, the ruins of Roman baths and a theater give a good idea of how the city looked in Roman times. Only a few kilometers away but only accessible by a winding road is the fishing village of **Zahara de los Atunes,** another spot where photographers and lovers of unusual patterns can stand and stare entranced at tuna-catching snares.

In **Barbata** too the fish is fresh and the beaches are clean and not crowded at all. The beach at **Caños de la Meca** is just beyond. At low tide a row of caves in the cliffs along the sea out of which freshwater springs bubble unexpectedly are accessible, but one has to be very careful not to be trapped by the incoming tide. This section of the coast is molded into romantic coves. This may be what has made it become a mecca for nudists. **Cape Trafalgar** recalls the famous sea battle here in 1805 where Nelson died while his fleet was fighting against the allied powers Spain and France for English supremacy in the Mediterranean. **Vejér de la Frontera** has remained Arab in ambience. Sprawling across several

COSTA DE LA LUZ

0   20 km

hills, it is reminiscent of the Moroccan city of *Chechaouen*. Both cities were founded in the 11th century by the Almohads. Narrow alleys with white, almost Arab-style, windowless houses concealing *patios* full of flowers around which household living centers lead to attractive Plaza de España. **Medina Sidonia** is inland, and this is indeed a city with an illustrious name. Dating back to Phoenician times, it played an important part in the Reconquista. Pl. Mayor is a testimony to its former grandeur.

CÁDIZ

After Conil, new *urbanizaciones* like Cabo Roche begin to line the beaches. A golf club has been built on the beach at Barrosa. There is a hatchery among the salt flats at **Sancti Petri**. On the promontory beyond Sancti Petri, built up with yet more holiday colonies, an old tuna fishery is decaying picturesquely. **Chiclana** is where *chiclanero* wine is made. It resembles sherry in taste, color and texture but it is made in smaller lots and is still sold at small family cellars. This is where the vast conurbation enclosing Cádiz Bay begins. A half million people live here. A welter of fisheries, shipbuilding, naval yard, cargo port and industry, all using the natural harbor, does not at first glance make a particularly good impression. **San Fernando** is a naval base. It is situated on a long sandspit which has

141

in the course of centuries almost been severed from the mainland. Known as *La Isla,* "the Island", it has produced famous flamenco singers like Camarón de la Isla. Charles III established a *Panteón* of 52 monuments to naval heroes here in the 18th century. In the early 19th century national interest focused on the city. During the resistance against the French occupation, parliament convened in the Teatro de las Cortes in 1810 and 1813. To the left of the Cádiz exit is the **Barrio Gallineras** with its small restaurants. A motorway runs along the beach for 15 km (9 mi) to Cádiz.

Cádiz is proud of being Europe's oldest city. Taxi drivers know the exact date of its foundation. According to their reckoning, the city is 3017 years old since 17 years ago the 3000th anniversary of its foundation by Hercules, the Greek mythical hero, was celebrated. There is no conclusive archaeological

Above: The port of Tarifa, the southernmost city on the Iberian Peninsula.

evidence from the most distant past, but the city's location on a peninsula jutting far into the sea and linked to the mainland only by a long narrow sandspit always has been a perfect spot for a fortress for any early civilisation not afraid of incursions from the sea. The bay is still an ideal harbor and a natural trap for fish, particularly tuna. When the new high-rise housing was built where low old buildings had stood, the detritus of millenia came to light: Phoenician burials, Tartesian shards, Roman amphorae, indefinable remnants of all the civilisations living on the Mediterranean littoral long before the interior was settled but which had ventured to this point. At all times in history venturesome and intrepid, seamen of Cádiz penetrated deep into the North Sea and the Baltic in search of amber. Traces of their far-flung exploration and colonizing exploits have been found on the African coast as far as Senegal. The praises of dancing girls from Cádiz, *puellae gaditanae,* were sung in Roman travellers' chronicles.

The age of New World maritime exploration reinvigorated the city. Many voyages of discovery to the South American continent set out from here. The harbor towns maintained ties with the young South American and Caribbean colonies and these links have never been severed. The inhabitants of Cádiz boast that their city is just like Havana and that Havana Cathedral is an exact replica of theirs. When trade began to flourish, merchants from Genoa, Tuscany and Flanders settled in the city, making it even more a magnet for the pirates who come to prey on them. Francis Drake and Lord Essex captured Cádiz in the 16th century. The sieges destroyed many buildings. It is said that they took over 150 *gaditanas* with them who had had enough of their husbands and found their religion onerous. In the 18th century the city was heavily involved again in the flourishing overseas trade.

Local merchants increased their wealth by means of a simple but effective form of speculation. Since the bay was usually crowded with ships lading and unloading cargo, it took time for a ship to receive permission to enter the harbor. Until its turn came, it had to remain at a safe distance from the sandbanks off shore. A merchant would keep a look-out from the high terrace of his house for a ship of his with the cargo he expected. Once he had spotted his ship, he had plenty of time to manipulate goods prices before it entered the harbor.

The at that time purely functional lookout turrets still give houses their distinctive appearance. By the late 18th century, 90 % of all overseas goods traded and reshipped in Spain arrived at Cádiz harbor. 125,000 people lived on that small spit of land.

Today Cádiz seems to have reached its natural limits with a population of 160,000. Yet high-rise buildings continue to mushroom parallel to the beach along 15 kilometers (9 mi) of road leading into the city. They have blocked out the view and with it the breeze. They even prevent sand from washing in and out naturally, which has had a detrimental effect on the beaches. Consequently, sand has to be brought by the lorryload to the four-kilometer-long (2.5 mi) city beach every year. The avenue leading into the **old city** ends at the Puerta de Tierra, the old city gate. The old and modern sections of the city have little in common. Old Cádiz is a gleaming, whitewashed 17th century city. The many Italian merchants who resided here have left their mark: narrow alleys opening out into quiet plazas and flat Italian-type roofs without tiles. Each plaza has its own appeal. Pl. de Candelaria is small with an intimate ambience. Pl. de San Juan is gregarious and full of terrace cafés. Pl. de Mina is well planted. Pl. de España and Pl. San Antonio are impressive. At the walls of the old fort are the inviting Alameda de Apodaca and Parque Genovés, leafy and refreshing parks with superb views over the bay.

Each of the quarters of the city is distinctive. Between Plaza Juan de Diós and Sta. María is the oldest quarter, the **Barrio del Pópulo.** Beyond Pl. de España and Pl. de Candelaria is the best residential area, opening on to the harbor and with the freshest air in the city. The old fishermen's quarter, **Barrio de la Viña,** is on the way to Playa de la Caleta beach. This is the most traditional part of the city. The center, Plaza Tío de la Tiza, is particularly lively during the Holy Week processions and at Carneval. Cádiz Carneval, a tradition observed since the 17th century, is a cross between Carneval at Venice and Carneval in the Caribbean. It lasts ten days. Everyone who lives in the city and throngs of visitors are on the streets at this time. Groups walk chanting through the streets mocking events and prominent people in pointed verses. Carneval goes on day and night. With their costumes, people assume a role they keep up the entire time.

Outstanding buildings are actually not what makes the city so impressive. It is its atmosphere. A stroll through the streets might end at Cathedral Square. The **cathedral** is Neoclassical but its golden dome give it an oriental air. In the crypt is the tomb of the city's most famous son, the composer Manuel de Falla (1876-1946). The big Falla Theater also recalls him. Adjacent to the Baroque del Rosario church is the round **Oratorio de la Santa Cueva** chapel. Its interior is covered with frescoes by Goya. It was consecrated to the strains of a work by Joseph Haydn which was composed expressly for the purpose, *The Seven Last Words of Christ*. A number of other Baroque churches should mark one's progress through the city: La Castrenser, Carmen, La Merced and San Antonio. Each conceals treasures of its own. The altarpiece in the chapel of Sta. Catalina is

Above: Great, threatening storm clouds gather over the already theatrically dramatic skyline of the town of Cádiz.

by Murillo. When he was working on it, he suffered such a serious fall from the scaffolding that he died soon after. The **Art Museum** contains a remarkable collection of Baroque painting: Murillo, Zurbarán, Ribera and Cano. Finds exhibited in the Archaeological Museum give convincing evidence of the city's antiquity. The oval-shaped **Oratorio de San Felipe Neri** is also of historic significance. In it, the liberal constitution of 1812 was read out. Cádiz thus also has valid claims to being the cradle of incipient Spanish democracy well ahead of similar events in many parts of Europe.

SHERRY TRIANGLE

One leaves Cádiz from the east via a bridge spanning the bay. **Puerto Real,** built by the Catholic Kings on the site of the Roman city of *Portus Gaditanus,* is an ideally conceived and laid out Renaissance city. Its architectural and urban planning significance lies further in the fact that its plan was a model for the young colonial cities. The Renaissance church of San Sebastian is particularly distinguished. It was here in the Guadalete estuary that Napoleon's heavy cannons got mired in the damp soil of the salt flats. The cannon balls fell short of Cádiz into the water, leaving the city unharmed. Today the area is racked by a shipyards jobs crisis, a universal problem of all nations renowned for the proud ships which left their slips and for the maritime trade their ports handled.

At the mouth of the river is **El Puerto de Sta. María.** From the harbor one can cross the bay to Cádiz by taking a scenic half-hour steam boat trip. The town became important in the 16th century when the owners of overseas merchant ships built themselves residences and haughty turrets here. The Municipal Museum is housed in one of these residences. The fortress of **San Marcos,** in which a Mozarabic chapel has been preserved, lodged Columbus and Juan de la Cosa. Rafael Alberti, a poet of the Generation of '27, was born here and a museum is dedicated to him. The town has a particularly handsome bullfighting arena.

The presence of so many wine cellars reveals that the sherry region starts here. Sherry, as Britons call the wine they so cherish from the wine-growing region of Jerez, is an apéritif wine. It is produced by a complex process and aged in casks in sheds also known as "wine cathedrals" because of their gloomy and solemn grandeur and size. *Bodegas* have left their mark on the skyline of the thirteen towns in the triangle-shaped wine-growing region of Jerez bounded by Sta. María, Trebujena and Sanlucar. Even **Rota,** the controversial NATO base at the end of Cádiz Bay, forms part of the sherry triangle.

Jerez de la Frontera looks as if it consisted entirely of *bodegas* when viewed from the outskirts by visitors driving into the city. Oldfashioned cellars, modern concrete storage sheds, wine vats, all stages and methods of wine ageing can be seen. The best known names in the international sherry export trade are emblazoned in large letters on the storage sheds, and each one of these is grander than the next. The royal Bodega La Concha was built by the French architect Eiffel. The "Gran Bodega Tio Pepe" is the world's largest with a storage capacity of 30,000 casks. Tasting rooms, stalls and salesrooms are all part of the complex and open to visitors.

Wine is not all that Jerez has to offer. With a population of 180,000 the biggest city in the province, it boasts an economy which can only be called vigorous. The old city is, however, relatively small. Some ruins and the mosque, converted into a church, are all that is left of the residence of the Caliphs of Sevilla. The Gothic Isabelline church of San Miguel is an elegantly airy structure. Further attractions at Jerez are the motor-racing track, the clock museum and the zoo.

The sherry triangle is famous for three things. Sherry, flamenco and horses are traditional here. The status Flamenco enjoys is demonstrated by a Flamenco school and the Andalusian Flamenco foundation in the Palacio de Pemartín. Broad steps lead up to the 17th-century collegiate church, which is impressive, with five aisles and an octagonal dome. On the steps, the official ceremony of the September wine harvest festival begins with the blessing of the must. It is consecrated to San Ginés, patron saint of wine-growing. Four weeks after Easter there is a festival in honor of Andalusia's horses. The magnificent animals, drawing carriages seating Andalusian girls in traditional costume, are presented at various performances. Time-honored clichés come to life again, revealing the haughty *caballero* as macho: His strong arms sweep a pretty girl up into the saddle to ride behind him ....

Since 1973, there has been a Court school of white Andalusian horses. It per-

forms all year in the **Palacio Recreo de las Cadenas.** Dressage is similar to that performed by the Viennese Riding School. The horses descend from the Cartuja bloodlines bred at the Carthusian monastery outside the city on the river. The monastery is only open to men visitors. Its Gothic church has a magnificently decorated Renaissance façade with figures made by Alonso Cano and a Gothic cloisters.

The third leg of the sherry triangle is closed by **Sanlucar de Barrameda** on the left bank of the Guadalquivir delta. By the 15th century it was a flourishing port with strong fortifications. Overseas trade enhanced its importance as a trading and lading port after the port of Sevilla had silted up. The town is divided into two sections. In the upper town are the tower and walls of the fortress of Santiago. Adjacent to it is the palace of the

Above: Showing off one's pride possessions at the Feria de Abril in Sevilla. Right: Preparing for a siesta to escape the noonday heat.

Countess of Medina Sidonia. Below the palace garden, towards the slope, are *covachas*, which are ornate Late Gothic wine cellars. Large *bodegas* have put their stamp on this city too. Many of them have bars or restaurants in which one can enjoy good *tapas* with one's wine. In the lower city, built on land reclaimed from the sea, are plazas, churches and Baroque monasteries. The ubiquitous and endless holiday resort colonies stretch down to the beach.

At the far end of the city is the fishermen's quarter of **Bajo de Guia** with lots of restaurants in which one can eat crayfish and drink the local sherry, *Manzanilla,* while gazing out over the sea. Riders might be frolicking about on the sand, training for the traditional races. On the far side of the river, however, nature is unspoiled. The Coto Doñana National Park extends down to the right bank. It covers the entire side of the Guadalquivir delta. **Chipiona,** at the end of a 15-kilometer-long (9 mi) beach north of Rota, is a popular seaside resort which has *bodegas* of its own.

WHITE TOWNS OF THE SIERRA

Many of the nice villages scattered throughout the mountains west of Jerez have the words "de la Frontera" appended to their names. Large areas of Andalusia were conquered in the 13th century by Ferdinand III and Alfonso X. It took 200 years for the last Moorish stronghold, Granada, to fall.

The towns on the border between Moorish and Christian territory were subjected to continual attacks and attempts at reconquest by either side. They were on the front and this is what the appendage to their names means. They still look as if the front were an imminent threat to them. Most are high up in the mountains, on steep escarpments or in steep river valleys protected on one side, and they are all guarded by strong forts and

towered over by churches, domineering and authoritative. These villages are all alike. Their white houses look like piled up cubes with romantic inner courtyards full of flowers. The main street is invariably the only street from which the mountains are fairly accessible. Along it are the most handsome façades and the strongest bars and grilles on the windows. All other streets and alleys are steep and difficult to ascend.

These are aesthetic villages. Their purity of line combines with whitewashed surfaces, red roofs and the verdant green of the hillsides to achieve austere perfection. From the outside they are fascinating. Once one is on the inside looking out, they are merely peaceful. Daily life is tranquil. Centuries of isolation have only recently and grudgingly yielded to the advent of new roads and tourism. In these villages the only objects of interest to sightseers tend to be the fort and the church. One has to ask for the key next door. It is now possible to spend the night in most villages in the area and there are

restaurants serving the regional dishes of the Sierra. The tourists who venture into this area, however, do not seek luxury. In the off season, the villages revert to normal, to all appearances remote from the world.

The best known and most accessible of the "White Towns" is **Arcos de la Frontera,** considered to be one of Spain's most beautiful towns. The narrow main street ascends endlessly before reaching the **Pl. del Corregidor**. From a balcony one can see where one has got to. At one's feet a wall of rock drops sheer 166 m (545 ft) to the Río Guadalete. All streets in Arcos are lovely, intriguing and enchanting. Some are spanned by buttresses supporting house walls. Many of the houses were residences of the gentry or monasteries.

The mayor's residence has been converted into one of the country's most distinguished *paradores*. The town hall, the fort and the Gothic church with its Plateresque façade are all on Corregidor Square. The choir of the church was

carved in the 18th century by Roldán. Choir and altar are said to be made of four types of wood: lemonwood, olivewood, walnut and mahogony.

Beyond Arcos, the Guadalete has been dammed to form two reservoirs. South of these artificial lakes the road leads into the mountains and to a tour of the most ravishing of the White Towns: El Bosque, Benamahoma, Ubrique, Grazalema, Ronda, Setenil, Olvera, Zahara and, farther south, Jimena de la Frontera. Above them all tower the peaks of the Sierra de Grazalema. The highest is **El Pinar** at 1654 m (5426 ft). Often snowcapped in spring, this range has more precipitation than the rest of Spain since advancing Atlantic fronts get trapped there and thus continually rain on it. The water has formed many limestone caves. In some of them, near **Benaoján** (El Hundidero, La Pileta, El Gato) prehistoric drawings have been found.

Above: A spectacular view of the imposing gorge of the Tajo in Ronda.

The **Sierra de Grazalema** is a protected area with distinctive vegetation. To the north of the Sierra, accessible from the road between Grazalema and Benamahoma, is the only *pinsapo* forest in Europe. These bristly trees have become fairly common in Central Europe as ornamental plants. The protected forest area is an ideal sanctuary for deer, mountain goats and many eagles and vultures. A favorite vulture nesting area is in the rocky walls of the **Gargante Verde Gorge,** which can only and with difficulty be reached from the narrow road between Grazalema and Zahara. While the young are in the nest from January to June, visitors are only permitted to enter the area with a guide.

Other rivers have cut deep into the soft rock to form breathtaking canyons like **La Butrera Gorge** on the Guadiaro north of El Colmenar. The train from Algeciras to Ronda goes through many tunnels on this scenic route through narrow valleys choked with rhododendron and the Sierra de Aljibe with its vast forests of cork oak. The village of **Setenil** near Ronda is built into the steep rock walls in defiance of all town-planning rationale. The most spectacular of these gorges is the one moulded by the Tajo at **Ronda.** The town is perched impregnably on a mountain cleft by a gorge nearly 100 m (328 ft) deep. It has been spanned since the 18th century by a remarkably constructed bridge. The Christians were only able to take the town from the Arabs by a clever ruse. The antiquity of the town is more than amply and convincingly evidenced by Stone Age drawings, excavations of a Roman settlement, and Arab baths. The Catholic Kings had the church of Sta. María built on the foundations of the mosque, and the monastery of Sto. Domingo was built by them too. The church of Espiritu Santo bears the more recent coat of arms of the Habsburgs. The ornate castle of the Marquis of Salvatierra is adorned with intriguing Baroque decoration imported from the colonies and incorporated into the architecture much as Modernist decor was used in defiance of seeming structural common sense in a larger age. Near the castle, the river is spanned much lower down by both an Arab and a medieval bridge.

The gorge has cleft the town into new and old sections. The main attraction of new Ronda is Spain's oldest **bullfighting arena.** Dating from the 18th century it is dedicated to Pedro Romero, the first modern torero, which simply means that he was the first torero who was not mounted. The town's cuisine has been adapted to the exigencies of tourism, yet few visitors linger more than a few hours. In "off hours" Ronda is a pleasant mountain village with bracing air and a cosy ambience. Half the tourist attractions mentioned in the brochure handed out by the tourist office are closed. The onslaught of tourism has been too much for the town. Its magnificent setting has, of course, always attracted writers. Cervantes stayed at the Posadas de las Ani-

mas. Rilke stayed at the Hotel Reina Victoria when he came. The town is proud of this. There is even a Rilke Driving School. At a distance of 12 km (7.5 mi) is "old Ronda", the remains of a Roman settlement with an amphitheater, 1000 m (3280 ft) above sea level.

SEVILLA

"Quien no ha visto Sevilla, no ha visto maravilla" ("He who has not seen Sevilla has never seen a marvel."), as the saying goes. **Sevilla**, the capital of Andalusia with a population of 700,000 is 10 m (33 ft) above sea-level on the broad stream of the Guadalquivir. The place with the hottest summers in Spain was once a major river port. Founded by the Phoenicians and taken by Julius Caesar, it was the capital of a subregion of the Province of Baetica under the Romans and the Visigoths. It was known then as *Hispalis* and the river was called *Baetis.* Ample and skilfully excavated traces of the Romans can be seen at Itálica north of the city. Under the Visigoths, the official conversion of Spain from Arian Christianity to Catholicism began here. The heir to the throne, San Hermenegildo, and Bishops San Isidoro and San Leandro spread the doctrine in the 6th century in writing and by word of mouth. The Arabs changed the face of the city, naming it *Isbiliat* and giving the river its present name. From the 11th century Sevilla was the seat of the Emirs of the Almohad dynasty. In the 13th century Ferdinand III of Castile took the city. Some of his Christian successors enjoyed to excess the luxury of the Arab city.

After the discovery of America, Sevilla became the richest city in Spain in the 16th century. Noisy and bustling, under the sway of trade and port, it was a magnet for all sorts of people-domestic and foreign merchants, charlatans, vagabonds and rogues, scholars and adventurers. A major port of reshipment for goods from

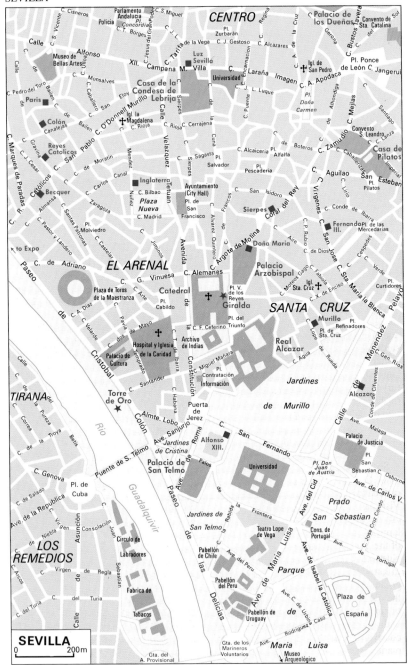

SEVILLA

0   200m

the colonies and Europe and for silver and gold, it became at the same time an important cultural center. That was the era in which the great cathedral was built. The distinguished sculptors Martínez Montañés and Nuño Delgado, the master woodcarver Rodrigo Alemán and painters like Murillo, Zurbarán, Valdés Leal and Velázquez rose to fame there. In literature, the Sevilla School flourished under the patronage of the House of Gelves, descendants of Columbus. The leading Renaissance poets, F. de Herrera, Aldana and de la Torre, wrote in the city. Four hundred years later the Generation of '27 took up the tradition.

Under the Bourbons, the first rash of colonial fever had subsided. Charles III, in the 18th century, was thinking of posterity. On the first floor of the old Merchants' Exchange built by Juan de Herrera in the 16th century, he had the **Archivo de Indias** established. Even today many a dust-gathering colonial document remains to be rediscovered by students and historians looking for virgin, primary source material in an unexhausted field of research. In the 18th century the city declined due to the silting up of the river port. Not until industrialisation did it regain its importance.

Sevilla Today

Seen from a distance, Sevilla looks like other Spanish big cities with vast new residential areas and industrial buildings. Visitors, however, are directed into the city center on the southern rim of the large inner city roundabout on the bend of the river. Here the main attractions are clustered in a relatively small area. To get to know the authentic Sevilla one has to go on foot. Cross the river or wander into the old Jewish quarter to find the Sevilla of many moods, lanes and alleys lined with yellow and white houses, inner courtyards (*patios*) with carefully tended plants, pretty tree-shaded plazas which turn into open-air restaurants on hot summer nights, picturesque corners with the Virgin painted on tiles and candles always burning before her, or restaurants in which one is overwhelmed by the sheer diversity of *tapas* delicacies on the counter.

One gets the best view of it all from the **Giralda,** the principat minaret of the old mosque, and today the city's emblem. Built in the Mauretanian style, it resembles minarets of the type familiar in Rabat and Marrakesh. It was added in the 12th century to Visigoth foundations which make up a few meters of the base. Intrepid visitors can ascend the tower by going through the cathedral and leaving it by the Puerta de los Palos to cross a small inner courtyard in which the tower stands. The Arab structure became a distinctive entity through Renaissance additions: the balconies, the belfry or weathervane, a personification of faith, *giraldillo*, which gave the tower its name. It is 100 m (328 ft) tall. One can reach 70 m by a ramp which Ferdinand III mounted on horseback after he took the city in 1248.

The more than 140 columns adorning the exterior are from the Medina Azahara Palace at Córdoba. From the top one has a panoramic view over the city: the island of Cartuja with the 1992 **World's Fair Grounds** between the canal and the river to the northwest; to the west, on the far side of the canal, the old fishermen's quarter of **Triana**; to the south of it, the modern residential section of **Remedios** adjacent to the park grounds on which the *Feria de Abril* is held annually; to the south, taking up a whole block, the **university** in what used to be the 18th century tobacco factory in which Carmen, the operatic heroine, worked, supposedly the second largest building in Spain after the Escorial; beyond it, **María Luisa** and **Prado de San Sebastain Parks** with the grounds of the 1929 Ibero-American Exposition: the semi-circle of Pl. de España

with the two slender Neo-Mudéjar towers and Modernist exhibition pavilions.

Farther south is the harbor which relieves the congestion of the large ports of Cádiz and Huelva. To the east, directly in front of the cathedral, are the buildings of the royal **Alcázar** with its inner courtyards and gardens enclosed by high walls. Next to it one looks down on terraces and busy streets in the **Santa Cruz quarter**, the old Jewish ghetto. Beyond stretches the new railway station, and as far as one can see, 20th century Sevilla, a monstrous agglomeration of traffic and industry relieved occasionally by large modern residential sections like the garden city of Ciudad Jardín or the Universid Laboral. To the north, finally, the city center is spread out, a tangle of streets, alleys and plazas, red roofs, domes and innumerable church spires, a few major thoroughfares and a sea of white houses.

Above: The altar of the cathedral of Sevilla, a golden sight for sore eyes. Right: Gypsies still perform the finest flamencos.

Historic Sights

The most important buildings from Sevilla's heyday are the cathedral, the Alcázar, Pilate's Palace, the Torre de Oro and the Archives. The **cathedral,** as a sign proudly proclaims, is in the Guinness Book of Records as the world's third largest, covering the largest area. When it was built it was intended to be a place of worship so enormous that beholders would be overawed and therefore not believe their eyes. It measures 116 x 76m (380 x 250 ft), has nine portals, five aisles up to 36m (118 ft) high, 45 apsidioles and radiating chapels and the most enormous *reredos* in Christendom behind the altar: an expanse so lavishly decorated that hardly more than a *mare magnum* of gold and silver meets the eye. The altar and choir by Nufro Sánchez (15th century) which is, believe it or not, one of the best of its kind, is scarcely visible behind the heavy grille blocking the approach to it. The Plateresque royal chapel in the ambulatory houses the catafalques of King

Ferdinand II, the Saint, his son Alfonso X, the Wise, and his wife, Beatriz de Suavia. This is where the patron saint of the city is venerated, the small 13th century Gothic statue of the Virgen de los Reyes. In the sacristy there are paintings by Murillo, Goya, Valdés Leal, Zurbarán, Ribera and Alonso Cano. Next to them a most unusual 16th century chapter house is oval in shape with Baroque frescoes in the dome. Through the Portal of Forgiveness one reaches the Orange Court, which is part of what remains of the mosque. The Columbinian Library, donated by the son of Columbus, opens on to it. Together with the chapter house library it contains an impressive collection of ancient works.

The **Alcázar,** once the residence of the Emirs, was rebuilt by Pedro the Cruel in the 14th century. He lived there like a sultan, which is what he had himself styled. Today one can see what remains of the extensive palace after devastation and fires. It is a blend of Mudéjar and Arab architecture. The tiles, stucco arabesques

and Atesonado ceilings of the inner courts are clearly Arab architecture at its best in the Patio de Doncellas (Court of the Maidens), where the ruler kept his harem, and the court of the Muñecas. The rooms, reminiscent of the Alhambra in decor, testify to the sophisticated taste of Pedro I of Castile who, in order to secure the throne, had his stepbrothers murdered one after the other. In the Ambassadors' Hall a spot on the floor is said to have been left by the blood of Don Fadrique, one of the murdered stepbrothers. The room with its elegant arch openings has a typical *almocárabe* ceiling. These are Mudéjar wooden ceilings which convey an almost cavernous illusion with their three-dimensional decoration. On the walls are portraits of the Castilian kings.

Pedro's successors also left their stamp on the building, as one can see in the rooms of Isabella the Catholic, the Gothic chapel and the hall of Charles V. The gardens have been much altered in the course of centuries, yet with their fountains and terraces of orange trees they re-

153

main an oasis from the heat of the city. Another secluded spot for a contemplative break is **Sta. María Square**, planted with jasmine and orange trees, a haven of shade and benches for the footsore traveller. The entrance to it is across from the cathedral. Beyond the Alcázar is the old Jewish quarter, the **Barrio Sta. Cruz.** In alleys which the sun seldom reaches, there are modest guesthouses, tourist shops and picturesque restaurants. There are two fairly large squares: Pl. de Doña Elvira, where plays by Lope de Rueda and his contemporaries were performed in the 16th century, and Plaza Sta. Cruz with its Baroque iron cross.

Cervantes set his Court of Monipodio, the gathering point for a gang of thieves and rogues, in Mesón del Moro Street. His description of contemporary locale and mores has lost nothing of its relevance. In C/Sta. Teresa is the convent of the same name, founded in the 16th cen-

tury by this reformer of the Carmelite Order. She is supposed to have said that anyone managing to live in the seductive city of Sevilla without sinning deserved particular respect. And C/Susona is named for the Jewess who, for love of a Christian, betrayed her faith and handed over her father, who opposed her, to the Inquisition. The decapitated head of the father is said to have hung in front of her house until well into the 18th century. Today no trace remains of the former ghetto occupants, who were murdered by the thousands in a notorious pogrom in 1391. The synagogue has become a church, **Sta. María la Blanca.** In it the entire history of Spanish art is represented, from Visigoth capitals to Arab decoration and Murillo.

North of the Barrio Sta. Cruz is **Casa de Pilatos,** a palace built in the early 16th century for the Dukes of Medinaceli as a replica of Pilate's palace in the Holy Land. The building with its magnificent arcaded court is a blend of Renaissance, Gothic, Flamboyant and Mudéjar stylis-

Above: The tiled Plaza de España. Right: The Torre de Oro, in Sevilla.

tic elements. Several rooms were decorated with frescoes by Pacheco, Velázquez' father-in-law. The original 16th
century tiles give visitors a good idea of
authentic Sevilla style, which has little to
do with recent imitations, an unfortunate
current fad. Greek and Roman statues
adorn the building, which also houses a
Roman museum. A similarly resplendent
16th century palace housing its own collection of notable archaeological finds
and in particular Roman mosaics is the
Palacio de Lebrija.

The **Torre de Oro**, which has pre-
sumably become a city landmark because
it invariably appears in the foreground in
romantic photos of the city skyline at
sunset, was a tower in the Almohad fortifications. It owes its name to the golden
tiles which used to decorate it. The
twelve-cornered tower today houses a
small maritime museum.

Beyond the Historic Monuments

A walk along or through the tobacco
factory, now the university, leads to the
gardens of the 1929 **Ibero-American
Exposition grounds**. They center around
Plaza de España. The semi-circular building is decorated with tile murals showing
typical scenes from all the Spanish provinces. Dainty bridges with ceramic rail-
ings span a narrow moat. At the end of
María Luisa Park, which one can drive
through in a horse and carriage, are the
Modernist but slightly decadent former
pavilions, now housing the archaeological and ethnological museums, surrounded by orange trees and flocks of
white doves. In the former, finds from the
early Iberian period, Roman sculpture,
mosaics and jewelry from Roman Itálica
are exhibited. The **Museo de Artes y
Costumbres Populare** exhibits tools and
ethnic costumes. In the basement are reconstructions of artisans' workshops.

Today the city centers around Pl.
Nueva and Pl. San Francisco. From here

the pedestrian shopping zone, **Sierpes,**
lives up to its name by twisting and turning like a serpent. In summer it is roofed
over by awnings affording relief from the
heat. In the west end of the city center
near the river and the old **Córdoba Station** which, like the Quai d'Orsay station,
is being converted into a cultural center,
is the **Sevilla Art Museum**. Known as
Spain's second largest art museum, it has
been undergoing renovation for years so
that very few rooms are open to the public. But it is well worth a visit. The building is a Baroque monastery. The rooms
opening on to the inner courtyards are remarkable in their own right. The collections include the works of Spanish and
Italian painters of the 15th - 18th centuries, particularly Murillo, Valdés Leal and
Zurbarán. From here it is not far to **La
Magdalena**, a distinguished Baroque
church which contains more paintings by
Zurbarán and frescoes by Valdés Leal.

If one crosses this arm of the river, the
Cartuja, the Carthusian monastery, is to
one's right. Since the 19th century it has

155

been used as a pottery factory. This is where the World's Fair grounds start, including the Cartuja and transforming the forbidding island into a park through which canals flow. To the left begins Triana which, as a fishermen's quarter, then a run-down section and now a restored restaurant section, has always been something special. Several modest two-storeyed houses line the streets. Pottery has always been a traditional craft here. Two local women potters, Santa Justa and Santa Rufina, refused to allow their wares to be used in heathen sacrificial rituals. In their stead they gave themselves up as hostages. The city of Sevilla subsequently made them its patron saints. In this quarter are the Gothic church of Sta. Ana with its Romanesque portal and the seat of the Inquisition, after which an alley behind the market has been named.

Another traditional quarter is the **Barrio de la Macarena** at the northern tip of the city center round the basilica of the same name, where there are remnants of the Moorish city walls. Others are the quarter north of Pl. de la Encarnación and the **Barrio San Lorenzo** round the church of the same name west of Alameda de Hercules, where fleamarkets are held on Sundays. This is where one is most likely to find the authentic Sevilla: This is the bailiwick of housewives chatting at the front door; at the corner there are bored prostitutes; here one cannot overlook the postman everyone knows who stops at every other bar; one encounters the priest queueing up with a plastic bag in his hand at the bakery.

Customs

The traditional way of life is dying out even in tradition-minded Andalusia. However, festivals keep old customs alive. *Fiestas* have always been more an escape from humdrum everyday living, the traditional form of holidaying at home with a touch of superstition and so-

cial event for good measure, than simply religious holidays on the Church Calendar. The biggest *fiesta* at Sevilla is the **Feria de Abril,** where nearly 1000 *casetas,* decorated festival tents, are set up for drinking and dancing. The most magnificent dress and ethnic costumes are donned for the occasion. One gives it all one's got. The crowds of people and horses are drowned out by lusty Sevillanas over hundreds of loudspeakers.

The second big festival in the year is **Holy Week**, a far cry from religious contemplation and atonement. Processions, which have become a national attraction, are the main event. At church doors particularly, where the *pasos* have to execute intricate manoeuvres, one has to fight for a place to stand. Brotherhoods, *cofradías,* in different disguises, (often in the penitential robes of the Inquisition, hooded apparel made notorious by the Ku-Klux-Klan), guilds and bands accompany the *pasos,* which are carved figures of the Virgin and Christ and Passion scenes, with a lugubriously spine-chilling roll of drums. The air is heavy over the procession with the scent of orange blossoms and incense. As many as 50 *costaleros,* swaying like dromedaries, carry platforms weighing tons. When they make the *paso* "dance", the public applauds. Penitents in robes with chains, crosses and candles shuffle barefoot through carpets of flowers. Silent processions thud at a trot through alleys, interrupted at intervals by *saetas*, religious outpourings in the form of flamenco songs performed by practised devotees to the applause of the crowd. Participants and spectators make liberal use of bars and restaurants, which are open all night.

Another festival is linked to the pilgrimage to the Virgin of El Rocío. On the Thursday before Whitsun at 11 o'clock a.m., the *Rocío Brotherhood of Sevilla* sets out from the church of San Jacinto in Triana in elaborately decorated ox-drawn waggons on the long and tiring journey to

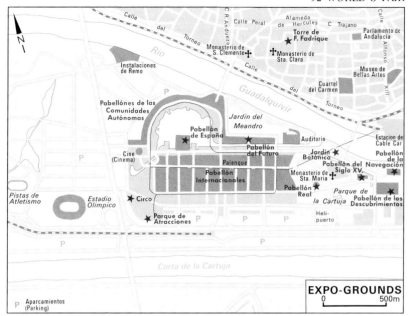

El Rocío. They return eight days later. First the outriders on their haughty horses leave the city, followed by the *simpecado*, the waggon with the Brotherhood's banner, and then the other waggons. The departure and the return are gladly exploited pretexts for unproarious festivities in the city and a mass is celebrated with flamenco songs.

The '92 World's Fair

For some years, everything in Sevilla has revolved around the '92 World's Fair. The 500th anniversary of the discovery of America will be celebrated all over Spain as the event of the dynamic and vibrant country's joining the great industrial nations of the world. Critical observations on the consequences of the events of 500 years ago – the persecution of the Jews, the expulsion of the Moriscos, the destruction of Indian civilisations – will not be heard.

With the Olympics at Barcelona and the selection of Madrid to be the cultural capital of Europe, Sevilla too will be in the international limelight. The inhabitants of Sevilla are not taking this as evidence of their region's importance and progressiveness, unlike the Catalans with regard to the Olympics. The residents of Sevilla are simply not being as pretentious about the honor awarded to their, admittedly, deserving city. Sevilla is taking things less seriously. The World's Fair is an opportunity in every sense of the word and everyone is well aware of all ramifications of this opportunity and the scope for development it offers. It will, first of all, mean economic growth: increased revenue and more jobs, an enhancement of Spain's image as a tourist country, an improved infrastructure, investment in the economy at large and in the hotel trade are expected. The Fair will bring Sevilla new streets, a new station accommodating the high-speed Madrid train, new bridges, millions of domestic and foreign visitors and six months of guaranteed broadcasting time on all TV channels.

157

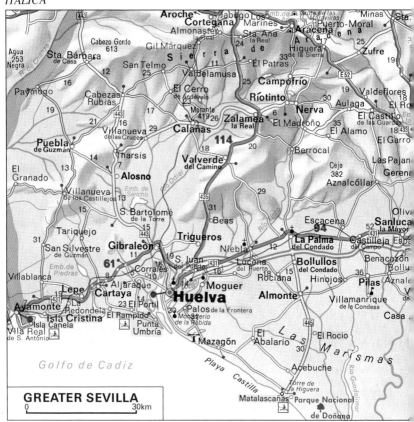

On 215 ha, 105 countries will exhibit their contributions to the twenty-first century. There is a pavilion for each of the *Communidades Autónomas*. This enables them to present themselves as largely autonomous and highly diverse cultural and social entities in a federation. The central complex comprising the monastery, the royal pavilion and the pavilion of the 15th century will, with the park, the botanical gardens and an artificial lake, remain in use after 1992.

The Ruins of Itálica

In North Sevilla the former Cistercian monastery of San Isidoro del Campo in **Santiponce** is a must. The massive fortified complex, where members of the House of Guzmán el Bueno were buried, has stood empty since secularisation. But the two churches, Early and Late Gothic, and the Mudéjar cloisters with lovely original tiles are still in good condition. Nearby is the excavation of the Roman settlement of *Colonia Aelia Augusta* **Itálica.** Founded in 206 BC for deserving legionaries who had fought in the Second Punic War, it was destroyed by the Moors in the 8th century after having declined in population and importance since the 6th century. The apparently quite prosperous Roman city had an amphitheater which is still in a good state of preservation, a theater, palaces and baths. Excavated treasures and mosaics are exhibited in a

National Park. The terrain was formed by the accretion of silt in what was the Roman lake of *Ligustinus*. Later it was a royal hunting preserve with hunting lodges scattered through it. The wetlands area, made up of the many interwoven mouths of the river, is one of the most important waterfowl sanctuaries in Europe. Due to its location between two continents it is an important stopping point for 250 species of migratory birds. Since wetlands farmers have been trying to drain parts of the area and have succeeded in reclaiming the entire eastern area for rice-growing, the drying out of the wetlands has become a threat to flora and fauna. The wetlands are further endangered by the encroachment of holiday resorts on all sides. The northern area of the park is an arid sandy upland with pine woods harboring lynx, deer and wild boar. A rather remote strip of land, it has a fascination all its own. The flickering glancing light which has given the coast its name combined with the monotonous flatness of the terrain produce a singular atmosphere. The area is, perhaps fortunately for visitors as well as the wildlife in the park, inaccessible by car and only in a few places on foot. In order to visit the interior of the park visitors have to book in advance for expensive Landrover excursions. Shorter walking tours on marked paths with bridges and vantage points are possible for visitors who are less energetic or have less time from the information centers along the road from Almonte to the coast.

The same road passes through **El Rocío,** a small village clustered around a modern pilgrimage church with the famous 13th century statue of the Virgin. Once a year at Whitsun it is sought out by a million pilgrims. This is the biggest sacred and profane pilgrimage spectacle in the western world, although this fact is not generally known. The houses of the pilgrimage Brotherhoods stand empty for the rest of the year, leaving the village

museum. Other finds are in the archaeological museums of Sevilla and Madrid.

HUELVA

Huelva can be reached quickly from Sevilla on the new motorway. Halfway there is the County of **Niebla**, which Enerique II of Castile gave to his illegitimate daughter Beatriz as a consolation prize. **Niebla** is a pretty wine-growing town surrounded by thick Arab walls and crowned by an Alcázar. The county, or *condado*, has its own version of sherry, quite like but not so renowned.

South of the motorway and west of the Guadalquivir stretch the 50,000 ha (125,000 acres) of the **Coto Doñana**

looking like a Texas ghost town. Nearer the coast at **Matalascañas** one is reminded again of the Wild West. Holiday accommodation mushroomed overnight until the protected zone around the national park was enlarged to put an end to land speculation, a bold and praiseworthy measure which will, one hopes, be widely imitated. Beyond it, the coastal road goes on to Huelva through relatively unspoiled dunes and marshlands.

Huelva's origins, like those of Tartessos, are mythical, but little about it recalls its past since it was completely destroyed in 1755 by an earthquake. From Roman times it was a major port from which copper and tin from the Río Tinto mines were shipped. Natural resources are still processed here. The petrochemicals and paper industries have had their share in turning the bay into what can only be termed a sewer. When the wind is blowing the other way, however, the town is pleasantly quiet, with some attractive pedestrian enclaves in which the lively provincial town life can unfold. From the monumental statue of Columbus by the American sculptress Whitney (1929), one can cross the bay by bridge to reach the spot where the voyages of discovery really began in 1492. **La Rábida,** an austere monastery across the bay, lodged Columbus. It is adorned with colorful paintings by Vázquez Díaz. The Pinzón brothers who provided the ships for Columbus' voyage were from **Palos de la Frontera.** The port where the voyage of discovery began and ended no longer exists. Inland from it is **Moguer,** which also boasts of having lodged Columbus. He is supposed to have prayed before setting out in the church of the convent of Sta. Clara. The 14th century convent is romantically decaying but is being converted into a regional museum. The re-

Right: The Coto Doñana National Park offers the beautiful coast protection from an overload of visitors.

stored church is a handsome example of the severe Mudéjar style. A small statue of Christ as a baby is the work of Luisa Roldán, *La Roldana*, whose little-known Baroque sculptures can be seen in the churches of the area. Connoisseurs of art, and not only feminists, are advised to seek out her work. Nobel Prize laureate Juan Ramón Jiménez was also born in Moguer. His philosophical dialogues with the donkey *Platero* have become famous worldwide. The house in which he was born is a small museum.

The towns that are profiting from Columbus' fame are today farming towns which, like many others near Huelva, grow early fruit, particularly the unbelievably big and tasty strawberries which have successfully taken a large share of the Central European market. The flats of the silted up harbor glisten anew – but with plastic forcing tunnels.

From the Marismas to Portugal

On the western landspit on the broad mouth of the Río Tinto and the Río Odiel is **Punta Umbría.** From here to the Portuguese border broad beaches, small holiday resorts, dunes and pine woods run into each other. Above Punta Umbría are the Odiel wetlands, known as the *marismas*, rather like the wetlands of the Coto Doñana. The terrain changes its configuration continually since it is regularly flooded by the tides, creating a flexible yet distinctive habitat for wetlands flora and fauna. Many migratory bird species stop here. Sea currents sweep the sediment washed down by the rivers to form long barrier islands parallel to the coast. The barrier island before the mouth of the Río Piedras is over 10 km (6 mi) long. A veritable paradise for bathers, it can be reached from the town of **El Rompido** which takes advantage of the ebb and flow of the tides in the long river mouth for extensive fish and mussel hatcheries. **Isla Cristina** and **Isla Canela**

are also popular seaside resorts, with beautiful beaches and good seafood restaurants. On the mouth of the Guadiana, which forms the border here between Spain and Portugal, is the last town in Spain, **Ayamonte,** an important fishing port. White houses rise in staggered terraces up a gentle slope. At the top is the *parador* in an old monastery with a view over the sea and the countless coves and sandbanks of the estuary.

Sierra de Aracena

Beyond Huelva, little-travelled roads lead north to the Portuguese border. After **Valverde del Camino**, the road climbs up into the foothills of the Sierra Morena. The chain of hills is interspersed with small villages. Some of them are mining towns, others are primarily the weekend retreats of Huelva and Sevilla residents. The vegetation consists of stands of holm and cork oak, mimosa and chestnut, and large areas covered with maquis and rock-roses (*gum cistus*).

At **Zalamea la Real,** there are copper mines. The red terraces of open cast mining cause the coloring of the Río Tinto, giving rise to its name. The main Sierra town is **Aracena,** overshadowed by an Arab fort and a Gothic church with a Mudéjar tower. The two casinos, one for the rich and the other for the poor, are conclusive evidence that Andalusia always has been a society of haves and have-nots. The ethnological museum is informative on customs in the Sierra Morena. Near town are the **Grutas de las Maravillas**. These are extensive limestone caverns with subterranean lakes and stalactite and stalagmite formations. They make a pleasant change from the heat outside. The town of **Jabugo** has lent its name to Spain's best mountain hams, made here from semi-wild black pigs which have from time immemorial been fattened on acorns. **Aroche** has, in addition to prehistoric finds and its city walls, a curious rosary museum. This is the gateway to the expanses of the Meseta and the Extremadura.

161

PROVINCE CÁDIZ

(Telephone area code: 956-)

Accommodation

TARIFA: *MODERATE:* **Hostería Tarifa**, Amador de los Ríos 22, Tel: 684076. **VEJER**: *LUXURY:* **Hospedería del Convento San Francisco**, Plazuela, Tel: 451001. *BUDGET:* **La Posada**, Los Remedios 21, Tel: 450258. **CÁDIZ**: *LUXURY:* **Atlántico**, Parque Genovés 9, Tel: 226905. *MODERATE:* **San Remo**, Paseo Marítimo 3, Tel: 252202. **SANLUCAR DE B**: *LUXURY:* **Tartaneros**, C/ Tartaneros 8, Tel: 362044. *MODERATE:* **Las Marismas**, Pl. la Salle 2, Tel: 366008. **PTO. DE STA. MARÍA**: *LUXURY:* **Los Cántaros**, C/ Curva 6, Tel: 864242. **Santa María**, Av. de la Baja Mar, Tel: 873211. *MODERATE:* **Hostal Gazpacho**, C/ Tortolas 10, Tel: 854611. **JEREZ**: *LUXURY:* **Royal Sherry Park**, C/ Alvaro Domecq 11, Tel: 303011. *MODERATE:* **Nuevo Hostal**, C/ Caballeros 23, Tel: 331600. **ARCOS DE LA FRONTERA**: *LUXURY:* **Parador Casa del Corregidor**, Tel: 700500. *MODERATE:* **El Convento**, C/ Maldonado 2, Tel: 702333. **OLVERA**: *MODERATE:* **Sierra y Cal**, Av. N. Sra. de los Remedios 2, Tel: 130303. **ZAHARA**: *MODERATE:* **Marqués de Zahara**, C/ San Juan 3, Tel: 137261. Hotel Gran Sol, Av. de la Playa. **RONDA** (Prov. Malaga): *LUXURY:* **Reina Victoria**, C/ Jeréz 25, Tel: 952-871240. *MODERATE:* **El Tajo**, C/ Doctor Cajal 7, Tel: 952-876236. *BUDGET:* **Hostal Rondasol**, C/ Cristo 11, Tel: 952-874497.

Museums / Sightseeing

SANLUCAR DE B: The Agencia de Viajes Ocio y Vacaciones, Calzada del Ejército, Tel: 360225, organizes guided tours through the **National Park Coto de Doñana**; Information Center in the town quarter Bajo de Guia.
RONDA: **Palacio del Marqués de Salvatierra**, 11 a.m.-2 p.m. and 4-6 p.m., closed Thur. **Sta. María la Mayor,** 10.30 a.m.-6 p.m. Pl. de Toros, 10 a.m.-7 p.m.
JERÉZ: **Museo Flamenco**, C/ Quintos 1. **Museo de los Relojes**, C/ Lealas, **La Atalaya,** 10 a.m.-1.30 p.m. **Cartuja Sta. Ma. de la Defensión,** 4-6 p.m., closed Mon, for men only. **Alcázar** and Mosque: 10 a.m.-1 p.m.
PTO. STA. MARÍA: **Iglesia Mayor Prioral**, 7.30 a.m.-12.30 p.m. and 10 a.m.-8.30 p.m. **Castillo San Marcos**, Saturdays 11 a.m.-1 p.m.
CÁDIZ: **Museo de Bellas Artes and Museo Arqueologico**, Tue – Sun 9.30 a.m.-2 p.m. **Museo Historico Municipal**, Tue – Fri 9 a.m.-1 p.m. and 4-7 p.m.; Sat and Sun 9 a.m.-1 p.m. only. **Oratorio de San Felipe Neri**, 10-11 a.m. and

7.30-9.30 p.m. **Cathedral**, 6-7 p.m., **Cathedral Museum**, 10 a.m.-1 p.m., closed Sun. **Oratorio de la Santa Cueva**, 10 a.m.-1 p.m., closed Sun. **Museo del Mar**, 10 a.m.-1.30 p.m.; 5-6.30 p.m.

Other Attractions

EL BOSQUE: Inform. Center **Nature Reserve Sierra de Grazalema**, Tel: 716063. Cuevas de la Pileta (25 km), 9 a.m.-2 p.m. and 4-7 p.m.
JERÉZ: **Real Escuela Andaluza del Arte Ecuestre**, Av. Duque de Abrantes, Tel: 311111. Horse shows Thursdays 12 noon, training Mon– Fri 11 a.m.-1 p.m. **Fundación Andaluza de Flamenco** (flamenco training courses), Pl. de San Juan 1, 10 a.m.-1 p.m.
Flamenco Bars: Peña Tio José de Paula, C/ La Merced. Camino del Rocío, C/ Velázquez 20.
Bodega Tours (weekdays): Sandeman, 12 noon and 1 p.m.; Williams, 12 noon and 1.30 p.m.; Harveys, 12 noon.
PTO. STA. MARÍA: Bodega tours after telephone appointment only: Osborne, Tel: 855211; Terry, Tel: 483000.

Information – Oficina de Turismo

SANLUCAR DE B.: Calzada del Ejércit: , Mon–Fri 10 a.m.-2 p.m. and 5-7 p.m., Tel: 366110. **RONDA**, Pl. de España 1, Tel: 871272. **Arcos**: C/ Belén, Tel: 702264. **JEREZ**: Alameda Cristina 7, Mon – Fri 9 a.m.-3 p.m. and 5-7 p.m., Saturdays 10 a.m.-1.30 p.m. **PTO. STA. MARÍA**: C/ Guadalete 1 (corner Av. Bajamar), 10 a.m.-2 p.m. and 5.30-7.30 p.m., Tel: 483144.

SEVILLA

(Telephone area code 954-)

Accommodation

LUXURY: **Canela**, C/ Pagés de Corro 90, Tel: 4342412. *MODERATE:* **Sierpes**, Corral del Rey 22, Tel: 4224948. **Murillo**, C/ Lope de Rueda 7-9, Tel: 216095. **Hostal Arias**, C/ Mariana de Pineda 9, Tel: 4218389. *BUDGET:* **Pension Sta Cruz**, C/ Lope de Rueda 12.

Bars / Tapas / Dance / Flamenco

Many locals select a specific quarter for a stroll through the bars. The generous helpings of *tapas* served with the drinks can make you forget all about a sumptuous dinner!
Triana: The road along the shore, C/ Betis, and the parallel C/ Pureza, are liberally dotted with bars (i.e.Napoleón) and good restaurants; Sevilla's top disco, the Disco Río, opens its doors here; on C/Castilla and C/ Salado you can find bars where you can drink and dance. Tapa Bars: Casa Manolo, San Jorge, 16; La Albariza, C/ Betis 6. Dulcinea, C/ San Jacinto; El Rinconcillo, Pagés del Corro 84.
Los Remedios: C/ Sebastian Elcano; the many

bars here are very popular with teens; especially on weekends this street is packed with strolling youngsters. Tapa Bars: Sebastian and El Riojano: C/ Virgen de las Montañas.

Center: Tabernitas in the streets C/ Argote de Molina and C/ de los Alemanes.

El Postigo: (area behind Correos between Puerta de Jerez and Pl. Nueva): Bodegas Barbiana, C/ Zaragoza. Rincón del Postigo, C/ Tomás de Ibarra 2.

Barrio Sta. Cruz: Casa Sergio, C/ Lope de Rueda 18A. Bar and Café Las Teresas, C/ Sta. Teresa 2. Mesón del Tenorio, C/ Mateos Gago 9. La Giralda, Mateos Gago 1., La Gitanilla, C/ Mesón del Moro. Bar La Carbonería, C/Levies. Bar Los Abades, C/ Abades.

Pl. Sta. Catalina: Taberna Quitapesares (Bar del Perejil = nickname of the proprietor, a flamenco singer); El Rinconcito (Sevilla's oldest bar).

Alfalfa: (area around Pl. de la Alfalfa and the streets C/ 7 Revueltas, C/ Empecinado): Bar Sopa de Ganso. Café Boteros, C/ Boteros. La Antigua Bodeguita, Pl. del Salvador. La Bodega, C/ Imgaen 8. Bar Pilar, C/ Morería 5. Bar Manolo, Pl. de la Alfalfa. Mesón la Fuente, C/ Odrero 4-6. El Refugio C/ Huelva 5, (*tapas*).

Flamenco: El Semáforo, C/Bormujos, 11. Casa Anselma, C/ Pagés del Corro 49. El Arenal, C/ Rodo 7. Patio Sevillano, Paseo de Colón 11. Those in the know drive to El Aljarafe, outside of Sevilla.

Other Attractions
Bullfighting: Adv. ticket sales: C/ Sierpes 50 A.

Post / Information / Transportation
Oficina de Turismo: Mon–Fri 9.30 a.m.–7.30 p.m., Sat 9.30 a.m.–2 p.m. Av. de la Constitución 21 B, Tel: 4221404. Paseo de las Delicias, Costurero de la Reina, Tel: 4234465.

Post Office: Av. de la Constitución 32. Telefonica: Pl. de la Gavidia. **Rental Cars**: Budget, Av. San Francisco Javier 9, Edificio Sevilla 2, Tel: 650703. Triana Rent a Car C/ Pagés del Corro 159, Tel. 4282979. Sevilla Car, C/ Almirante Lobo, Edificio Cristina, Tel: 4222587. Hertz, at the Airport and at Av. Rep. Argentina 3, Tel: 4514720 and 4278887. Avis, at the airport and at Av. de la Constitución 15, Tel: 4514314 and 4216549. **Rail Terminals**: Estación Cordoba, Pl. de Armas (closed). Estación San Bernardo. Estación de Santa Justa (from April 1992).

Bus Terminals: C/ Manuel Vázquez Sagastizábal. **Airport**: San Pablo, 12 km outside of town; the airport bus leaves at the Bar Iberia, C/ Almirante Lobo.

Car Sharing Agency: Compartecoche S.A. C/ Amparo 22, 2º D, Tel: 4215494.

Steamboat Cruises to Cruceros del Sur, jetty below the Torre de Oro.

Museums / Sightseeing
Museo de Bellas Artes: Tue–Fri 10 a.m.-2 p.m., 4-7 p.m., Sat and Sun 10 a.m.-2 p.m., closed on public holidays. **Casa de Pilatos**: daily 9 a.m.-6 p.m. **Museo Arqueologico**: 10 a.m.–2 p.m., closed Mon. **Museo de Arte Contemporaneo**: 10 a.m.-2 p.m., closed Mon. **Museo de Artes y Costumbres Populares**: 10 a.m.-2 p.m., closed Sun and Mon. **Reales Alcázares**: 10.30 a.m.-5.30 p.m., Sun 10 a.m.-1.30 p.m., closed Mon. **Casa Murillo** (under renovation). **Cathedral and Giralda**: 11 a.m.-5 p.m., Sun 2-4 p.m. **Torre de Oror/Museo Naval**: Tue –Fri 10 a.m.-2 p.m., Sat and Sun 10 a.m.-1 p.m. **Archivo de las Indias**, 10 a.m.-1 p.m., closed Sun. **Convento de Sta. Paula**: 9 a.m.-1 p.m., 4.30-6.30 p.m. **Basilica de la Macarena**: 9 a.m.-1 p.m., 5-9 p.m. **Iglesia del Salvador**: 6.30-9 p.m., Sun additional opening 10 a.m.-1.30 p.m. **Museo de Cofradías** (brotherhoods partaking in holy processions), C/ de Jamerdana, 9 a.m.-12 noon and 4.30-8 p.m. **Itálica** (outside of town): Tue – Sat 9 a.m.-5.30 p.m., Sun 10 a.m.-4 p.m.

PROVINCE HUELVA
(Telephone area code: 955-)

Accommodation
HUELVA: *LUXURY:* **Tartessos**, Av. M. Alonso Pinzón 13, Tel: 245611. *MODERATE:* **Hostería de la Rábida** (outside of town), Tel: 350312. **ALMONTE**: *LUXURY:* **El Flamero**, Rd. Maestro Alonso, Tel: 430000.

AYAMONTE: *LUXURY:* **Parador Costa de la Luz**, El Castillito, Tel: 320700. *MODERATE:* **Don Diego**, C/ Ramón y Cajál, Tel: 320250. **MATALASCAÑAS**: *MODERATE:* **El Cortijo**, Sector E 159, Tel: 430259.

ISLA CRISTINA: *MODERATE:* **Paraíso Playa Hotel**, Camino de la Playa, Tel: 331873.

EL ROMPIDO: *MODERATE:* **La Galera**, Ctra. to Cartaya, Tel: 390276.

ARACENA: *MODERATE*: **Sierra de Aracena**, Gran Vía 21, Tel: 110775.

JABUGO: *BUDGET:* **Aurora**, C/ Barco 9, Tel: 121146.

Museums / Sightseeing
HUELVA: **Museo Provincial**, Alameda Sundheim. Monastery de la Rábida (outside of town). **COTO DOÑANA**: Reservations for landrover tours, Visitors' Center El Acebuche, 8 a.m.-7 p.m., Tel: 430432; **Palacio del Acebrón**: 9 a.m.-6 p.m.; Center La Rocina 8 a.m.-7 p.m.

Information – Oficina de Turismo
HUELVA: Av. de Alemania 1, Tel: 257403.

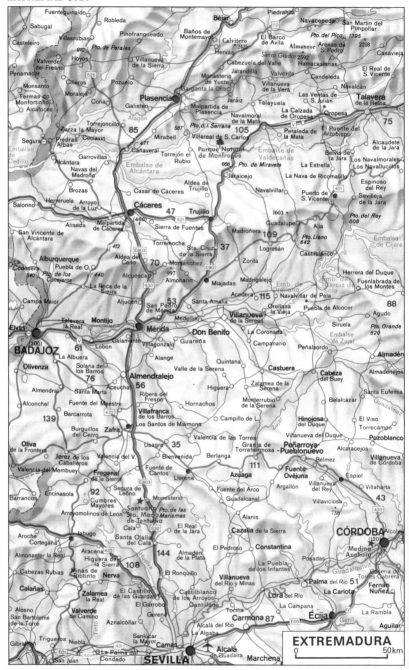

EXTREMADURA

0   50km

THE EXTREMADURA

BADAJOZ

CÁCERES

SIERRA DE GREDOS

The territories which formed the front lines in the battles of the various medieval Christian kingdoms against the Moors were called "Extremadura". There were "estremadurs" on the Duero and there is one in Portugal. The Spanish one was formed by the southern boundary of the kingdom of León. The name has kept its significance as the southernmost point reached by the *transhumance*, the seasonal migration of the herds which wintered in the plains and sought summer pasturage in the cool of the mountains. "Ya se van los pastores a la Extremadura, ya se queda la sierra triste y oscura ...", the northeners sing: The shepherds migrate to the Extremadura and the Sierra remains bleak and dark.

Even today, the character of the region is moulded by livestock breeding. Bold fighting bulls, *toros bravos*, black pigs and sheep populate the wide expanses of the *dehesas*, as the estates, sparsely wooded with holm and cork oak, are known here. The large individual estates are a legacy from the Middle Ages, when the countryside, remote from events of national importance, was under the sway of orders of knights.

Preceding pages: Moorish artistry, demonstrated in the intricately woven arches of the Mezquita in Córdoba.

The Extremadura is still remote from the usual tourist haunts. Yet it is a region well worth discovering.

It is not, however, a land of superlatives. There are few high mountains or deep gorges. The villages are far apart but many an unpretentious town may conceal a surprise or two and many a stream is a small paradise.

The climate of the region, however, suits the name. Temperatures are extreme, the winters harsh and the summers hot. Travellers are advised to find a shady spot for the early hours of the afternoon: a vine-covered terrace, a reservoir, a stand of oak, a riverbank ...

The two provinces comprising the autonomous region of Extremadura, Cáceres and Badajoz are Spain's largest, yet together they have a population of a million at most. Both are watered by great rivers, the Tajo and the Guadiana, which have been dammed at many points. They pass hydro-electric and nuclear power plants and are saturated with fertilizers used in the agrarian regions they flow through.

The inhabitants of the region are friendly and hospitable, as if they had not yet had enough of tourism. Many of them are only visitors spending the summer in their native villages before returning to work in France or Switzerland.

167

The White Villages in the South of Badajoz

The south of the Extremadura is hardly distinguishable in many respects from Andalusia. There are the same villages with low houses, relatively plain and centered upon inner courtyards, glaring white, empty, forbidding, yet full of bustling crowds and lively in the evenings. The churches are a blend of Gothic, Andalusian Baroque and, as is particularly noticeable in the towers, Moorish architecture. Monasteries, sometimes decaying, usually dilapidated and with about a half a dozen monks or nuns left who seldom leave their walls, are generally at the heart of the old towns. Then there is the central square with one or two casinos, and rural clubs which are a blend of social institution and café, bars in this region just like the others. Such villages are

Above: An unusual sight, snow in a southern landscape. Right: The best place for keeping an eye on the world at large.

168

as peaceful and tranquil as the paintings of Zurbarán, who was a native of this area.

Fregenal de la Sierra is one of these typical villages: Overshadowed by a massive Templars' fort, it has a small park, the house in which the local painter, Eugenio Hermoso, was born, the square in front of the church full of noisy children charging about, the austere church of Sta. Catalina, bars around the plaza which prepare *tapas* with great care and serve the cloudy resinated local wine, *pitarra*. The remains of the Roman settlement of *Nertobriga,* 6 km away, are nearly overgrown.

The road to Jerez de los Caballeros goes through small valleys and vineyards bordered by cork oaks. The bark of these versatile and useful trees is stripped off every 7 to 10 years. The trunk turns yellow and then reddish brown, until it finally regaines its original colour. The *dehesas* near Fregenal boast the largest stands of cork oak in the entire Extremadura. What is not generally known is

that they are highly valued by environmentalists as bird sanctuaries, especially since in other areas trees have been uprooted to make room for easier mechanical farming.

Jerez de los Caballeros has a long history, as evidenced by the dolmen of Toriñuelo and a Roman road and settlement. A column in the church of San Bartolomé carries the date of the early Christian basilica which once stood here: 556. Once they had been conquered, the surrounding lands were entrusted by Ferdinand III to the Templars, after whom the town was named.

The last of the *caballeros* were beheaded in the 14th century in the Torre Sangriente (Bloody Tower) of the fort, after the order was outlawed. The churches, most of them Churrigueresque Baroque, are worth a visit. The sexton might even let one climb one of the richly ornate belfries. At any rate, one should take the trouble because this is the most contemplative way of visiting such churches. Great seafarers and explorers,

descubridores, came from many southern Extremadura towns. For example, the explorers Nuñez de Balboa and Hernando de Soto came from Jerez.

West of Fregenal, in the Sierra, not far from Monesterio, is **Sta. María de Tentudia,** a monastery of the Knights of Santiago with a Mudéjar cloister and an austere church. The epic story of the hero, Pelayo Pérez, who fought here against the Moors, is told on tiles. The sun is said to have stood still in its course to prolong the bloody day until the battle was won.

Llerena was the seat of the Inquisition. The palace of the *Santo oficio* is still standing. Through the Monleón gate one reaches the impressive central square where the town hall and church are. The latter is a blend of all known styles with an astonishing façade. Francisco Zurbarán (1598-1664) had his studio on this square. In the 17th century the well known, in fact notorious, sect of the Illuminati had many adherents in the area: In Llerena there were eight monks who

169

interpreted the mystical doctrine in their own way, making it their goal to "dissolve in libidinous ecstasy for the love of God". Through hands-on physical contact penitents were imbued with the Holy Spirit. One Mari-Gómez de Barcarrota opened a "monastery" in Llerena which was a magnet for the bourgeoisie and the clergy. It all ended with one of the most famous auto-da-fés which were enacted by the Tribunal of the Inquisition.

Zafra is known as "little Sevilla". In Roman times it was a major junction on the Silver Road. Large livestock fairs take place here. On the outskirts of the town is the original Arab fort, now one of the most beautiful *paradores* in the entire country. It was built by the Dukes of Feria, who are entombed in state in the church of the convent of Sta. Clara, and immortalised in alabaster statues (15th century). In the Sta. Clara church, there is also a reliquary chamber, tiled from floor to ceiling and closed off by a grille. In it all imaginable parts of the mortal remains of countless saints are preserved in costly shrines. Rather incongruously, perhaps, the nuns sell tasty pastry across the cloister turnstile. The richly ornamented Gothic portal of the Hospital de Santiago at the end of a cul-de-sac is also noteworthy.

But the two plazas, **Plaza Grande** and **Plaza Chica**, are the most beautiful sights in the town. The large square is bustling, palm-shaded and lined with shops and street cafés. The smaller square next to it is quieter, more straight forward and almost forgotten. Once bullfights and markets were held here. One of the columns still has an incised yardstick, point of reference to the merchants who used to sell their wares here and now a concise historical pointer to the tourist who takes time to look.

Right: The Plaza Grande, indeed the more lively of the two main squares in Zafra.

The Guadiana Valley

From Zafra to the Guadiana Valley stretches a monotonous plain on which wheat and grapes are grown. The resounding names of the towns are the only diversion here: Salvatierra de los Barros with a tadition of pottery work, the spa of Alange with Roman baths and, finally, **Mérida.**

By crossing a Roman bridge with 60 arches, "eyes" as they are called in Spanish, one reaches *Emerita Augusta,* founded in 25 BC by Augustus as yet another of the Roman retirement colonies in outposts of the Empire for deserving legionaries. Later it was the capital of Lusitania, the third Roman province on the Iberian peninsula, incorporating present-day Portugal. Mérida has the most extensive and best preserved Roman buildings in Spain. In addition to the great bridge spanning the Guadiana over which the Baetic Road ran, there is a well-constructed bridge crossing the Albarregas, which once formed part of the Silver Road. At the edge of town the first thing one sees on arriving, is the Moorish **Alcázar**, which was built here on the foundations of a Roman dyke. Beyond is a triumphal arch, the **Arco de Trajano**.

The core of Mérida looks like an overgrown white village. At the center is the *parador* in an old monastery. Round the Plaza de España cluster the town hall, restaurants and a church. The comprehensive and well-labelled archaeological museum records the town's entire history. It even has Visigoth finds. The center of the Roman town was actually off to the north of what is now the old town. Here the theater, the amphitheater, excavated villas and the Circus Maximus in which the famous Roman chariot races were run are all adjacent to one another. The theater seated about 6,000. The two-storeyed stage, each fronted by 16 Corinthian marble columns, is well preserved. Behind them one can visit the ar-

tists' dressing-rooms and the imperial shrine, a reminder that all this was part of a vast imperial network. In the ellipsoidal amphitheater spectators would watch gladiatorial combats with wild animals whose cages were under the stands. Now classical theater festivals are staged annually in July. Even if one doesn't know the language, the ambience of the performances on hot summer nights is worth coming for, and one is still able somehow to understand what is going on.

In addition to the remains of temples and villas, the town has an outstanding museum of Roman artefacts. It is impressive for the way finds and its reconstructions are displayed, and it is an exemplary modern building. Mérida is now a commercial center with a cork factory and a modest tourist industry. Since the 1983 administrative reforms, it has been capital of the district and the seat of the Junta of Extremadura. This reform represents a political compromise on the part of the provincial capitals of Cáceres and Badajoz. On the northern edge of town

there are remains of an aqueduct which once had up to three tiers. It led to the **Proserpina Reservoir** and supplied Mérida with water. After 2000 years the reservoir is still intact and a welcome source of refreshment. A second Roman reservoir, the **Embalse de Cornalvo,** is situated in a small stand of cork oak, now a protected area, 15 km northeast of the town.

The part of the Guadiana Valley between Badajoz and Don Benito became one of the country's largest irrigation projects in the 1960s. The **Plan Badajoz** project passed in 1952 provided for the promotion of a more intensive agriculture through the building of dams, irrigation canals and new villages in the alluvial plain, all conceived as comprehensive measures to halt emigration and produce energy. The project has cost a fortune since then. Fallow land was dispossessed, divided up into allotments of 4 ha each and reallocated to farmers. However, the allotments proved too small. Farmhands were allotted 1/2 ha for their own use. Irrigation had to be paid for. Since the recommended new special crops did not yet have a market, farmers soon returned to the traditional dry farming of wheat and barley on the irrigated land. This caused a concentration of allotments in the hands of a few landowners since grain farming is not profitable under 30 ha. Today three quarters of the area is again owned by 6 % of the population, so that the land reform has in effect failed. Of the projected 150,000 ha about 100,000 are irrigated. Entire new villages of standardized housing stand empty.

Eastern Extremadura

In the northeastern part of Badajoz Province, an area once known as the Siberia of the Extremadura, large artificial lakes: **Orellana, Zújar, García de Sola** and **Cijara** are extending. Depending on water levels and how much the water has warmed up during the summer, they are quite inviting places to swim. In any case they are suitable for water sports and enhance the scenery. In recent years attractive holiday resorts have sprung up. One is advised to take the longer route to Guadalupe along the Guadiana (N-430).

The towns in this area are what they have always been: farming towns, yet they have retained their share of aristocratic residences, handsome churches with unexpected treasure troves of art and pretty plazas. **Medellin** is the birthplace of Hernán Cortés, the conqueror of Mexico and destroyer of the Aztec kingdom. The small town is overshadowed by a massive fort of the Knights of Santiago. The Roman bridge is also an indication that the town was more important 2,000 years ago. In November a bell-ringers' competition takes place here. **Villanueva de La Serena,** a small city with intriguing Renaissance buildings, is the birth-

place of Pedro de Valdivia, the discoverer of Chile.

In the wilds of the Sierra of the same name the vast monastic complex of **Nuestra Señora de Guadalupe** can be seen from a great distance. It is one of the most important places of pilgrimage in the entire Hispano-American world. Guadalupe is a small and picturesque Moorish village which is entirely geared to regional and national tourism. Still it has retained its characteristic 15th century architecture. Right in front of the plaza with its restaurants under the *porches*, or arcades, a widestair leads to the monastery entrance. The massive 14th-century edifice is in the Mudéjar style blended with Gothic, Renaissance and Baroque elements. The world famous and universally venerated Romanesque **Black Virgin of Guadalupe** was, according to legend, carved by Luke the Apostle and found by a shepherd. The conquerors of the Americas asked for the blessing of the Virgin of Guadalupe before setting out on their voyages. They took the name of their patroness to the colonies where she is the patron saint of Hispanidad today. After his successful return voyage from America, Columbus came here on a pilgrimage. He even made a point of having the Indians he had brought back with him baptised here. The immense treasures amassed in the Hieronymite monastery at Guadalupe were looted in 1808 by Napoleonic troops during the occupation. The monastery was disbanded as a consequence of secularisation in 1836. Not until the 20th century did it open its doors again as a Franciscan monastery.

Parts of the monastery as well as the church and the Mudéjar cloister with the "fountainhead temple", the sacristy with paintings by Zurbarán and others, various museums, the chapel of the relics, the library pavilion and the "chamber" of the Virgin with Baroque paintings by Luca Giordano are open to the public.

Right: In this procession the statue of the Virgin Mary is decorated with necklace.

The **Hospedería Real** with a Mudéjar cloister built in 1512 for the Catholic Kings and the pilgrims' hospice are now first-class pilgrimage and tourist accommodation adjacent to the monastery.

From Guadalupe one can go on to Toledo, turning off on the way to **Talavera** or **Puente del Arzobispo.** Both are rather unattractive towns but they make the distinctive pottery sold all over the area and nowhere else. Puente ware is green, often with hunting scenes, and Talavera ware is decorated with delicate colourful patterns.

On the Portuguese Border

The towns along the Portuguese border, regardless of size, all have the same atmosphere: One seems to smell the sea in the distance, to taste the *viño verde* and the fish dishes, and one recalls the ancient tales of gypsies and smugglers. Tourists who come here are all just passing through and unluckily they are missing something.

Badajoz, the Moorish kingdom of *Batalvoz*, the biggest city in the Extremadura, looks back on an eventful history during which it changed hands between Spain and Portugal several times.

Luis Morales (17th century), called the Divine, whose pictures hang in the country's major museums as well as in the small churches of the Extremadura, was born in Badajoz. His works and those of Zurbarán hang in the art museum here. The city landmark familiar to tourists is the crenellated city gate, the **Puerta de Palmas**, leading to the bridge across the Guadiana. The long Renaissance bridge was built by Juan de Herrera on extant Roman piers. On the other side, between the river and the border, is the modern campus of the new university. It is the result of further efforts to halt emigration, which have yet to produce the desired results.

The massive Late Romanesque fortified cathedral is at the center of the old city. Its interior, a blend of all styles, is a treasure trove: a handsome choir, a

Palacio
de Justicia
Pl. de
Santiago
C. de Niдos
C. Chaves
C. de Sande
C. de Codoy
C. de Villalobos
de
Rivera
de
Curtidores
Tenerias
† Igl. de
Santiago
C. de Sancti Espiritu
Casa de los
Toledo -
Moctezuma
Arco del
Socorro
Caleros
C. de Andrada
Casa de Pl. del
Galarza
General Palacio
Arco de Episcopal
la Estrella
Información
Mola
Torre de
los Espadero
Torre de
Carajal
Igl. de Sta. Maria
(Concatedral)
C. Gral. Ezponda
Estrella
Palacio de la Isla
Palacio de los
Golfines de Abajo
Palacio de
Mayoralgo
Pl. S.
Jorge
Museo de
Bellas Artes
Igl. de
San Francisco
Javier
C. de los Pintores
Arco de
Sta. Ana
C. de Moret
Ad.
del Alcázar
Igl. de
San Mateo
Residencia
"Luisa de
Carvajal
Palacio de
las Cigüeñas
Museo de Arte
Contemporaneo
Palacio de los
Golfines
de Arriba
Igl. de
San Juan
C. del Rosario
C. de Olmos
C. Ancha
Casa del
Comendador
Casa de
las Veletas
(Museo Provincial)
Parador
Puerta de Merida
Puerta
de Mérida
Pl. de
Sta. Clara
Muralla
Ronda del Mira El Rio
Ronda de Macarena
C. D. L. Sergio
C. Cortes
C. de Hornos
C. Consolado
C. de S. Ildefonso
C. de S. Ildefonso
Damas
Fuente Nueva
Pl. San
Francisco

CÁCERES
0   150m

Gothic cloister, a Morales in the radiating chapter of the ducal house, and additional treasures in the Diocese Museum. Narrow alleys lead from here uphill to the old city core. Since the houses get more dilapidated on the way up, one may be surprised on reaching lovely **San José Square** below the fort. The houses are empty, the doors bolted: a ghost town. In some of the archways dwell the poorest of the poor. Begging children swarm around one. Above, accessible by narrow paths, is the **Alcazaba**, housing the Archaeological Museum.

To the south is the white unadorned town of **Olivenza.** It has been nominally and politically Spanish since the Orange War, but it is still Portuguese in spirit. Churches and sacred buildings are Manueline in style. Good examples of this are the charity hospice donated by Manuel I in 1501, or the church of Santa María Magdalena with its twisted columns.

Right: The old town of Cáceres, a combination of narrow streets and austere towers.

The border towns to the north are all fortified. They were under the sway of the Knights of the Order of Alcántara. **Albuquerque** with its massive fort looks from a distance like a picture in an old-fashioned, expensively illustrated children's book. The small town has many Gothic buildings. Even more picturesque is **Alcántara** is even more picturesque on the Tajo gorge, which of course is the Tejo from here on. The famous Roman fortified bridge, 71m above the river and ending in a temple, is in marked contrast to the massive barrage of the Alcántara dam in the background. The long trip to this remote spot is worth it: a 16th century fortress; the astonishing ruins of the monastery of San Benito with its exterior cloister, which was built in the 16th century as the seat of the Order of Alcántara and then turned into a barracks in the 19th by the French occupation forces; the Romanesque-Gothic church of Santa María where a painting by Morales hangs. The route to these remote sights will soon be shortened. The motorway linking Spain with Portugal as far as Lisbon is under construction.

CÁCERES

North of Mérida, on a small by-road to Trujillo, a white village gleams on a hilltop. Lovely **Montánchez** makes the best hams in the area, the famous *pata negra.* In village restaurants the heavy local white wine, *vino de pitarra*, is served. The castillo is in ruins, but from this "balcony of the Extremadura" one can see as far as Portugal and Cáceres.

Cáceres was called "Al-Kazris" by the Arabs, or Alcázar. Their fortifications live up to the name, as usual. Nevertheless Alfonso IX took Cáceres in 1299. From the chapel of the Virgen de la Montaña south of the city, one sees the three rather disjointed sections of modern Cáceres: the modern city around Calvo Sotelo Square; the section outside the

walls around Plaza Mayor, long, like a village on which the busy and crowded pedestrian zones converge; and the old city, on a rise, reached through the Arco de la Estrella from the square. The old city is an entity dominated in the usual Spanish way by the residences of the rural gentry, who demonstrated their status by erecting towers, and surrounded by closed city walls with 12 towers. Every building is remarkable and each has its own story.

The **Casa de las Veletas** houses the provincial museum and the Arab wells, which are said to have been nearly as large as the famous ones at Istanbul. The **Casa del Comendador de Alcuéscar** is a *parador*. In the **Palacio de los Golfines** General Franco was made Head of State on 29 October, 1936, after his first victories in the Civil War. **Casa de las Ciguenas** is the only one of these palaces to have retained its crenellation when the Catholic Kings decreed that all such structurally demonstrative decor be removed as a sign of subjection. The churches of Sta. María and San Mateo and the monastery of San Francisco are still Gothic. Oddly enough, they have undergone less alteration than other Spanish churches. Outside the walls are more residences and the church of Santiago with an altar by Alonso Berruguete, a reminder that the Order of Knights of Santiago was originally established at Cáceres. It would be pointless to list all the palaces and residences of the aristocracy. Strolling through the city while looking up to catch sight of the decoration of the buildings, which appear merely overpowering in the narrow alleys, one can see them all.

Towards evening, the old city goes utterly dead. Life goes on in the restaurants on Plaza Mayor. One can easily imagine the ghost of the Moorish lady of local legend haunting the abandoned buildings, who a long time ago opened the door to her Christian lover and killed her own father because he was against the affair. Supposedly she returns as a hen on Midsummer's Eve.

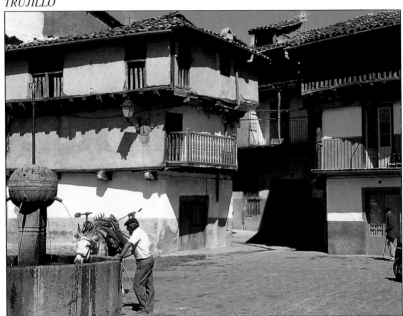

Cáceres is in good repute among environmentalists because it is one of the largest stork refuges. These ungainly and beloved endangered birds can nest here undisturbed on all the roofs.

As in Cáceres, the Plaza Mayor at **Trujillo** is at the foot of a walled precinct. Through one of seven gates one enters the old city by steep lanes. Here, however, the residences and churches are less overpoweringly monumental. One is immediately aware that a quiet late medieval quarter has been preserved. To visit the Romanesque church of Sta. María one must knock next door. The monasteries are only occasionally open to the public. At the top is the wall around the Arab **Alcazaba**. What was once a Franciscan nunnery, today houses the **Museum of the Conquest of the Americas**. The pivotal point, though, is Plaza Mayor. A Baroque and a Gothic church as well as the old town hall and several Renaissance

residences frame the square. But its dominating feature is the monument to Pizarro, the city's most famous son. An apocryphal story has it that Pizarro was a swineherd. When he lost one of the animals in his charge, he went to sea to avoid the penalty and thus discovered Peru. The discoverer of the Amazon, Francisco de Orellano, also came from here.

The land between the Tajo and the Tietar is now the **Monfragüe Nature Reserve.** The road from Cáceres to Plasencia and a small road along the Tietar go through it. The views are best from the Santuario de Monfragüe, once the seat of the Order of Monfragüe. The area is covered with evergreen trees and bushes, rock-roses, buckthorn and maquis. One of the largest animal and bird reserves in western Spain, it has a lot to offer, even for inexperienced birdwatchers. Flashy hoopoes, orioles, blue-throats and green bee-eaters can be found everywhere. Song-thrushes and nightingales are heard even if not always seen. In the water

Above: A quiet afternoon on the village square of Garganta la Olla in the Vera.

meadows there are various species of heron, ducks and greyleg geese. Even some of the last pairs of black storks nest here. From all vantage points one sees majestic birds of prey riding the air currents, gliding eagles, red and white kites, several species of vulture, imperial eagles and lesser species, falcons, sparrowhawks and hawks. All these elsewhere endangered bird species feed on the myriads of tiny rodents and reptiles seldom visible to the naked eye. If one leaves the road one may spot an Iberian lynx or, by the water, aquatic tortoises, otters and watersnakes.

A particularly scenic footpath runs parallel to the road along the Roman road and the *cañada,* the path taken by herds during the *transhumance* from the mountains to the plain. It intersects the road at **Villa Real de San Carlos.** Attempts are being made to turn the entire area of the Tajo reservoirs from the nature reserve and on into Portugal into a protected area without borders, an undertaking without precedent in European environmentalism and one which could well be emulated by other European nations.

SIERRA DE GREDOS

The unprepossessing town of **Coria** in the Vega of the Río Alagón boasts one of the best-preserved Roman fortification walls (480m, hexagonal and up to 8 m thick). The four gates can still be closed. This happens each year at the fiesta, when a bull is let loose in the town accompanied by young men. The 13th-century tower of the single-aisled Gothic cathedral collapsed in the 18th century earthquake which destroyed a great part of Lisbon. Cracks are still visible in the church façade but they seem to be no cause for alarm.

Plasencia lived by the motto "rather free than rich". From the 13th century it enjoyed a privileged status, which was comprehended in the old legal concept of

fueros. The whole city on the hill in the middle of the plain of Jerte has monumental palaces, churches and residences around its central squares. The half Romanesque, half Gothic cathedral has a Renaissance choir by Rodrigo Alemán (15th century) which is by anyone's standards the match of the one in Toledo. The lewd scenes on it are obviously aimed at the licentious clergy of the time. The master was arrested by the Inquisition. A true man of the Renaissance, he attempted to escape by flying from the cathedral tower by means of a flying apparatus he had contrived of wood and feathers. He died as a second Icarus. The long main square is vibrant with life in the early hours of evening. Seated at a table in front of a café one has a box from which to watch the drama of small-town life unfold.

The small town of Plasencia is a junction for no fewer than eight national roads. The various feeder roads from the western Extremadura, the roads going north into the Sierra de Francia and along the Río Jerte, as well as the connecting roads leading east to Madrid at the foot of the Gredos Range all converge here. The northbound road goes into the mountains and Salamanca Province to the old Jewish settlements of **Hervás** and **Béjar.** What is really fascinating is that the descendants of the Jews who went into seclusion here to escape persecution by the Catholic Kings still live where they alway have. To the west lies the **Hurdes,** a mountainous region considered the most backward in Spain. There Moriscos hid from persecution for a long time. Luis Buñuel made his first documentary film about the area, *Land without Bread.* The whole region is now a cool summer resort area. When one has crossed the Béjar Pass in midsummer, one has the feeling of being able to breathe again.

It is advisable to travel the road to Avila through the **Jerte Valley** in March when the whole valley is white with

177

cherry blossoms. This is a bucolic landscape, inviting one to walk and bathe in the cool clean streams rushing down from the **Gredos Range.** On the other side of the range, which divides the Meseta into north and south, is the **Tiétar Valley,** a wide fertile drainage basin. Here the main crop is tobacco and one sees the drying sheds everywhere. The district beyond Plasencia between the river and the mountains is called **La Vera.** It comprises 15 villages located on the first or second terrace above the river. The cool streams rushing down from the mountains, called *gargantas*, "gorges", form green swirling pools which are marvellous for bathing. If one leaves the road on foot for only a few hundred meters one is sure to find a secluded spot. The streams are spanned by the original bridges of the Roman road which ran parallel to the modern one. The villages of the Vera are all charming. The road

Above: Orange is the color of the freshly pealed cork oaks.

passes them by, surely a blessing in some respects. Therefore one has to make the effort to reach their town squares on foot. From the balconies of the white houses red peppers are hung to dry. Figs are laid out in front of the houses. Honey and raspberry jam are offered for sale.

The most important town is **Jarandilla,** with a palace of Charles V, now a **parador.** This is where the emperor lodged until his apartments in the nearby monastery of **Yuste** were ready to receive him. He spent his last years there in contemplative retirement. The monastery is higher up in the mountains in a sparse oak forest. When one has seen the view, one understands the emperor. His bedroom, still decorated with black hangings and equipped with his special gout stool, seems to have been left just yesterday. From the monastery a road goes on to **Garganta la Olla,** another typical village where a few houses are still painted blue. In garrison towns, where the soldiers and officials of Charles V resided, this was the prescribed way of indicating a house as a brothel. From here a small road climbs high into the mountains to **Piornal,** then down the other side into the **Jerte Valley.** Ballads tell the story of "Serrana de la Vera", a wild woman who lived in these mountains in a cave after soldiers of Charles V had raped her. She seduced every man who came by and then she murdered him.

The loveliest villages in the Vera are at the far end: **Villanueva** and **Valverde.** Below the peak of Almanzor, at 2,592 m the highest in the range, is a protected area in which there are chamois, ibex and many species of bird of prey. It is advisable to go there via **Arenas de San Pedro,** a summer resort boasting the castle of the sad countess, the widow of a nobleman killed by King John II of Castile. East of Arenas one is not far from the region accessible at weekends from Madrid, an area which extends all across the foothills of the Sierra.

PROVINCE BADAJOZ
(Telephone area code: 924-)
Accommodation
MÉRIDA: *LUXURY:* **Parador Vía de la Plata**, Plaza de la Constitución 3, Tel: 313800. *MODERATE:* **Emperatriz**, Pl. de España 19, Tel: 313111. **Cervantes**, C/ Camilo José Cela 8, Tel: 314901. **ZAFRA**: *LUXURY:* **Parador Hernán Cortés**, Pl. Corazón María, Tel: 550200. *BUDGET:* **Pension Rafael**, C/ Virgen de Guadalupe 7a, Tel: 552052.
MONESTERIO: *BUDGET:* **Pension Puerta del Sol**, Po. de Extremadura 63, Tel: 517001.
DON BENITO: *MODERATE:* **Miriam Hotel**, C/ Donoso Cortés 2, Tel: 801500.
BADAJOZ: *LUXURY:* **Gran Hotel Zurbarán**, Paseo de Castelar, Tel: 223741. *MODERATE:* **Lisboa**, Av. Elvas 13, Tel: 238200. **Cervantes**, C/ Tercio 2, Tel: 225110. *BUDGET:* **Hostal Victoria**, C/ Luis de Camoens 3, Tel: 237662.
OLIVENZA: *BUDGET:* **Heredero**, Tel: 490835. **MÉRIDA**: **Rufino**, Pl. STa. Clara 2. Bocao, C/ Atarazana 6. **Nicolás**, C/ Felix Valverde 13.

Information – Oficina de Turismo
ZAFRA: Pavilion in the park at Pl. España: 11 a.m.-2 p.m. and 6-8 p.m. **BADAJOZ**: Pasaje de San Juan, Tel: 222763, weekdays 9 a.m.-2 p.m. and 5-7 p.m. (in winter 4-6 p.m.). **MÉRIDA**: C/ del Puente 9. Tel: 315353.

Museums / Sightseeing
MÉRIDA: **Museo de Arte Romano**: 10 a.m.-2 p.m. and 5-7 p.m., in winter 4-6 p.m., Sundays 10 a.m.-2 p.m., closed Mon. Advance tickets for the **Theater Festival**: Oficina del festival Tel: 317612, 315915. Viajes Emérita, C/ Santa Lucia, Tel: 300952. (in Madrid: C/ Evaristo S. Miguel 17, Tel. 91- 2485854).
BADAJOZ: **Museo Arqueologico**: 10 a.m.–3 p.m., closed Mon. **Museo Provincial de Bellas Artes**, C/ Meléndez Valdés 32: 9 a.m.–2 p.m., closed Sundays.

PROVINCE CÁCERES
(Telephone area code: 927-)
Accommodation
TRUJILLO: *LUXURY:* **Parador de Trujillo**, Pl. Sta. Clara, Tel: 321350. *BUDGET:* **Mesón La Cadena**, Pl. Mayor 8, Tel: 321463. **Hostal Trujillo**, C/ Francisco Pizarro 4, Tel: 322274, 322661.
GUADALUPE: *LUXURY:* **Parador de Guadalupe**, C/ Marques de la Romana 10, Tel: 367075. *MODERATE:* **Hospedería del Real Monasterio**, Pl. Juan Carlos I, 367000.
CÁCERES: *LUXURY:* **Parador de Cáceres**, C/ Ancha 6 (Old Town), Tel: 211759. **Extremdaura**, Av. Virgen de Guadalupe 5, Tel: 221604. *MODERATE:* **Ara**, C/ Juan XXIII 3, Tel: 223958. *BUDGET:* **Hostal Hernán Cortés**, Trav. Hernán Cortés 6, Tel: 243488.
ALCÁNTARA: *BUDGET:* **Hostal El Arco**.
MONTANCHEZ: *BUDGET:* **Hostal Montecalabria**, C/ Gral. Margallo 2, Tel: 380216.
PLASENCIA: *MODERATE:* **Alfonso VIII**, C/ Alfonso VIII 32, Tel: 410250. *BUDGET:* **Hostal Rincón Extremeño**, C/ Vidrieras 6, Tel: 411150.
HERVÁS: *BUDGET:* **Hostal Montecristo**, A. de la Provincia 2, Tel: 481191.
JARANDILLA DE LA VERA: *LUXURY:* **Parador Carlos V**. Tel: 560117. *MODERATE:* **Hostal Jaranda**, Av. Calvo Sotelo, Tel: 560206.
MADRIGAL DE LA VERA: *BUDGET:* **Las Palmers**, Ctra. to Plasencia 16, 565011.

Museums / Sightseeing
CÁCERES: **Museum of the Province**, Casa de las Veletas: 9.30 –2.30 p.m., closed Sun, Mon.
TRUJILLO: **Palacio de San Carlos**: 10 a.m.-1 p.m., 4-6 p.m. **Iglesia de San Martín**, 10 a.m.-1p.m., 4-6 p.m. **Palacio de la Conquista**, 11 a.m.-2 p.m., 4.30-6.30 p.m. **Sta. María**: Keys at the first house in front of the church. **Museo didactico sobre la Conquista**: weekends, 11.30 a.m.-2 p.m.
CORIA: **Cathedral**: 9 a.m.-12.45 p.m and 4-6.30 p.m. **Real Monasterio de Nuestra Señora de Guadalupe**: 9.30 a.m.-1.30 a.m., 3.30-7 p.m.
PARQUE NATURAL DE MONFRAGÜE:Information Pavilion in Villareal de San Carlos; for further information: Dirección General de Medio Ambiente: 924-301662, 315962.
CUACOS DE LA VERA: **Monasterio de Yuste**: 9 a.m.-12.45 p.m. (Sundays and public holidays until 11.45 a.m.) and 3.30-6.45 p.m. Church service weekdays 1 p.m., Sundays and public holidays 12 noon.

Information – Oficina de Turismo
CÁCERES: Pl. Mayor 33, Tel: 246347; **PLASENCIA**: C/ Trujillo 17, Tel: 412766; **TRUJILLO**: Pl. Mayor 18, Tel: 320653
Festivals
VALVERDE DE LA VERA: *El Empalao* (a penitent reenacts Christ's carrying the cross on his way to Golgotha), Holy Thursday midnight.
CUACOS DE LA VERA: September 14 to 16, *Christo del Amparo*, with folkloristic shows.
VILLANUEVA DE LA VERA: *Pero Palo* (the inhabitants of the village give chase to a doll), in the carnival season.
PLASENCIA: Sunday after Easter: Pilgrimage to Nuestra Señora del Puerto.
CORIA: *San Juan.*

THE SOUTHERN MESETA

CÓRDOBA
LA MANCHA

When travelling from Sevilla to Córdoba one should rest for a while in **Carmona**. The Alcázar of Pedro the Terrible overlooks the town and is one of the country's most beautiful *paradores*. A great deal of alterations have been carried out since it was built.

There are no less than three fortresses in the town. Traces of the Roman period can still be found among the ruins. The Roman *carmo* must have been large and significant in its time. A necropolis containing over 1000 elaborately decorated underground tombs and cult rooms was discovered. A bridge on the outskirts of the town, the mosaic in the town hall courtyard and parts of the city wall also bear witness to the Roman period.

The church of Santa María La Mayor offers a cross section of architectural achievements. Integrating Visigothic elements, it has nevertheless also retained the Arab orange-tree courtyard. Its foundations are Gothic, but it was extended during the Renaissance. The main altar is in Plateresque style, whilst the choir stall is Baroque. From the Baroque gate, Puerta de Córdoba, there is a good view of the plain.

Left: The striped appearance of the arches in the mosque of Córdoba comes from the alternate use of brick and chalk.

Two roads lead to Ecija through the plain. One follows the Guadalquivir to **Palma del Río**. The village is situated at the edge of the protected Hornachuelos cork oak forest, containing ancient specimens. The road leading to the motorway gets one there much faster. The ten steeples of **Ecija** emerge from a basin on the banks of the Genil. Four of them are lookout towers, and were at one time part of the Arab city wall. The others are Baroque church steeples which were restored after an earthquake in 1755. The Santa María steeple is a replica of the Giralda of Sevilla. The Plaza Mayor with its surrounding arcades and numerous Renaissance and Baroque palaces give the town an air of dignity. According to Arab tradition the interior is the most important part of the building. The San Francisco and Santo Domingo cloisters, as well as the shady courtyards, offer a pleasant refuge from the intense afternoon heat.

CÓRDOBA

If you manage to catch the early morning mass in the **Mezquita** of Córdoba before anybody else and you take a stroll through the forest of pillars, you will be taken back to the days of the 10th century caliphate. You will also become aware of the fact that the Christian cathedral is sit-

uated right in the middle of the mosque. Only the Alhambra grants more imposing testimony to the architectural achievements of the caliphs. The mosque, like the Alhambra, was desecrated in part by the ill-advised modifications of Christians. Until today the Christians insist that it belongs to them. The Moslems in the town are not permitted to use any part of the buildings for their prayers.

After walking around the built-in church, through the forest of pillars you begin to understand the layout: built in the 8th century, it had almost doubled in size by the 10th century. Its 23,000 square meter vastness made it the world's third largest mosque. The double-tiered and scalloped arches, characteristically patterned in alternating bands of stone and brick, separate no fewer than nineteen aisles, each 175 meters long. Imagine how many believers must have prayed here to necessitate continual ex-

Above: The richly decorated interior courtyards in Córdoba are a sight for themselves.

pansion work to the building. Up to a million inhabitants are said to have lived here in the 10th century. The pillars reflect the various building phases. The Visigothic and Roman church capitals are situated in the first part, the front third, looking onto the entrance to the orange-tree courtyard. Pillars were brought from the Roman theatre of Merida for the extension to the present-day cathedral area. Blue and pink marble from the region was polished and worked for the third extension, and only Corinthian capitals were used. This is the most exquisite part of building. The *mihrab*, a prayer niche pointing to Mecca, is situated along the aisle, on the far side of the wall. It has a remarkable dome, exquisitely carved and sheathed in tiles and mosaics. A mere 26 years passed before the 11 aisles were extended to 19 under Almansor.

Parts of the Gothic **cathedral**, erected by Charles V, now tower above the simple low roofs. During the first 200 years of Christian rule there had only been a pulpit and a royal chapel. The

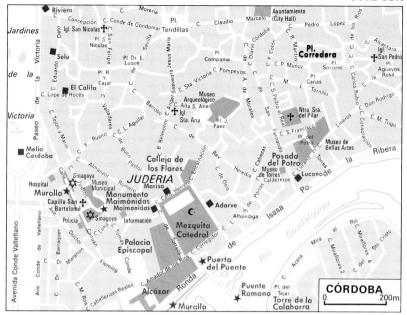

cathedral has a beautiful choir stall and its high dome makes it seem very bright compared to the gloomy mosque. The splendid chapels Real and Villaviciosa are next to the choir. Additional chapels and the vestry are built into the exterior wall of the mosque. The minaret still functions as the belfry and looks onto the orange-tree courtyard.

Alcázar with its beautiful grounds is siutated behind the mosque on the banks of the river. This is where the Inquisition and the Catholic kings resided during the Granada conquest. The Roman bridge spans the Guadalquivir in front of this. The defense tower, **La Calahorra**, where the town's past is presented to you in a multi-media show, is at the other end of the bridge. The city wall is still in good condition behind the Alcázar and leads to the **Puerta de Almodóvar**. It is the entrance to the Jewish quarter which extends from here to the mosque, one of the largest Spain ever had. The narrow winding lanes with simple whitewashed houses bedecked with flowers spilling

from their window boxes is a very picturesque sight indeed. One of the synagogues is still in good condition. The **Maimonides monument** is nearby. The great theologist, scientist and philosopher was just one of the city's learned men. Very early in its history the city had a university and a library. Poets and philosophers have a long-standing tradition here. Both Senecas and the Roman poet, Lucanus, came from Córdoba. The bridge and the Roman temple next to the city hall bear witness to this period.

The parts of the city bordering the mosque and *Juderia* are obviously Arab in character. Their narrow, meandering streets made it necessary for the new part of the city, present-day Córdoba with its 300,000 inhabitants, to expand beyond the avenues and plazas. A lot of churches in the old town have transformed the minarets into belfrys. The alleyways open on to beautiful plazas, among them the Plaza de las Bulas, in the heart of the Jewish quarter, and the **Plaza del Potro**, named after its fountain with its colt sculpture. There is an inn of the same name where Don Quixote is said to have stayed; the Plaza de los Dolores, narrow and simple in style, is behind the monastery with the famous **Cristo de los Faroles**, the Christ figure, which is romantically lit up at night; the Plaza de la Corredera is surrounded by arcades and balconies bedecked with flowers and, contrary to tradition, not painted white.

The numerous monasteries and palaces throughout the city are reminiscent of past splendor. The Palacio de Merced, the Medinaceli, the Casa de Carpio or the Villalones are but a few examples. The archeological museum is situated in the Palace of Paéz de Quijano, the city hall is is also housed in one. The art museum is the former Hospital de la Caridad. The most impressive palace is that of the of Marquis de Viana with its numerous courtyards and gardens. A completely different type of palace is to be found on the outskirts of the city. In 936, Abderraman III had the magnificent palace **Medina Azahara** built for his favorite wife Azahara. Later it became Abderraman's residence. It's a huge complex with terraced gardens and was built in a very short time. It was destroyed in less than 50 years, however, by rival Berber tribes who took over from the caliphs. Thereafter, parts of the building were used to extend the mosque and other parts were taken as far afield as Sevilla to be used in the Giralda. Sections have been reconstructed and the foundations excavated to give visitors an idea of the enormous size and splendor of the place.

The Campiña of Córdoba

There are many typical Andalusian villages on the way from Córdoba to Bailén, where Napoleon was defeated in Spain for the first time. The white houses surrounding the Mudéjar fortress in El Carpio, the old part of Andújar and Montoro are well worth visiting.

To the south of the road towards Jaén and Granada, the **Campiña**, a huge agricultural area extends. The soil changes colour in this treeless landscape with amazing effects. There is a large wine-growing region to the south, near Montilla. The wines are produced according to the same *solera* and *criadera* process used in Jerez. A different type of grape is used, however, and the climate is much drier. They taste similar to Jerez wines, but they are less expensive. You still find *bodegas* in Montilla, Doña Mencía, Lucena, Aguilar de la Frontera, Moriles, Puente Genil and Cabra without English names. Elaborate 16th-century churches and monasteries indicate that these vineyard towns were more influential at the end of the *Reconquista* than they are today.

A surprise awaits bird watchers to the southwest of Aguilar, in the middle of the vineyard region. A large number of *lagunas*, salt-water lagoons, form a perfect breeding ground for many rare species of water birds. The small lagoons dry up in summer and all of them are shallow. The **Fuente Piedra**, largest of these lagoons, lies farther south, almost in Antequera. In spring up to 3000 pairs of flamingos nest here. Apart from the Camargue, it's the only such nesting ground in Europe. Farther east, Jaén's endless olive-tree plantations come into sight. Amid the sprawling white villages of Baena, Martos and Alcalá la Real, spectacular castles are prominent in the hilly landscape.

The recently widened national road leading to the motorway crosses the mountains at **Linares**, a town hit by the coal-mining crisis. In the past this was a difficult journey, made dangerous by bandits and the notorious "Seven Rascals of Ecija". Charles III and his minister Olavide brought life to the region by establishing German settlements here in the 18th century. Villages like La Luisiana, Santa Elena, La Carlota or Las Navas de

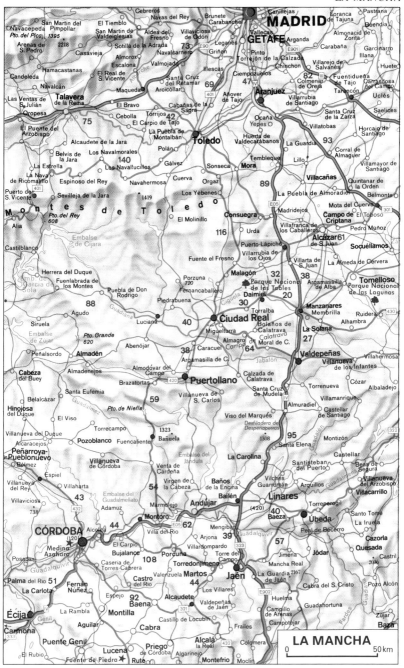

LA MANCHA

0   50km

Tolosa developed. The largest of these settlements is **La Carolina**. Its sweeping avenues, plazas and parks are a good example of Baroque town planning.

LA MANCHA

Beyond **Desfiladero de Despeñaperros** the vast southern Meseta, La Mancha table-land, expands. Mancha means "dry land" in Arabic. The name of the largest agricultural region in entire Spain now refers to the whole area. Very sparsely populated and bare, irrigated only in parts by Artesian wells, it is an arid strip of land. The sunsets in this part of the country are spectacular. The villages are large and little attractive, with small and brilliant, whitewashed houses and *corrales,* cattle enclosures located at the edge of the village. Village life takes place in the plazas. The most beautiful is the Plaza Mayor in **Tembleque**, built in the 17th century and once used as a bullfighting arena.

There is a mining area in the south of the province, but the economy is mainly geared to agriculture. Winter crops are harvested in May or June. Huge herds of sheep are grazed on the harvested fields. Famous Manchego cheese is made from their milk. The vast vineyards that produce the dry Mancha wine are also found in this region as well as the enormous onions that are fed to cattle if the EC fails to take them. Tasty melons that store the soil's only moisture are grown here.

The lack of water in the region is a serious problem. The two remaining marshes are now conservation areas. The situation in the **Tablas de Daimiel** national park is downright alarming, however. This onetime huge marsh, constantly underwater during the winter months, is almost dry today. Rare species of birds, reeds and rushes are in danger of

Right: Don Quixote was the person who made the windmills of Consuegra famous.

becoming extinct. There is a high price to pay for La Mancha's agriculture. Excessive pumping means that the ground water level sinks, so that more and more rivers are drying up. Complicated ways to divert the rivers are now being discussed. It is less dry in the **Lagunas de Ruidera** nature reserve. Some theories suggest that the underground source of the Guadiana forms the tiny lakes, linked together by small streams that flow into the reservoir at Peñarroyal. This oasis is a bird's paradise. During the La Mancha summer drought, it serves as a sanctuary for birds from the Daimiel region.

Coming from the south, the first village one arrives at is **Viso del Marqués**. The splendid 15th-century Renaissance palace belonging to the aristocratic de Luna family is situated in this arid region. They have transformed it into a maritime archive. **Valdepeñas** is a market town situated in the vineyard region of the same name. Its *bodegas* are open to the public.

The entire region was conquered from the Moors at the Battle of Navas de Tolosa in 1212. Thereafter, it was divided between the Calatrava military order, the Templar and the Santiago Knights for colonization and defense purposes. The area around **Ciudad Real**, deridingly referred to as La Mancha's New York, is thus called **Campo de Calatrava**. The best *tapas* between Madrid and Sevilla can be sampled in one of the town's many restaurants. Calatrava la Vieja, the remains of the Order's first seat of residence, is north of Carrión de Calatrava, by the Guadiana. The river functions as a moat.The residence was later moved to Calatrava la Nueva near **Calzada de Calatrava**, where impressive fortress ruins bear witness to its importance. From the surrounding villages, special emphasis should be given to **Almagro**. An influential town at the time of the Knights of the Order with numerous monasteries and churches, it owed its wealth to the Fugger family. The merchant family from south-

ern Germany established itself here because Charles V transferred his silver and quicksilver mines to it to cover his huge debts. They also administered the wool trade in the region. The unique town square with its glassed-in balconies is reminiscent of a nordic village. The small streets, the Renaissance and Baroque façades, the splendid Sto. Domingo monastery and the impressive town hall attest to the town's past glory. During the demolition of an old inn, an original 16th-century theater courtyard was discovered. Even the trapdoor from where the devil appeared can still be seen. A festival of classial theater takes place here every summer, and is becoming increasingly popular.

But not many people would know about La Mancha were it not for Don Quixote, the strange anti-hero created by Cervantes. A poor descendant of the *caballeros*, the knights, the 50-year old Don Quixote spends his time reading tales about knights. He identifies so much with the main characters in his books that he thinks he is a knight himself. In Sancho Pansa, a level-headed swineherd, he finds a submissive country squire, who doesn't seem to mind his master's eccentricity. Together, they journey through the land confronting the corruption and avarice inherent in the contemporary social system – Sancho on a donkey and Don Quixote on an old nag. The irony in this novel lies in the fact that the author transforms the bleak region of the La Mancha plain into a landscape full of adventure à la Lancelot du Lac. Out of politeness, the author doesn't name Don Quixote's hometown. No less than eight villages now claim to have this honor. Rumor has it that Cervantes wrote his novel while imprisoned in the Cueva de Medrano in **Argamasilla de Alba**. This is reason enough for Argamasilla de Alba's claim to be the only legitimate one.

Don Quixote allows himself to be knighted in an alleged castle that is in actual fact an inn. The knighthood is bestowed upon him by the inn keeper in the presence of two "ladies-in-waiting" – the

local prostitutes. A barber's bowl serves as a helmet. There is an inn in Puerto Lápice which serves the simple, country food commented on by Don Quixote. Spicy, with a high cholesterol content. As the hero needs a lady he chooses an uneducated farmer's daughter and calls her Dulcinea del Toboso. There is a museum in **El Toboso** named after her. **Qintanar de la Orden**, **Mora** and **Yepes**, situated amid vineyards, olive groves and saffron fields, also claim to be Don Quixote's hometown.

Don Quixote's escapades are observed sceptically by his cousin, the village priest and the barber. In the end, they burn his library. The adventures of the unfortunate hero begin with the famous battle with the windmills which he mistakes for giants, and on the sails of which he remains hanging. Only a few windmills have been preserved as tourist attractions in La Mancha. Their construc-

tion is of Arab origin, dating back to the 11th century. They weren't used on a large scale in La Mancha until 1575, however. The best examples are in **Campo de Criptana**, **Mota del Cuervo** and **Consuegra**.

In the further adventures of Don Quixote, he encounters monks accompanying a Basque lady whom he believes to be a victim of a kidnapping. He attacks a herd of billygoats, in the belief that they are soldiers, and he attempts to free some prisoners who are being taken to serve at the galleys, convinced that they are victims of a miscarriage of justice. After many entertaining adventures which take the two heroes throughout Spain, they return to their hometown where the *cabellero* finally comes to his senses before his death.

Tomelloso not only became famous through Don Quixote, but was also made famous by its village policeman, Plinio, who popularly lives in the novels by Pavón, set in the fifties. The contemporary painter Antonio López was born in Tomelloso, where he has opened a museum. He depicts the La Mancha landscape very aptly. To the north, the Johannine Order region borders the main town of **Alcázar de San Juan**. The archeological museum in the town has many beautiful Roman mosaics.

Part of the La Mancha continues into Cuenca Province. There is an impressive fortress in **Belmonte** not far from Mota del Cuervo. Belmonte was the birth place of Fray Luis de León. One can stroll through the characterstic lanes in the Jewish quarter and visit the collegiate church. The Roman ruins of **Saelices**, which include a theatre and an amphitheatre, are farther north, near Tarancón. The Escorial de la Mancha, a Renaissance monastery of the Santiago Order, istands in the vincinity, in **Uclés.** Today it functions as a seminary; Juan de Herrera and Francisco de Mora were both involved in its construction.

Above: The raw materials for basketry are harvested by hand in La Mancha.

PROVINCE SEVILLA

(Telephone area code 954-)

Accommodation

CARMONA: *LUXURY:* **Parador Alcázar del Rey Don Pedro**. Tel: 4141010. **ECIJA**: *MODERATE:* **Ciudad del Sol**, C/ Miguel de Cervantes 42, Tel: 4830300. *BUDGET:* **Hostal Santiago**, Ctra. Madrid–Cádiz at km 450, Tel: 4830162.

Sightseeing

CARMONA: **Necropolis Romana**: Tue–Sat 9 a.m.–2 p.m. and 4–6 p.m, Sundays 9 a.m.–2 p.m.

PROVINCE CÓRDOBA

(Telephone area code 957-)

Accommodation

CÓRDOBA: *LUXURY:* **El Califa**, C/ Lope de Hoces 14, Tel: 299400. *MODERATE:* **Abucasis**, C/ Buen Pastor 11, Tel: 478625. **El Oasis**, Av. de Cádiz 78, Tel: 291350. *BUDGET:* **Seneca**, C/ Conde y Luque 7, Tel: 473234.
LUCENA: *MODERATE:* **Baltanas**, Av. José Solís, Tel: 500524.
MONTILLA: *MODERATE:* **Don Gonzalo**, Ctra. Madrid–Malaga at km 447, Tel: 650658. *BUDGET:* Los Felipes, C/ San Francisco Solano 27, Tel: 650496.
PALMA DEL RÍO: *MODERATE*: **Hospedería San Francisco**, Av. Pio XII. 35, Tel: 644185.

Museums / Sightseeing

Mosque/Cathedral: 10.30 a.m.-1.30 p.m., 4-7 p.m, in winter 3.30-5.30 p.m. **Alcázar de los Reyes Cristianos**: 9.30 a.m.-1.30 p.m., 5-8 p.m, in winter 4-6.30 p.m. **Torre de la Calahorra**: 10.30 a.m.-6 p.m, in summer 10 a.m.-2 p.m., 6-8 p.m. Multivision show in various foreign languages: 11 a.m., 12 noon, 1, 3.30 and 4.30 p.m. **Synagogue**: 10 a.m.-2 p.m., 6-8 p.m, in winter 3.30-5.30 p.m., Sun 10 a.m.-1.30 p.m., closed Mon. **Museo Taurino** (Museum of Bullfighting): 9.30 a.m.-1.30 p.m., 5-8 p.m, in winter 4-7 p.m, closed in the afternoon on Sun, Mon and public holidays. **Museo Provincial de Bellas Artes**: 10 a.m.-2 p.m., 6-8 p.m, in winter 5-7 p.m, Sun 10 a.m.-1.30 p.m., closed Mon and public holidays. **Museo Julio Romero de Torres** (undergoing renovation). **Museo Diocesano de Bellas Artes**: 9.30 a.m.-1.30 p.m., 3.30-5.30 p.m., closed Sun and public holidays. **Palacio de los Marqueses de Viana**: 10 a.m.-1 p.m, 4-6 p.m, in summer 9 a.m.–2 p.m. only, Sun and public holidays 9 a.m.–2 p.m., closed Wed. **Posada del Potro**, Sala de Cueros (leathercrafts): 9 a.m.-2 p.m., 6-9 p.m. **Medina Azahara** (outside of town, 8 km to the east): 10 a.m.-2 p.m., 4-6 p.m, in summer 6-8 p.m, Sun and public holidays 10 a.m.-1.30 p.m., closed Mon.

Post / Information / Transportation

Córdoba: Oficina de Turismo: Palacio de Congresos y Exposiciones de Córdoba, C/ Torrijos 10, Tel: 471235. Pl. de Juda Levi, Tel: 472000-209. **Post Office**: C/ Cruz Conde 15. **Rail Terminal**: Av. de América. RENFE Bureau: Ronda de los Tejares 10. **Bus Terminal**: Av. de la Victoria.

PROVINCE JAÉN

(Telephone area code: 953-)

Accommodation

BAILÉN: *LUXURY:* **Parador**, Ctra. Madrid–Cádiz at km 296, Tel: 670100. *MODERATE:* **Zodiaco**, Ctra. Madrid – Cádiz at km 294, Tel: 671058. **LA CAROLINA**: *LUXURY:* **La Perdiz**, Ctra. Madrid –Cádiz at km 269, Tel: 660300. *MODERATE:* **Los Caballos**, Ctra. Madrid–Cádiz at km 265, Tel: 661830.

PROVINCE CIUDAD REAL

(Telephone area code 926-)

Accommodation

CIUDAD REAL: *MODERATE:* **Almanzor**, C/ Bernardo Balbuena, Tel: 214303.
ALMAGRO: *LUXURY:* **Parador**, Ronda de San Francisco, Tel: 860100. *MODERATE:* **Don Diego**, Ejido de Calatrava 1.
ARGAMASILLA DE ALBA: *BUDGET:* **Na. Señora de Peñarroya**, Ctra. to La Solana.
DAIMIEL: *MODERATE:* **Las Tablas**, C/ Virgen de las Cruces 5, Tel: 852107.
PUERTO LÁPICE: *MODERATE:* **Aprisco de Puerto Lápice**. Ctra. Madrid – Cádiz at km 134.

Museums / Sightseeing

CIUDAD REAL: **Museum of the Province** (Bellas Artes and Arqueologico), C/ Prado 3: 10 a.m.-12 noon and 5-6.30 p.m., Sun 10 a.m.-12 noon, closed Mon.
TOMELLOSO: **Museo Antonio López Torres**: 11.30 a.m.–1.30 p.m. and 5-7 p.m, Sun 12 noon– 2 p.m., closed Mon. **Museo de Carros**: keys at the city hall. Posada: open afternoons.
VALDEPEÑAS: **Museo Gregorio Prieto**, Av. G. Prieto: 12 noon-1.30 p.m. and 4-6 p.m, Sun 12 noon-3.30 p.m. **Museo Municipal**: 10 a.m.-1 p.m. and 5-8 p.m, Sun 12 noon-2 p.m., closed Mon. **Information Center Tablas de Daimiel** (11 km out of Daimiel): 11 a.m.–7.30 p.m., in summer 9 a.m.–9 p.m. **VISO DEL MARQUÉS**: **Palacio** (Marine War Archives): 9 a.m.–1 p.m. and 4–6 p.m, closed Mon. **ALMAGRO**: **Corral, Museo Teatro**: 10 a.m.-2 p.m. and 4.30-8 p.m.

Post / Information / Transportation

CIUDAD REAL: Oficina de Turismo: C/ Alarcos 21, Tel: 211081. **Rail Terminal**: C/ Ferrocarril. **Bus Terminal**: C/ Larache.

MADRID
In the Heart of Spain

With a population of three million, an additional million live in the suburbs, **Madrid** is the largest city in Spain. It lies in the center of the Iberian peninsula, amid the arrid Castilla and La Mancha landscape. Far away from any of the other large cities, Madrid attracts the region's commercial and economic interests. It is rapidly developing into a conglomeration of industries, administrative buildings, highrise office blocks, large ring-roads, sweeping avenues and busy fly-overs.

Madrid, capital since the time of Philip II, has met the challenge of modern Europe with considerable success. The advent of new buildings and new districts is more apparent here than in any other city. Madrid has also become obsessed with the automobile fetishism other European cities experienced 20 years ago. Under Franco's rule it was a moderate city, outflanked by the European oriented city of Barcelona. Madrid broke free of its shackles and revamped its image after Franco's death. Nightlife, festivals and theater, boutiques and galleries, artists and globetrotters conquered the city at the same time as banks, insurance companies and big business.

Left: The Rastro, Madrid's great flea market, takes up an entire city district on Sundays.

The way into the city takes one automatically to the north-south axis, the **Castellana**. This sweeping boulevard with its green strip forms a time bridge between the blossoming period under the Bourbons and the modern EC-era, as represented by the administrative district of Azca. Castellana leads to the north from the Atocha railway station. The ethnological museum is on the large square in front of the station. A renovated former hospital houses the modern cultural center of **Reina Sofía** with the modern art museum. The first part of the Castellana is called **Paseo del Prado**, after the walking rondell that Charles II had established near a stream on the outskirts of the city. The Castellana is widest here and even the busy traffic dosen't spoil the illusion of being in a park. The fountains, so well-liked by the king, still stand in their original place. The **Botanical Gardens** are situated on the Paseo and next to them is the **Prado Museum** which was first planned as a natural science musem. On its completion it was irreverently misused by Napoleonic troops as a stable and barracks. It was finally opened as an art museum in 1819. Today it is a repository for one of the largest art collections in the world, and displays unique and abundant art treasures belonging to the Spanish school. Every day thousands of visitors

admire the masterpieces by Murillo and Velázquez, El Greco and Goya, Zurbarán and Ribera, as well as Titian, Tintoretto, Rubens, Dürer, Bosch and Rembrandt. Apart from 19th-century paintings exhibited in the Neoclassical building, **Cason del Buen Retiro**, the principal attraction is Picasso's *Guernica*. He created the work for the World Exhibition in Paris, 1937, to immortalize the beastly bombing of a Basque mountain village by a commando of the German Luftwaffe, and as a warning against civil war. The boulevard stretches farther north like a green corridor, expanding every now and then onto large beautiful plazas that are unfortunately mostly packed with cars. The old fashioned luxury hotels and

the stock exchange building are situated on the Pl. de la Lealtad with its Neptune fountain. The exhibition of the **Thyssen-Bornemisza** collection is in the Palacio de Villahermosa. The main post office's neo-gothic palace is on the square named after the Cibeles fountain. On the opposite side large bank buildings line the elegant Alcalá Street. A look at the classical **Puerta de Alcalá** indicates how far the city wall went until the last century.

Columbus Square, where numerous blocks of flats were demolished to make room for the "Park of Discovery", is situated a little farther on. Embassies, luxury hotels, banks, elaborate buildings and expensive cafés line the streets of this part of Castellana. Farther to the north are

gant old buildings and ultra-chic shops. Going west, it takes us to the **Puerta del Sol**, Sun Gate Square, formerly in front of the medieval city wall. The square was transformed to what it looks like today during the secularization in the last century . The underground junction, the great bus station and the pedestrian precinct, which commences at the square, make the Puerta del Sol the hub of Madrid. Night and day, the square is full of tourists, loafers, lottery ticket and newspaper vendors, and people selling titbits and souvenirs. The city's landmark, a bear munching on the fruit of a strawberry tree, has been erected on the square. It symbolizes the lush forests and hunting grounds that once upon a time surrounded the city, and that the Habsburg monarchs found so attractive.

On the opposite side of the square, there is a milestone sunk into the ground outside the **Comunidad Autónoma**, Madrid's administritive headquarters. The distance of all of Spain's highways is measured from this point.

The Comunidad Autónoma building used to house Franco's security police. There is a plaque on the building commemorating the uprising on 2nd May, 1808, against seizure of power by the French. Josephe Bonaparte, Napoleon's brother, was installed on the throne and remained king for six years. He resided in the King's Palace and tried to impose the principles of the French Revolution here. During his reign, churches and monasteries were demolished. Graveyards and slaughter-houses were moved to the outskirts of the city for the sake of hygiene, creating more residential room in the narrow part of the old town, and early industrial manufacturing was established.

Gran Vía also had to make its way through the maze of buildings in the old part of the city. It was not until the turn of the century that this avenue was formed, brunching off from Calle Alcalá and making its way through the lanes, passing

examples Franco's sombre buildings: the Nuevos Ministerios. The Natural Science Museum is here as well. Behind the **Bernabeu football stadium** and the congress building with the Miró mosaics come the highrise office blocks of **Azca**.

This cross section of Castellana is only a small part of Madrid, however. Its history did not begin with the Bourbons and present-day Madrid doesn't only consist of highrise flats and office blocks. You get to the heart of the city from the Cibeles fountain. The elegant **Alcalá**, and **Gran Vía**, a street branching off from Alcalá, are the two most famous streets leading to the heart of the city. Towards the east, the Calle Alcalá leads to the residential area of **Salamanca** with its eleby the old city center, which was already bursting at the seams. The new elegant street was designed according to European and North American standards; grand and stately, with ornate art deco buildings, street cafés and palatial cinemas. At weekends people streamed into the city from the country and strolled along the Gran Vía, intoxicated by the glistening cars and the neon signs. The hotels and ultra-chic shops, the bars and cafés were enticing.

At the far end, the Gran Vía opens out onto the **Plaza de España** bearing a Cervantes monument, in front of which are the mounted figures of Don Quixote and Sancho Pansa. They are dwarfed by two highrise apartment buildings built in the fifties. Although they don't compare with present-day skyscrapers, they were the highest housing buildings in Europe at one time. Gran Vía has lost much of its glamor. In recent years, however, an attempt has been made to recapture some of its flair. The solid old buildings are being renovated, the ornate details are being restored; while country folk no longer admire the cinemas and street cafés, they are crowded with people from the suburbs seeking entertainment and a taste of city life.

The actual **old town** in Madrid is relatively small. The best way to discover it is on foot. Whilst the original Moorish settlement of *Mayrit* extended to the crags above the river Manzanares near the present-day King's Palace, the Christian settlement extended farther east to the Puerta del Sol, after it was conquered in 1085. During the 14th and 15th centuries the town's importance increased. The Castillian city and guild parliaments, the *Cortes*, met here a few times. When Philip II made Madrid the capital in 1561, it had 25,000 inhabitants living in crammed conditions in one-storey mud

dwellings. The Arab fortress, Alcázar, was transformed into a royal residence. Noblemen's palaces and administrative buildings were erected nearby. The Duke of Uceda's palace, today the army headquarters; the palaces of the Condes de Barajas and de Miranda; and the court goal, now the Ministry of Foreign Affairs, all form part of the **Madrid of the Austrias**, the Habsburg district. The trading area for various goods and crops was then located, on the south edge of town (Pl. de la Paja, de los Carros, de la Cebada). Today the *Rastro* fleamarket takes place here every Sunday. Both the **Pl. de la Villa** with its early Baroque town hall (1664) and the Plaza Mayor date back to the time of the Habsburgs, as well.

The **Pl. Mayor** was opened in 1620 during the reign of Philip III to celebrate the canonization of San Isidro. The expansive layout of this square, based on Italian landscape architecture, was quite unknown at that time. It served as an open-air theatre for an audience of up to 50,000. They watched theater productions, bullfights and equestrian events from the balconies and tribunes. It was also established amid the existing maze of winding lanes in the old town. The up to ten-storey high buildings on the southwest corner indicate how difficult it must have been to regulate the level differences in order to attain a suitable form for the square. The square owes its present-day form to the Prado architect, Juan de Villanueva. It was reconstructed after one of the many fires in 1790. The city traffic pulsated here until the 60s. Thereafter, it functioned once again as a place for cultural events, festivals and gatherings.

Only a few monasteries have been preserved. During the secularisation in the 19th century, 60 monasteries were pulled down or put to a different use. The royal nunneries, the **Real Monasterio de la Encarnación** and **Las Descalzas Reales**, were preserved, however. Both of them contain many art treasures from the

Right: The central point of Madrid's old town is the Plaza Mayor.

Habsburg era. The Trinity Monastery in the Calle Lope de Vega with Cervantes' tomb has also been preserved.

The old town became overcrowded during the Habsburg era due to the many members of the royal entourage. A law was passed whereby all houses with more than one storey had to accommodate court officials. This led to the construction of the so-called *malicia* houses. They had a one-storey façade at the front of the building and numerous floors and living quarters at the back. Lots of poor people moved into the area outside the city wall, which was eventually extended in 1624. The new city wall runs across the vast squares and *rondas*, which were reconstructed in the 19th century.

Some of the suburbs originating from the Habsburg era are still here today. The artists, painters, poets and actors sponsored by the court, who took part in the daily theater extravaganza, lived in the artists' quarter near the streets of Cervantes, León and Lope de Vega. **Lavapiés**, the part of the town leading to the river, was the Jewish quarter at that time, whilst the area around the **Calle de Toledo** and the **Calle del Pez** was the craftsmen's quarter. All these structures are still preserved in present-day Madrid. Construction work was carried out during the rule of the Bourbon monarchs in the 18th century, turning Madrid into a city. After the Alcázar had been burned down, a new grand and elaborate royal palace was erected. Artists were brought from Italy and France to work on its interior. Gardens and parks were created around the royal palace. Elegant streets and elaborate gates were constructed, canalization and street-lighting installed, and vast squares adorned with ornate fountains laid out.

Parks and plazas and wide streets are essential to counteract the smog and intense summer heat in the polluted city. The weary visitor should look for a shady bench and observe the city from there. Young and old throng the Pl. Sta. Ana, Pl. Olavide, Pl. Mayor, Pl. Dos de Mayo during the hot summer months. There is

195

always something happening in the **Retiro Park** around the Glass Palace or on the **Estanque**, the lake where the royal boat races used to take place. And on weekends Madrid's inhabitants take their dogs, grandmothers and children for a walk. One can pass the time at the summer cinema or in a terrace restaurant in the **Parque del Oeste** at the **Templo de Debod**, the Egyptian temple that was moved to Spain before the flooding of the Assuan Damm, and at the **Paseo del Pintor Rosales** until the small hours of the morning in the hope that the temperature will drop. One will also find a shady spot a little farther on, in the **Casa del Campo** royal hunting grounds, easily accessible by metro or cable car. In this vast park area there are numerous outdoor restaurants, a lake, a zoo and a fairground. In the evenings, it's customary to stroll from bar to bar in the city center, staying only

Above: The glass pavilion in the Retiro Park is the site of special exhibitions. Right: Street life alone can be exciting to watch.

long enough in each place to drink a coffee, a beer (caña) or a *tinto* (red wine).

One doesn't aim for any place in particular, but simply goes on a pub crawl through one of the city's districts, where every second building is a pub. There are lots of good eating places around the Pl. Mayor and the Cava Baja, places with live music and modern pubs around the Pl. Sta. Ana and the Calle de Huertas, trendy places around the Pl. Chueca, the Calle Libertad, the Pl. Dos de Mayo as well as Palma Street and Vicente Ferrer. There are also numerous small *tapa* pubs around the Pl. Olavide and Calle Cisneros. There is a wide choice of concert and theater performances.

The Zarzuela Theater, the Theater Royal which is presently being turned into an opera house, the Teatro Español, the Albeniz Theater or the smaller fringe theaters like the Comedy or the Teatro María Guerrero are only a few of the many stages.

Madrid is not a city of extremes from the point of view of sightseeing. Discover and experience the many bustling parts of the city, the large number of street cafés, the markets and the plazas.

Exursions from Madrid

The Guadarrama Mountains extend a day's drive from the north of the city. There are weekend houses, nature parks and reservoirs on the south side of the Castillian mountain slopes, which reach a height of up to 2400 meters. The sonorous-sounding names of the famous castles **El Pardo**, **La Granja de San Ildefonso** or **Riofrío** sound inviting. The **El Escorial** monastery, preserved by the Habsburgs, represents Philip II's splendour. Not far away, in the wonderful mountain landscape, is the **Valle de los Caídos** monument commemorating all those who lost their lives in the Civil War, the **El Paular** monastery and the **Manzanares El Real** fortress.

To the south, one quickly arrives at the great, flat La Mancha region. **Chinchón**, with its picturesque village square, at the same time bullfighting arena, is situated a little off the main road to **Aranjuez**, the splendid royal country residence on the green banks of the Tajo, surrounded by beautiful parks, hunting pavilions and fountains.

The ancient and very beautiful Visigothic capital of **Toledo**, a medieval huddle of roofs, domes, towers and minarets, stands bold on its granite hill, near the banks of the Tajo. This site was erected by the Romans under the name of *Toletum* and it was later occupied by the Visigoths, who then made it their capital in 554.

It also became the religious capital after the conversion of King Reccared to Catholicism in the year 587, and the archbishops of Toledo have been the primates of Spain since this time.

Its history embodies all that has contributed to developing modern Spain and it is truly a living museum of Spain's past

glory. Iberians, Romans and Visigoths have all left their mark here albeit their traces are somewhat pale. Arabs and Jews had a stronger influence on the town, however. Toledo fell to the Moors in 711 and it later became an independent Moorish domain. The city was captured in 1085 by Alfonso VI and he moved there with his entire court. Toledo then remained capital of Spain until the transfer to Madrid in 1561 under Philip II.

There are still quite a few traces of mosques and synagogues, baths and bridges, palaces and houses, bazaars and markets, fountains and water mills. The Alcázar, the grand cathedral and the many of Toledo's churches and palaces date back to the Christian period after the *Reconquista*.

The Catholic Kings gave Toledo a landmark with the **San Juan de los Reyes** church. Toledo is a symphony in stone. On the surface it appears to have a very reserved life style, but Toledo does not disappoint – a surprise awaits one around every corner.

MADRID
(Telephone area code: 91-)
Accommodation

LUXURY: **Gran Hotel Reina Victoria**, Pl. del Angel 7, Tel: 5314500. **Hotel Tryp Ambassador**, Cuesta de Sto. Domingo 5, Tel: 5416700. **Ritz**, Pl.de la Lealtad 5, Tel: 5212857.
MODERATE: **Ramón de la Cruz**, C/Don Ramón de la Cruz 94, Tel: 4017200. **Nuria**, C/Fuencarral 52, Tel: 5319208. **Tryp Asturias**, C/Sevilla 2, Tel: 4296676. **Londres**, C/Galdo 2, Tel: 5314105. **Los Condes**, C/Libreros 7, Tel: 5215455. **Embajada**, C/ Sta. Engracia 5, Tel: 4473300. **Laris**, C/Barco 3. **Reyes Catolicos**, C/del Angel 18, Tel: 2658600.
BUDGET: **Teran**, C/Aduna 19, Tel: 5226424. **Europa**, C/Carmen 4, Tel: 5212900.

Tourist Information / Post

Oficina de Turismo: Pl. Mayor 3, Mon – Fri 10 a.m.-2 p.m., 4-8 p.m., Sat 10 a.m.-2 p.m., closed Sun and public holidays, Tel: 2665477. At the **Airport Barajas** and the **Chamartin Rail Terminal**, weekdays 8 a.m.-8 p.m., Sat 8 a.m.-1 p.m., **Plaza de España** in the Torre de Madrid, Tel: 5412325, weekdays 9 a.m.-7 p.m., Sat 9.30 a.m.-1.30 p.m.; **Duque de Medinaceli** 2, Tel: 4294951, weekdays 9 a.m.-7 p.m., Sat 9 a.m.-1 p.m. POST: Pl. de Cibeles. **Telefonica – Locutorio**: Gran Vía 30 and Paseo de Recoletos 41 (9 a.m.-midnight).

Transportation

Metro – Underground: Your ticket is valid for travel on all underground routes; a *diez viajes* – a multiple ride ticket (10 rides on one ticket) – is a real money saver: buying ten separate tickets would cost you about double the price! All metro stations offer 3- or 5-day tickets (Metrotour) too.
Bus: Buy your ticket for a single ride in the bus; the *Estancos* (tobacco shops) sell *Bonobus* multiple-ride tickets (10 bus rides on one ticket at a reduced price); the network of buses is a closed book to outsiders, route maps and timetables being virtually non-existent.
Rail Terminals: Estación del Norte for short-distance trains to the north and east; Atocha, for long-distance trains to the south and west; Chamartín, for long-distance trains to the north, east and southeast; the rail terminals Chamartín and Atocha connect with an underground train. RENFE-information, Tel: 4290202.
Taxi: The fastest way to get a taxi in town is to wave one down in the street. Watch out for a sticker on the inside of the rear window, listing (in Spanish and English) the various supplementary charges which may be added to the fare displayed on the taxometer.

A motorway runs straight to the **Airport Barajas**. Taxis are allowed an extra charge for the ride to and from the airport. The Airport Bus runs from/to the basement garage on Pl. Colón every 15 minutes. Airport information, Tel: 4112545, Iberia National, Tel: 411011; international Tel: 4112011, Iberia flight confirmation, Tel: 4111895.
Town Buses: Estación Sur de Autobusses: C/ Canarias 17, Tel: 4684200.
Teleferico: (Cable cars to the Casa del Campo) Paseo del Pintor Rosales on level C/Marques de Urquijo; runs during dailight hours only, daily in summer, weekends only in winter.

Car Hire / Automobile Club

Hertz, Gran Vía 88, Tel: 2485803. **Avis**, Gran Vía 60, Tel: 2472048. **American Express**, Pl. de las Cortes 2, Tel: 4295775. **Rentalauto**, C/García de Paredes 57, Tel: 4413602. **Unión Rent a Car**, General Margallo 29, Tel: 2796317. **Real Automobil Club de España**: C/ José Abascal 10, Tel: 4473200/4779200.

Museums

Circulo de Bellas Artes de San Fernando, C/ Alcalà , Mon – Fri 7 a.m.-7 p.m., Sat – Mon 9 a.m.-3 p.m. **Museo del Prado**, Paseo del Prado, and **Cason del Buen Retiro**, C/Alfonso XII 23: 9 a.m.-7 p.m., Sundays and public holidays 9 a.m.-2 p.m., closed Mon. **Museo Nacional de Artes Decorativas**, C/Montalbán 2, 10.30 a.m.–1.30 p.m., closed Mon. **Museo de la Real Academia de Bellas Artes San Fernando**, C/ Alcalá 13, Tue – Fri 9 a.m.-7 p.m., Sat – Mon 9 a.m.-3 p.m. **Museo Nacional de Ciencias Naturales**, C/José Guitiérrez Abascal 2, Tue – Sat 10 a.m-6 p.m., Sundays and public holidays 10 a.m.-2.30 p.m., closed Mon. **Museo Nacional Ferroviario**, Paseo Delicias 61, 10 a.m.-5.30 p.m., Sundays and public holidays 9 a.m.-2 p.m., closed Mon. **Museo Soralla**, Paseo General Martínez Campos 37, 10 a.m.-3 p.m., closed Mon. **Museo Taurino** (Museum of Bullfighting), Plaza Monumental de las Ventas, Tue – Fri 9.30 a.m.-1.30 p.m., Sundays 10 a.m.-1 p.m. **Museo Thyssen-Bornemisza**, Paseo del Prado 8 (from autumn 1991). **Museo Arqueológico**, C/Serrano 12, Tue – Sat 9.30 a.m.–8.30 p.m., Sundays and public holidays 9.30 a.m.-2.30 p.m., closed Mon. **Casa de Lope de Vega**, C/Cervantes 11. **Centro de Arte Reina Sofía**, C/Sta. Isabel 52, 10 a.m.-9 p.m., closed Tue. **Museo Cerralbo**, C/Ventura Rodríguez 17, 10 a.m.-3 p.m., closed Mon. **Museo Lazaro Galdiano**, C/Serrano 122, 10 a.m.–2 p.m., closed Mon. **Museo Municipal**, C/ Fuencarral 78, 10 a.m.-2 p.m. and 4.45-8.45 p.m., Sundays 10 a.m.-1.45 p.m., closed Mon.

Sightseeing

The **Palacio Real** is open from 9.30 a.m.-5.15 p.m., Sundays and public holidays 9 a.m.-2.15 p.m.(closed during state visits). **Monasterio de las Descalzas Reales**, Plaza de las Descalzas 3, weekdays 10.30 a.m.-12.30 p.m. and 4-5.30 p.m.; Sun and public holidays 11 a.m.-1.30 p.m., closed Mon. **Real Monasterio de la Encarnación**, Plaza de la Encarnación 1, 10.30 a.m.-1 p.m., closed Mon and Fri. **San Ginés**, side chapel 10 a.m.-1 p.m. **Panteon de Goya**, Paeso Florida (closed for reform). **Panteon de Hombres Ilustres**, C/Gayarre 3, weekdays 9 a.m.-2 p.m. **San Francisco el Grande**, C/San Buenaventura 1, Tue – Sat 11 a.m.-1 p.m. and 4-7 p.m., in summer 5-8 p.m. **Botanical Gardens**, 10 a.m.-8 p.m. **Templo de Debod**, 10 a.m.-1 p.m. and 4-7 p.m. **Museo Colon de Cera**, Museum of Waxworks, Paseo Recoletos 41, daily 10.30 a.m.-2 p.m. and 4-9 p.m. **Real Fabrica de Tapices**, C/Fuenterrabía 2, weekdays 9.30 a.m.–12.30 p.m. **Parque Zoologico**, Casa de Campo, open all day, Metro: Batán. **Sala de Exposiciones del Canal Isabel II**, C/de Sta. Engracia 125, temporary exhibitions with varying opening hours. **Monasterio de los Trinitarios**, C/Lope de Vega 27.

Restaurants

CASTILIAN: **La Bola**, C/La Bola 5; **Casa Lucio**, Cava Baja 35; **Casa Paco**, Puerta Cerrada 11; **La Cacharrería**, C/Morería 9; **Mi Pueblo**, Costanilla de Santiago 2; **Posada de la Villa**, Cava Baja 9; **Aroca**, Pl. de los Carros 3; **Botin**, C/Cuchilleros 7;

FISH: **El Bonar**, C/Cruz Verde 16; **Aymar**, C/Fuencarral 138; **Korynto**, C/Preciados 36; **Tres Encinas**, C/Preciados 33; **El Pescador**, Jose Ortega y Gasset 75; **Casa Rafa**, Narváes 68; **Bajamar**, Gran Vía 78.

VEGETARIAN: **Casa Marta**, C/Sta. Clara 10; **Restaurante Vegetariano**, C/Marqués de Santa Ana 34; **La Biotika**, C/Amor de Diós 3; **El Granero de Lavapiés**, C/ Argumosa 10.

NORTH COAST CUISINE: **Peña Arriba**, Francisco Gervás 15; **Moaña**, C/Hileras 4; **Casa Gallega**, C/Bordadores 11;

BASQUE: **Jai-Alai**, C/Valverde 2; **Irizar Jatetxea**, C/Jovellanos 3; **Pagasarri**, C/Barco 7; **Guria**, C/Huertas 12; **Balzac**, C/Moreto 7.

ANDALUSIAN: **Los Borrachos de Velazquez**, Principe de Vergara 205; **Berrio**, Costanilla de los Capuchinos/corner San Marcos; **Don Paco**, Caballero de Gracia 36; **Jose**, Castelló 61.

RESTAURANT ALLEYS: **Pasaje de Matheu**, C/Manuel F. González; **Travesía de Arenal**, C/Ventura de la Vega.

Madrid Specialities

The typical dish of Madrid, the *cocido*, is only served at lunchtime. This tasty casserole, prepared with a multitude of ingredients, gets its unique flavor from stewing for hours over a charcoal fire. According to local custom, the stew's sauce is served as an appetizer, followed by the vegetables and chick-peas as a first course, and the meat as second course.

Public Holidays / Festivals

The public holiday on May 2 celebrates the resistance against the Napoleonic Army. Second week in May: *San Isidro*. Second week in August: *San Lorenzo, San Cayetano* and *La Paloma*. October 12: *Virgen del Pilar*, miltary parade to the Dos-de-Mayo-Monument on the Paseo de Prado. November 9: public holiday in Madrid in honor of the *Virgen de la Almudena*.

Bullfighing

Every Sunday from March to October in the bullring of Las Ventas; in May during the Festival of San Isidro every day for ca. 24 days; advance booking C/Victoria 9.

At the Casa del Campo (Metro-Station Batán) the bulls are held in a coral during the morning preceeding the fight; at 12 noon lots are drawn to decide which *torero* is going to fight against which bull.

Shopping

Department stores and clothing stores in the city cluster around Gran Vía and Puerta del Sol; look for shoes, handbags and furs at bargain prices on the C/Fuencarral; department stores and more elegant fashion shops around the metro-station Goya.

Boutiques: On the C/Almirante and vicinity, also on C/Conde de Xiquena and around C/Ayala; creations of well-known fashion houses on C//Serrano; genuine Spanish *capa*: Seseña, C/Cruz 23. Discover **quaint, traditional shops** in the city centre on the streets C/del Pez, Corredera Baja, Alta de San Pablo and Santi Espiritus; or in Lavapiés on the streets Mesón de Paredes, Valencia, Lavapiés.

Antiques: C/del Prado around the Plaza de las Cortes; in the Rastro-Quarter around the Plaza Grl. Vara del Rey and in the two courtyards on the left and right hand side half way up the Ribera de Curtidores; market at the Puerta de Toledo.

Flea Market: The Rastro takes place every Sunday from ca. 10am–3 p.m. in the quarter south of the Plaza de Cascorro. It is absolutely essential to leave all your valuables at the hotel and keep a sharp eye on your purse or wallet. Stamp and coin collectors shouldn't miss the Sunday morning market on the Plaza Mayor.

BALEARIC ISLANDS

MALLORCA
MENORCA
IBIZA
FORMENTERA

MALLORCA

Largest of the *Islas Baleares*, and populated by over half of the inhabitants of the archipelago, Mallorca has the best tourist facilities. The whole of the northwest region is girded by the magnificent Sierra de Tramuntana with peaks like the Puig Major (1445 meters) or the Massanella (1349 meters). From here it becomes flat, stretching into a fertile coastal plain towards the southeast and to the arid region in the south of the island, where visitors can enjoy the many coves and splendid beaches. A walk down by the seaside either out in the wilderness or in one of the picturesque harbors on the islands, is among the most pleasant activities here.

Palma de Mallorca is the capital of the autonomous Baleares region. The city offers a cross section of various periods in history which influenced the island's life style. It was founded by the Romans, but its golden age came with the Moors. A section of the **Moorish town** wall is still preserved. It runs along the coast from Palacio de la Almudaina and the

Preceding pages: The promenade along the harbor of Palma de Mallorca. Left: Taking time off from the harvest in La Puebla for a bite and a rest.

cathedral to the Avenida Gabriel Alomar Villalonga.

The Moors also extended the Medina Mayurka and laid out magnificent gardens parks and narrow streets, a number of which still exist today. The **Arab baths** date back to this period. One can visit them in the Calle Serra in the Gothic quarter.

Jaime I's troops conquered the island in 1229 and integrated it into Christian Aragón. After the death of Jaime I, Palma figured as the capital of the independent kingdom of Mallorca until 1349, to which the islands of Ibiza, Menorca and Formentera also belonged, along with southern France's Montpellier and Roussillon. It was during this time that the **Seo**, the cathedral opposite the old Moorish **Almudaina** was built. The latter was transformed into the King's Palace. The **Bellver Fortress** which dominated the entire bay was erected in the 13th century. It is the only fortress which has a completely circular outline.

Another important building in the Mallorca capital is the **Lonya**, the early medieval goods exchange built by Guillem Sagrera – an outstanding example of secular late Gothic architecture. There are many typical Mallorcan courtyards in the old palaces where social life has been concentrated since Gothic times. The

S

Menorca

Punta Nati
Cala Morell
16
Ciudadela
Cabo de Caballeria
Playa Tirant
Fornells
Agueda 244
728
San Juán
El Arenal
d'en Castell
Santandrié
Cala Blanca
St. Galdana
Naveta dels
Ferrerias 8
Mercadal
Monte
Toro 21
Santuario
24
Cala Mezquida
Cabo Dartuch
Sto. Tomás
11
Alayor
Playa Arenal de Son Bou
Playa Mesquida
Cala'n Porter
Cala Coves
721
Maó
14
9
La Mola
San Luis
Cala Alcaufar
Cala Punta Prima

Cabo de Formentor
Bahía de Pollensa
Cabo del Pinar
6
Pto. de Pollensa
Pollensa
lobra 20
710
Monasterio 11
de Lluch
Escorca
org Cuevas de
Blau Campanet
x 15
11
Alcudia
Puerto de Alcudia
12
Playa de Muro
713
11
Bahía de Alcudia
Cabo Farruch
La Puebla
12
8
Cala
Picafort
Playa Son Serra
Playa Estretd
Playa Mesquida
Muro
Sant Pere
10
Artá
Cala Ratjada
Capdepera
Inca 19
lubi
Sta. Margarita
12
715
ro
13 11
13
Costitx
Maria de Salut
14 Cuevas de Artá
Binissalem
sell
Sancellas
Sineu
13
Puig Calicant 472
Son Servera
a
Lloret
Petra
S. Lorenzo
10
15
Cala Millor
Pina
13
14
Manacor
aida
7
Montuiri
7
Cuevas de Hams
Porto Cristo
9
hal
13
9
Cuevas del Drach
Mallorca
Porreras
13
714
luchmayor 10
Felanitx
14
Calas de Mallorca
Cala Murada
15
13
Campos
San Salvador
9
Porto Colom
orb
13
16
15
Playa Marçal
La
Rapita
13
717
Cala d'Or
Santanyí
Porto Petro
ala
Ses Covetes
Playa Es Trenc
Salines
12
Cala Figuera
Playa Es Carbo
Cabo de Salinas

Pto. de Cabrera
abrera

MEDITERRANEAN   SEA

BALEARIC ISLANDS
0   20km

205

Palau Solleric court yard is a good example. Today, it functions as a center for contemporary art.

The city hall, known as **Cort** in the local dialect, the **Consulat de la Mar** and the **Santa Eulária** church are also worth a visit. The tomb of the well-known Mallorcan philosopher and mystic, Ramon Llull, is in the **Sant Francesc** church.

City life is centered around the grand boulevards like the **Paseo Marítimo**, Palma's real façade, with its modern **Parc de la Mar** in front of the cathedral. **El Born**, a popular promenade during the romantic period, is now one of Palma's busiest streets. The majority of shops are situated along the modern **Jaume III Street**. The large **El Arenal** beach girdles one side of Palma and the suburb of **El Terreno** the other. This is where the city's night life is concentrated around the famous **Gomila Plaza**.

El Poniente – the West Coast

If you leave Palma on the motorway heading for Andraitx, you will arrive at a number of popular beaches. **Cala Major**, **Illetes**, **Bendinat** and **Portals Nous** beaches are virtually situated on the outskirts of town.

Puerto Portal's modern and fashionable water sports harbor is nearby. This is where the yacht crews and the jet-set meets in the summer months. The adjoining **Marineland Park** with its many aquatic animals is a worthwhile attraction, especially worth seeing are the antics of the tame and trained dolphins.

Of the many holiday resorts on this coast, which boast a veritable smorgasbord of beautiful beaches, **Palma Nova** and **Magaluf** are the most popular.

Right: The beach of El Arenal is one of the great favorites. Far right: Getting dressed up for the procession in San Juan in Ciudadela on Menorca.

The latter is frequented mainly by young English people. Mallorca's Casino, situated in an *urbanización* right above the **Cala Xada Bay**, is a good place where one can try one's luck.

The holiday resort of **Santa Ponça** with its extensive beach is a little farther on, going towards Andraitx. There is a monument on the beach, commemorating the landing of Christian troops. The **Paguera** and **Cala Fornells** beaches are also very popular. The harbortown of **Port d'Andraitx** is another favorite spot for water sports fans.

A number of luxury estates straddle the hill-slopes, overlooking the bay. A narrow mountain road, curvy and fairly bumpy, leads into the hills to the remote valley of **S'Arracó**. Going downhill from here, you come to the small **Sant Elm** harbor that offers perhaps the best view of the unusually shaped island of **Sa Dragonera**. It is shaped like a dragon that appears to be keeping watch on ships arriving at the island.

Sierra de Tramuntana

One of the most scenic spots on Mallorca is, without a doubt, the **Tramuntana** mountainous region in the north. These mountains stretch the entire length of the island so that they can be seen from any point on the island. A number of roads leads to this region, but the majority of people take the road that goes via the mountain resort of **Valldemossa**, made famous by Chopin's and George Sand's stay at the cloister in 1838/39.

The erstwhile **Carthusian monastery** lies in an enchanting environment, in the midst of a terraced landscape bearing olive trees, almond trees, carob trees. In her autobiographical book *A Winter on Mallorca*, the French author carefully describes her stay here with her children and lover Chopin. For his part, the composer was not so thrilled with the environment, it was cold, damp, he had

nightmares and daymares. The sound of rain on the roof and morbid thoughts, however, inspired him to write his *Prelude in D-flat-major, Opus 28 Nr. 15*, the later-named *Raindrop-Prelude*. The Carthusian monastery contains many souvenirs relating to this stay, and every summer a Chopin piano festival takes place, in which many musicians living in the Sierra participate.

Most visitors usually follow the road towards Deià from Valldemossa. **Son Marroig** manor is on this road. It overlooks the impressive **Sa Foradada peninsula** which extends into the turbulent waters of the north coast. The entire region, including the bulk of the farms and estates on the coast of Valldemosa and Deià, once belonged to the Grand Duke Luis Salvator of the house of Habsburg and member of the Austrian-Hungarian line. Luis Salvator (1847-1915) was an educated man and a great environmentalist. He wrote a comprehensive monograph entitiled *The Balearic Islands*. A large portion of the agricultural land near

the Valldemossa and Deià coastal region also belonged to him.

San Marroig is an interesting place for a brief sojourn. You can visit the small museum and the small marble temple where Luis Salvator watched the sun set over Sa Foradada, a sight beyond compare almost anywhere in the Mediterranean region.

A little farther on, you come to **Deià**, the place where the English author, Robert Graves, spent most of his life. Shortly after leaving the village, a turnoff leads to **Cala de Deià**, which is reminiscent of earlier times when only fishermen frequented the bay.

Driving past the enchanting *caserío* (hamlet) of Lluc-Alcari, the road leads us to the valley of **Sóller**, which reaches way up through the orange plantations to the highest peaks of the northern range. There is also a tourist train from Palma to Sóller which runs along one of the most picturesque landscapes of Mallorca. A tram then carries passengers from the station to the harbor.

207

You shouldn't forget to stop by at the villages of **Biniaraix** and **Fornalutx**, both situated at the edge of the valley. Their natural stone buildings make them quite unique to the island. From Sóller, the road winds its way up into the mountains and leads to the **Cúber** and **Gorg Blau** reservoirs. The ruins of a prehistoric temple – partially covered in water – are at the bottom of the latter.

A little farther on, in the shade of the Puig Major, the winding road from Sa Calobra to **Torrent de Pareis** begins. This is the kind of scenery that creates a lasting impression. The deep river gorge twists its way through the barren desert-like mountains until it reaches the sea. You can also enjoy views of it from a boat. Trips to this unspoiled part of the Mallorcan north coast are available at the Sóller harbor. Farther north, you come to **Santuario de Lluc**. The monastery has

Above: The northern reaches of Mallorca are very mountainous. Right: The monastery of S. Salvador dominates the flat south.

one of Mallorca's most treasured statues of the Holy Virgin in its safekeeping. People come here from Palma on foot each year. This hike is a strange hybrid between a pilgrimage and an athletic event. Lluc has been Mallorca's religious center since pre-Christian times. There is evidence that the moon and the bull were sacred here in prehistoric times. The road continues its crawl through these remote mountain regions until reaching **Pollença**.

There is another itinerary leading in westerly direction from Valldemossa, and going to the little harbor towns of **Port de Valldemossa** and **Port d'es Canonge**. The road to **Esporles** goes to **La Granja**, an old Mallorcan estate, where traditional Mallorcan utensils of days gone by are exhibited. The two villages of **Banyalbu-far**, with its numerous stone walls and the Mirador de ses Animes lookout point, and **Estellencs** link the north range with the town of Andraitx.

Heading due north to the mountains towards Sóller from Palma, you will pass

through the village of **Bunyola** and the beautiful **Alfabia** gardens, as well as the **Raixa** country estate.

The Center of the Island

The center of Mallorca has little in common with the standard Mallorcan clichés and touristy image of the island. Many regions and villages are the same as they were hundreds of years ago and allow us to enter a world that is the complete opposite of what you would expect of a holiday resort.

The road to Inca, which has partly been developed into a highway, marks the axis of the region. Driving from Palma, the first towns you come to are **Santa María** and **Consell**, from where the road branches off to **Alaró**. This town has Moorish origins. It lies in a valley which is guarded by the two twin-like mountains: the Puig del Castell and Puig de s'Alcadena.

A branch-off from the road to Orient leads to the ruins of the **Alaró fortress** which are situated on a mountain of the same name. It is not the ruins of this medieval fortress in which the Moors defended themselves against the advancing Christians that make this trip especially worthwhile however, but the wonderful views that you can enjoy from this point.

Anyone who has carne this far should continue their journey to **Orient** at all cost. It sits secluded between the mountain slopes. Heading towards Inca, the road goes through the lovely town of **Binissalem**, well-known for its wines and its Acualandia grounds.

Inca's leather and shoe industry make it the island's second most important town. From there the road continues on to **Sineu**, right at the heart of the real Mallorca. Just outside Sineu a turn off leads to the village of **Costitx** where the famous bronze bulls' heads were found. These are now exhibited in the archeological museum in Madrid.

The scenery changes at this point. In the distance the town of **Sineu** cuts an elegant silhouette against the sky with its

209

churches that stand on a hill. The town was founded by the Romans and was, for a time, the seat of the Mallorcan monarchs. It has managed to retain its regal character until the present day. From here, you have access to the villages of **Lloret**, **Sencelles**, **María de la Salut** or **Llubí**. They bear witness to the fact that there is still a part of Mallorca that hasn't changed since the days when the island was known as the "Island of Tranquility".

The South

Whilst the central inland region of the island is fertile farming country, the south is arid and sparsely populated.

Some of the island's most beautiful beaches are nevertheless in this region. You can by-pass the Arenal and Palma beach holiday resort complexes when coming from Palma if you drive along the motorway. **Cape Enderrocat** and **Cape Blanc** lie beyond this. Steep cliffs stretch along the sparsely populated coastline for miles. Not far from the Cape Blanc lighthouse a turnoff leads to the small **Cala Pi** bay, one of the characteristic scenic spots along this coastal region.

The prehistoric ruins of **Capocorb** with remains of the famous Mallorcan *talayots*, megalithic stone towers, are nearby. Farther along this road, you come to **Sa Ràpita**, where the landscape becomes a coastal plain with sandy beaches and crystal-clear water. **Ses Covetes** and **Es Trenc** rank among the island's most beautiful beaches.

Boat trips are available from the Colònia de San Jordi to the **Cabrera** archipelago that can be seen on the horizon. These islands earned somewhat infamous fame during the War of Independence when they were used as a prisoner-of-war

Right: Such clear blue water, a rarity in the Mediterranean, is one of the reasons why so many people flock to the Balearic Islands.

camp for thousands of Napoleonic soldiers. They are to turned into a national park in the near future.

The **Colònia** marks the starting point of the expansive sandy beaches that begin at Es Carbó and line the extreme south of Mallorca. Our journey concludes at **Cape Ses Salines**, with the lighthouse of the same name. The most important towns in this region are **Campos** and **Santanyí**.

The island's most beautiful bays and coves are situated in the coastal area of the latter towns: Cala Mondragó, Cala Figuera or Cala Santanyí.

The East Coast – El Levante

One of the most important roads on the island is the one from Palma to Manacor, continuing on to the east coast. Before arriving at **Manacor**, famous for its artificial pearl manufacturing, you arrive at the famous Gordiola glass factory just outside **Algaida**. After Manacor, the coastal road leads on further to Porto Cristo, which boasts a special sight: the **Coves del Crac** caves. There is an underground lake and an entire forest of stalagtites to visit within the caverns.

The region of **Calas de Mallorca** stretches from here to the south. Heading south, you find one bay after the other from here to **Porto Colom** and the highly recommendable **Cala Marçal** beach. The adjoining resorts of **Cala d'Or** and **Porto Petro** have become the favorite vacation hang-out for German tourists. Thereafter, the route winds on back to the Satanyí region again.

The Northeast

The northeastern part of the island, with its generous bay, is another popular tourist region. Traveling down the road from Inca you first come to **Pollença**, a town with a lot of character and the chosen home of many artists.

Excursions from here to the marvellous bay of **Sant Vicenç** are especially recommended. The mighty peaks of the Cavall Bernat mountain range tower in the background. They continue on to the **Formentor** peninsula, which juts out into the sea between mountains and forests. The Formentor luxury hotel, the first of its kind in this category, is situated here.

The popular town of **Port de Pollença** lies between two piers – **La Victòria** and **Cap Pinar** – in the bay of the same name. **Alcúdia**, with its impressive city walls lies on a slope beyond.

These very walls bore witness to a siege of the town in the 16th century, after the poverty-stricken peasants rebelled against Charles V and the townspeople remained loyal to the king. Here, too, are the ruins of the old Roman town of **Pollentia**, with, among other special items, a Roman theatre.

The expansive bay of Alcudia is a huge sandy beach lined with dunes and woods, which has become almost entirely urbanized. The most important tourist resorts are **Muro**, **Can Picafort** and **Son Serra de Marina**.

It pays to visit the **Albufera nature reserve**. It is a marshland area where many migrant birds stop to rest. Here, on the outskirts of Can Picafort, there is a large camping site. The small urbanizations of **Sant Pere** and **Es Caló** beach lie at the opposite end of the bay.

Continuing our journey along the main road we arrive at a town called **Artà**. Surrounded by majestic mountains, it is the site of the *talayot* complex of **Ses Països**.

A few less commercialised bays like the **Cala Mesquida** or the **Cala Estreta** can still be found in the north. Beyond **Capdepera**, however, with its Moorish fortress, you will find yet another tourist resort – **Cala Ratjada**. Farther south lie the well-known **Coves de Artà**, a series of fascinating, bizarre rock formations, and from here the road leads to **Cala Millor** where the typical Levant coast coves abound all along the shore.

MENORCA

Although the second largest Balearic island is very close by it has very little in common with Mallorca. It lies to the north of Mallorca, so that it is exposed to the strong *Tramuntana* winds coming from the Gulf of León. This, together with the extremely flat nature of the island, always made it difficult for the islanders to cope with the extreme conditions of wind and water. Menorca's three periods in history when it was under British and French rule for a short period in the 18th and early 19th century is another factor that makes it different from Mallorca. A few lingustic features remain from those times, as well as the great liking for *gine,* a locally distilled spirits made from juniper-berries. Other typical traits of the Menorcan character are said to include unwieldliness, meticulousness and good business sense.

Above: Salt marshes are part and parcel of the landscape and economy of Ibiza.

Maó (Mahon) is the capital, located at the end of a fjord-like natural harbor basin, which is regarded as the best Mediterranean harbor after La Valetta (on Malta). The architecural achievements of the English fuse with the white Mediterranean structures. The harbor, with its numerous bars, is by far the best place to enjoy the town's night life. The **Plaza de la Esplanada** is the most vibrant part of the city.

One of Menorca's special features is the significant Megalithic excavation sites, which have earned it the title of an "open-air museum". The most important finds are the so-called *taulas*, table-like structures made from a horizontal stone slab supported by a vertical stone slab. Until now, scientists have not been able to agree as to their function. There is often a *talayot* in the vicinity of these finds.

A *talayot* is a watchtower made of large rocks that, like the *taulas*, date back to between 700 BC. and the time of the arrival of the Romans in 122 BC. The most impressive of the *taulas* are those of Torrauba de Salort (Alaior), Trepucó (Maó) and Talati (Maó).

Cala Alcaufar and **Punta Prima** beaches are situated on the outskirts of Maó, in the south. **Cala Mesquida** beach lies to the north, on the way to the **La Mola** fortress which keeps watch over the bay.

The road from Maó to Ciutadella divides the island into two almost equal halves. In the northern part, the coast is rugged. The harbor in **Fornells**, famous for its lobster fishing, or the **El Arenal d'En Castell** or **Cala Tirant** have accessible beaches in parts, however.

In contrast, the southern part of the coast is charming, with several expansive beaches and many *barrancs*, gorges formed by the water's effect on the limestone. **Cala en Porter**, **Arenal de Son Bou**, **Sant Tomás** and **Santa Galdana** beaches in the Algendar *barranc* estuary are highly recommendable. The **Cales Cove** caves were once used as a burial ground.

Monte Toro with its monastery marks the center point of the island. It is the only mountain on the island that rises to a height of 357 meters. There are wonderful, spreading views of the island and the not so distant Mallorcan coast from its summit on a clear day.

Farther to the west, you come to famous **Naveta dels Tudons**, a prehistoric burial place that is said to be the oldest construction of this type in Europe. It is, like most of the excavation sites, clearly sign posted and in very good condition, considering the fact that it dates back to 1400 BC.

Ciutadella is the second-largest town on the island and the principal settlement of the western part. The town was founded by the Carthaginians and later proclaimed capital of the island by the Moors, which it remained until the English, for strategic reasons, made Maó the capital. The bishop's residence and the cathedral are still situated in Ciutadella, however. The town has managed to retain much of its erstwhile monumental and aristocratic character.

One of its most typical characteristics are the *voltes* (arcades), and the narrow winding lanes, which are reminiscent of centuries gone by. A monument on the **Born** commemorates the devastating Turkish invasion, which took place at a rather unpleasant time when marauding pirates kept the islanders in a constant state of fear with their lethal sallies for booty.

Ciutadella is well-known for its town festival, **Festes de Sant Joan**, in which the Menorcan horses also play a role. The riders participate in all kinds of competitions, which take place in the old part of the former capital, amidst the crowd. It is one of Spain's most colorful and popular festivals.

Cala Santandria, **Cala Blanca** or **Cala Morell** beaches all lie close to Ciutadella. Apart from their beautiful surroundings, these beaches also have crystal clear water.

IBIZA

Together with Formentera, Ibiza forms the Pitiuse archipelago, which differs widely in morphology and history from the Baleares (Mallorca, Menorca and Cabrera). Ibiza is, on the whole, very smooth with its rolling hills and numerous pine forests. Because it is situated close to the mainland, Ibiza has traditionally played an important economic role. It was one of the principal Carthaginian colonies in the entire Mediterranean region, and it retained its customs and traditions after Carthago was ultimately and decisively destroyed by Rome.

The city of **Eivissa** (Ibiza) is situated on a mountain slope, from where it dominates the entire harbor basin. It has retained its charm to the present day. The upper part of the town, **Dalt Vila**, is sit-

uated behind the fortifications erected by Charles V, scattered picturesquely around the **Seo** (cathedral).

Farther down are the **Sa Penya** and **Sa Marina** quarters, no longer individual fishing villages but a conglomeration of boutiques, bars, restaurants and exotic shops. The so-called *Ad lib* fashion emerged in Ibiza when hippies frequented the island back in the flower-wiebling days of the 60s and 70s. It is still a lucrative source of income.

The town center is the boulevard **Vara de Rey** with its well-known hotel and Cafetería Montesol – both important meeting places for real Ibizans. Some night-clubs, like **El mono desnudo** (the naked ape) or **La oveja negra** (the black sheep), have become legends of their time, reminiscent of the late sixties, when Ibiza was a hippies' paradise. During the eighties, they became popular with all

Above and right: La Mancha is not the only site for windmills, as demonstrated by these specimens on Formentera.

types of jet-setters, yacht owners, snobs and last but not least the curious throng that comes to watch the nightly spectacle in Eivissa. It is quite an experience just sitting on one of the terraces observing the different types in their way-out costumes go by.

If you have other priorities, the most important places to visit are the necropolis museum on the **Puig des Molins** and the archeological museum, in which the most significant finds of the Punic period are exhibited.

The **Talamanca**, **Figueretes** and the **Platja d'en Bossa** beaches are close to the town. The most famous beach on Ibiza is, undoubtedly **Ses Salines** however. It is situated under a promontory, orientated towards Formentera. It was, for many years, the only nudist beach in Spain. In the meantime, it has lost something of its special charm. Just as beautiful is **Playa des Cavallet**. It is close-by, on the other side of the peninsula. In the southwest of the island, near **Sant Josep** there are a number of charming bays, among them **Cala d'Hort**. From here you can see the tiny island of **Es Vedrà**.

On the eastern shore, around **Santa Eulària del Riu** is another holiday resort. In the vicinity is the camping site of **Es Canar**, where a colorful market still takes place that dates back to the hippie era. **Cala Sant Vicenç** and **Portinatx** in the north offer a pleasant atmosphere for a quiet summer holiday. **Sant Antoni de Portmany** on the west coast is, on the other hand, the liveliest town on the island after Eivissa. The numerous bars and discos frequented by young, well-healed people make it a real nightlife spot. The large harbor, with beautiful views of **Conillera Island**, is reminiscent of the time when it was a quiet fishing and trading port.

To get to know the other side of Ibiza, you have to visit the small hamlets in the central part of the island. **Santa Agnés**, **Sant Mateu** or **Santa Gertrudis** are a few of the places where there are still many examples of traditional architecture said to have African roots. The low buildings and their extreme simplicity support this theory.

FORMENTERA

The island of **Formentera**, only 14 km long, and very flat, lies to the south of Ibiza, separated by a narrow strip of water. Boats operate from Eivissa to **La Sabina** harbor. The journey takes about one hour and the boat goes via the tiny islands of **Espardell** and **Espalmador**.

Because the islanders were not able to defend themselves from the constant pirate atttacks, Formentera was almost uninhabited for hundreds of years. This may be the reason that it has managed to retain its simplicity and gaiety, which failed to attract hippies in the 60s. It has remained unaffected by the hubbub of modern times.

The waters of the beaches in **Illete** almost match the Caribbean in color, a fact

that makes them unique in the Balearic archipelago. Apart from **Sant Francesc Xavier**, the island's main town, and **San Ferran**, there is only the tourist resort of **Els Pujols**. The visitors who come to Formentera cherish the peace and hospitality that the smaller of the Pitiuse islands has managed to retain.

A megalithic burial ground has been discovered on Formentera, in **Ca Na Costa**. The site lies on the shores of **Lake Estany Pudent** and reveals a kind of prehistoric burial place that is otherwise unknown in the Balearic islands.

La Mola and its surroundings is especially worth visiting. From here, you have views of the entire island. You should also visit **Berbería** with its lighthouse pointing toward the African coast. There are beaches on both the north and the southern shores. They are often situated opposite one another on narrow strips of land so that one has an unusual natural vista of the calm sea on one side and the waves crashing against the shore on the other.

MALLORCA
(Telephone area code: 971-)
Accommodation

PALMA: *LUXURY:* **Son Vida Sheraton**, Urbanización Son Vida, Tel: 790000. **Valparaíso Palace**, C/ Francisco Vidal, Tel: 400411. **Palas Atenea Sol**, Paseo Marítimo 29, Tel: 281400. *MODERATE:* **Jaime III Sol**, Paseo Mallorca 14 B, Tel: 725943. **Palladium**, Paseo Mallorca 4, Tel: 713945. **Saratoga**, Paseo Mallorca 6, Tel. 727240. **Villa Río**, Av. Joan Miró 115, Tel: 233346. *BUDGET:* **Portixol**, C/ Sirena 27, Tel: 271800. **Corona**, C/ José Villalonga 22, Tel: 231935. **Hostal Archiduque**, C/ Archiduque Luis Salvador 22, Tel: 751645.

DEIÀ: *LUXURY:* **La Residencia**, Son Moragues, Tel: 639011. *BUDGET:* **Costa d'Or**, C/ Lluch Alcari, Tel: 639025.

Post / Tourist Information

PALMA: **Post Office:** C/ Constitució 6, 9 a.m.-1.30 p.m. and 4-5 p.m. Telefonica: C/ Constitució 8 a.m.-3 p.m. **Police Headquarters**: C/ Hölderlin 1. Tel: 280400. Police emergency call: 091 and 092.

Oficina de Turismo: Avda. Jaime III 10, Tel: 712216. C/ Santo Domingo 11, Tel: 724090.

Museums / Sightseeing

PALMA: **Museo Municipal de Historia** in the Castillo de Bellver: 8 a.m.-8 p.m. **Museo de Mallorca:** C/ Portella, 5: 10 a.m.-2 p.m. and 4-7 p.m, Sundays 10 a.m.-2 p.m, closed Mon. **Museo de la Catedral**, C/ Palau Reial 29: 10 a.m.-12.30 p.m. and 4-6.30 p.m., Saturdays 10 a.m.-1.30 p.m., closed Sundays and public holidays. **Palau de Almudaina** (museo del Patrimonio Nacional), Baños Arabes, C/ Serra 3: 10 a.m.- 1.30 p.m. and 4-6 p.m. **Museo de Bellas Artes** in the Palau Solleric, C/ San Cayetano 10: 11 a.m.-1.30 p.m. and 5–8.30 p.m., Saturdays 11 a.m.-1.30 p.m., closed Sundays and public holidays. **Pueblo Español**, C/ Capitán Mesquida Veny 39: 9 a.m.–8 p.m.; workshops: 10 a.m.-6 p.m. **Flea Market:** Baratillo, Polígono de Levante, Saturdays until 3 p.m.

ALGAIDA: **Casa Gordiola** (Glass Factory), Highway Palma – Manacor at km. 19: 9 a.m.-1.30 p.m. and 3-8 p.m., Sundays 9 a.m.-12 noon.

ESPLORES: **La Granja**, daily 10 a.m.-6 p.m.

MANACOR: **Perlas Majórica**, 9 a.m.-12.30 p.m. and 3-7 p.m., Sat and Sun 10 a.m.-1 p.m.

Caves: Cuevas de Artà: 9.30 a.m.-7 p.m. Cuevas del Drac: 10 a.m.-5 p.m. (with concerts).

VALLDEMOSSA: **Palacio del Rey Sancho** (Folk Dancing): Mondays and Thursdays 11 a.m.

Sports / Diving

CALVIÁ (Diving): CIAS, C/ Obispo Cabanellas 29a. Escuba Palma, Av. Rey Jaime I, 69; Estrella del Mar, C/ Monte.

PALMA (Tennis): Club Natación Palma, C/ Teniente Oyaga; Club Tenis Playa de Palma, Av. Son Rigo. Mallorca Club de Tenis, C/ Artillería de Muntana.

Rental Cars

PALMA: Hertz, Paseo Marítimo 13, Tel: 232374. Iberocars, C/ Marqués del Palmar 11, Tel: 236077; Baleares, Paseo Marítimo 19, Tel: 280317.

MENORCA
Accommodation

MAÓ: *LUXURY*: **Port Mahón**, Avda. Fort de l'eau, Tel: 362600. **Capri**, C/ San Esteban 8, Tel: 361400. *BUDGET:* **Jume**, C/ Concepción 6 y 4, Tel: 363266.

CIUTADELLA: *MODERATE:* **Ses Voltes**, Cala de Santandria, Tel: 380400. *BUDGET:* Alfonso III, Cami de Maó 53, Tel: 380150.

VILLACARLOS: *MODERATE:* **Hotel del Almirante**, Fonduco Puerto de Mahon, Ctra. Villacarlos, Tel: 362700.

IBIZA (Eivissa)
Accommodation

IBIZA: *LUXURY:* **Los Molinos**, C/ Ramón Muntaner 60, Tel: 302250. **El Corso**, Playa de Talamanca, Tel: 312312. *MODERATE:* **Montesol**, C/ Vara de Rey 2, Tel: 310161. **El Corsario**, C/ Poniente 5, Tel: 301249. **Victoria**, Playa Talamanca, Tel: 311912. *BUDGET:* **Marigna**, C/ Al Sabini 18, Tel: 304912. **Hostal Estrella del Mar**, C/ Felipe II, Tel: 312212.

SAN ANTONIO ABAD: **Pikes**, Camí de Sa Vorera, Tel: 342222.

Museums

Museo Arqueológico in the old university, Pl. de la Catedral: 10 a.m.–1 p.m.

Museo de Arte Contemporaneo, Ronda Narcis Puget in Dalt Vila.

FORMENTERA
Accommodation

PLAYA MIGJORN: *LUXURY:* **Iberotel Club La Mola**, Tel: 328069. **Formentera Playa**, Tel: 320000. *BUDGET:* **Costa Azul**, Tel: 320024.

CALA SAHONA: *MODERATE:* **Hotel Cala Sahona**, Tel: 322030.

EL PILAR: *BUDGET:* **Entrepins**, Tel: 320023.

PUERTO LA SABINA: *BUDGET:* **La Sabina**, Tel: 320279.

CASTLES AND FORTRESSES

When the Phoenecians and the Greeks settled on the Iberian peninsula they always chose places that were by nature located so as to provide a maximum in defence. They fortified these places with stone and cyclopean walls so that they controlled the way of access to the town. There is evidence of this in Gerona, Tarragona or Ibros. Very little of these fortifications has been preserved. It was the normal procedure for each conqueror to extend or to make changes on the existing fortresses. The pre-Roman coastal fortresses (Segorbe, Alicante, Peñíscola, Sagunto) ultimately derived their specific appearances from the Romans, the Arabs and finally from the Christians.

Up until the 10th century, medieval castles in Spain were built over the re-

Previous pages: A monk in an old monastery. Ready for fishing. Vines in La Mancha. Above and right: The fortresses in Baños de la Encina and Segura de la Sierra.

mains of Roman *castri*. The word *castillo* is dervived from the latin diminutive form for *castrum*. These walled-in settlements were erected primarily as defense outposts along strategic places such as intersections of overland roads or bridges and not intended to last forever. They were simply made of mud and wood. The Romans erected lookout towers all along the Mediterranean coast, making it easy for news of the first signs of approaching danger to be passed on immediately.

The city walls of Barcelona, Tarragona or Segorbe, and the fortresses of Coria and Morella date back to the same period and still reveal their defensive origins.

In the 8th century, the Arabs brought their own more sophisiticated defence strategies with them. They used the older Byzantine fortifications as models for their own fortresses, adapting them to the peculiarities of the land. They chose strategic rises from where they were able to control large areas. Some still offer splendid views (Zahara, Olvera, Alcalá la Real, La Iruela and Montanchez). Also

dating back to this period are the square lookout towers in Martos, Lucena, Trujillo, Tarifa or Badajoz; the *corazas*, multi-walled systems without a fortress, such as in Almería or Lorca; *alcazabas* or citadels, fortifications with a fortress as in Mérida, Almería, Cullera, Málaga or Guadix; and *alcázares*, or fortified palaces like Granada, Sevilla or Córdoba.

The fortresses which also functioned as military barracks, seat of government as well as courts of law, were erected during the numerous disputes between the nobles in the 11th century. The clergy also erected its fortresses in order to defend church property (San Pere de la Roda, Ripoll) and to give shelter to the peasants of their region.

A large part of Andalusia was conquered by Fernando III in the 13th century. He and his son, Alfons X, further fortified the conquered towns and enlarged the fortresses: the Castillo de Sta. Catalina in Jaén, the Alcalá de Guadaira, Lorca, Arcos de la Frontera, Niebla – which laid under siege for six months –

and the Castillo de San Marcos in Puerto de Sta. María. A large part of the mountain region remained unstable for a long period of time, however, and changed hands many times between the Moors and the Christians. The villages which developed here still reflect their defense nature: Vejer, Castellar, Zahara, Olvera, Setenil and all of those villages bearing the name of "de la Frontera".

Towards the end of the *Reconquista*, the military knights were assigned the task of protecting the conquered regions. For this purpose fortresses were erected, especially in La Mancha and in the Extremadura. These fortresses had a strong Byzantine influence due to the crusaders of the Knights Order: Fregenal de la Sierra, Jerez de los Caballeros, Medellín, Trujillo, Carrión de Calatrava. A similar thing happened in Levante, in Peñíscola or Oropesa after Jaime I conquered the country in 12 years and placed his trust in the Montesa order.

During the Nasrid era in Granada, in the 14th century, the Arabs fortified the

223

alcazabas in Málaga and Granada. The Christians had already begun to erect grand fortresses which looked similar to fortified palaces. This style was fully established during the Renaissance. The first of these fortified palaces is said to have been *La Calahorra* (Granada).

Apart from being a nobleman's residence, fully equipped with all the luxurious furnishings one would expect to find in a nobleman's palace, it had a defence function as well. Examples of this type of fortified palace are Perelada, Jarandilla, Zafra, Escalona, Maqueda, Guadamur, Oropesa, Canena and Villena. The Marquis of Villena, by the way, translated Dante's *Divine Comedy* into Castilian.

Despite new techniques in military defence systems, Charles V (Almuñécar) and Philip II (Antequera, Altea) fortified

Above: The lonely fortress of Consuegro.
Right: Political parties with regional programs are often more popular than their national counterparts.

former Arab fortresses. A new fortress was erected in San Sebastián in Cádiz. It played an important role in the Battle of Trafalgar against the English. The fortresses in Olivenza and in Alburquerque on the Portuguese border were fortified as late as the 19th century in an attempt to win the Orange War.

Although the fortresses adorn many hillsides, they are threatened with decay. The aristocracy often does not have the means to preserve them. For many, the simplest form of upkeep was to turn former luxury chambers into *paradores* for tourists. Freely translated, *paradores* means stopping place. Over a third of the 80 or more *paradores* are former castles, convents, or palaces. Whatever their origin, they all offer comfortable and spacious accommodation. The first *parador* was opened in Gredos in 1928. The intention was to bring tourism to the regions that didn't have good hotels. Since then the popularity of the *paradores* is ever increasing, and they are still remarkably good value.

Nationalism and Separatism

Apart from Castilian, that is, the actual Spanish as we know it, three other languages are spoken in Spain: of these, Galician (*Gallego*) and Catalan are similar to Castilian and they all have common Latin roots. Basque, on the other hand, does not even belong to the Indo-European family of languages and is thus quite distinct. Although these languages were spoken in regions that were independent monarchies in medieval times, the Galicians, the Basques and the Catalans always considered themselves to be Spanish.

It was only in the middle of the last century, in the wake of the Romantic era, that a plethora of nationalist movements emerged, but they did not establish themselves as an actual political force until the lid was taken off of Spain's political life with the departure of Generalissimo Franco in 1975. The strongest nationalist tendencies ultimately developed in the Galician, Basque and Catalan regions.

The Basque Country – Euskadi

The violence people associate with ETA makes the Basque separatist movement the most famous and notorious. The main source of support for the movement comes from the Basque Nationalist Party, the PNV, founded in 1894 by Sabino Arana. Arana developed Basque nationalist ideology, and it was he who designed the Basque flag with its white and green cross and the Basque symbols. His ideology was based on two main principles: a return to traditional religious values bordering on theocracy, and the firm belief that Basques are a "superior race" that has degenerated through miscegenation. Strange enough, Arana became founder of a Spanish nationalist party during the latter part of his life.

Most social scientists maintain that the PNV's popularity increased with the Basque country's industrial revolution, which, under the strong influence of the clergy, destroyed the rural way of life based on fishing and farming. The new

225

opponents of Franco. At the end of the sixties, however, ETA terrorism commenced. Although it claimed to be a national movement, it became extremely left wing, influenced by Castrism and events in Algeria. ETA terrorism began in the latter years of the Franco era, but most of its victims were killed in the years of democracy. Bombings in department stores and residential areas, claiming the lives of innocent people, among them women and children, has weakend ETA's stand, especially after one of its former members was murdered after being smuggled into the government.

The Catalans

Catalan separatist fervor has a completely different character. It is partly geared to independence, there is at the same time a strong wish to transform Catalonia into a modern, prosperous region. It has always been more or less a federal movement. During the Civil War the Catalan separatists lost a lot of support, whilst the Anarchists became very popular. Unlike the Communists and the Anarchists, the separatists offered little resistance to the Franco regime after the conclusion of hostilities. Some of the left-wing terrorist groups gained support after democracy was established. But, unlike in the Basque country, terrorism didn't spread here as it found no solid support among the Catalans. If there are any terrorsist attacks in Catalonia today at all, they are usually carried out by the Basque ETA.

The strongest nationalist party in Catalonia is the *Convergencia i Unió*. It is considered the most important stabalizing element in Spain's democracy and in the regional government.

society with its factories and urbanization process and the loss of traditional religious forms brought much social unrest so that people began to nostalgically idealize the distant past. Many people believed that a return to their old life style could only be achieved if the region became independent of the mother country. At this time the Spanish Socialist Workers Party (PSOE) gained support in the Basque country. Their aims were in fact contrary to those of the PNV, but they did form an organized opposition to the reactionary forces in Madrid.

Although the majority of Basques were right wing and religous, they fought on the side of the anticlerical revolutionaries in the Civil War because they supported their claim to independence, while the Franco supporters did not. In the years immediately following the war, the Basque nationalists were not very active

Galicia

The third region, and one that has a very strong nationalist movement, is Ga-

Above and right: Two personifications of the political atmosphere in Spain today, optimism and critical uncertainty.

licia. The Galicians base their nationalist leanings on their Celtic origins, although historians are convinced that the evidence of Celtic culture in Galicia is no stronger than in other regions of the peninsula where the Celts were present before the arrival of the Romans. Galician is a Romance language and was at one time Spain's most important written and spoken language.

Similar to the Basque Country and to Catalonia, part of the nationalist movement here sees terrorism as a legitimate weapon in their struggle for independence, even to the point of justifying atrocities, like the bombing of a discothèque. Unlike in the other regions, however, the separatist movement here has little social importance.

There have been some very violent outbursts indeed by irredentist groups on the Canary Islands in recent years. They favor the reunification of the Canaries with the Magreb – an option which finds very little support among the islanders, however.

Nationalist regional identy became popular in other regions as well after the 1981 autonomy statute. Andalusia, Asturia, Cantabria, Castilla, even down to places as small as El Bierzo, place much importance on their roots, not so much for political reasons, but more to improve their image in the field of commerce as well as in the tourist industry.

In general – despite the very different historical backgrounds of the various regions – the nationalist phenomenon has only become popular in the last 20 or 30 years. It was greatly encouraged by the democratic government's autonomy statute. Although violent attacks do make the headlines occasionaly, they are few and far between. The various national groups, like the Catalans, who have been striving for decentralization since the time of the Bourbons, are much more concerned about winning support for their national customs, language and traditions than with establishing another political order which could in turn lead to a real separatist movement.

CATALAN CULTURE

Although it wasn't always easy, the Catalan people managed to preserve their culture down through the centuries. The most significant cultural basis was certainly the Catalan language, varieties of which are also spoken in Valencia and on the Baleares. Derived from the common roots of Langue d'Oc, it had its golden era during the reign of Aragon, until the central power of the Bourbons, who were in favor of Castilian, restricted its use in the 18th century.

The 19th century *Renaixença* movement demanded a revival of Catalan, reminding people of its golden age in the Gothic era. During this time Catalan became so widespread that some time later Pompeu Fabra was able to compile a first Catalan grammar. Following the Republican defeat in the Civil War, Catalan was officially forbidden until, after the democratic constitution of 1976, it again became a symbol of national identity and a basis for reviving Catalan traditions.

Catalan Culture and Art

Barcelona has always been the center of this movement. Thanks to its cosmopolitan character and to its broad-minded bourgeoisie, Barcelona has been able to meet modern and progressive cultural demands.

Fine Arts: Two of the most important personalities in modern art, Joan Miró and Salvador Dalí, were Catalan by choice, even if the former did choose to live on Mallorca and the latter moved about all over the world. The Miró Foundation Fund in Barcelona and the Dalí Museum in Figueres keep the memory of both artists alive. Pablo Picasso spent part of his youth in Catalonia and a museum in Barcelona now honors the

Right: Modern Catalan architecture, the Palau de la Musica Catalana.

famous exile Catalan, who undoubtedly was *the* painter of the 20th century.

Architecture is another major form of Catalan aesthetic art. Barcelona became the center of the modern movement – *Modernismo* – at the end of the last century. Names like Antoní Gaudí, Domènech i Montaner or Puig i Cadafalch represent elaborate buildings in a style which reflects the Gothic elements revived by the *Renaixença* as well as the Mediterranean love of color.

Architects like Ricardo Bofill keep up the Catalan architectural traditions today. The buildings being erected for the 1992 Olympics will set new trends.

Music: Folk music is still alive in many parts of Catalonia. People dance the Sardana everywhere. It is accompanied by trumpeters and is a strange blend of Arab and Baroque music.

Habanera is sung in coastal regions. It is reminiscent of the soldiers' melancholic feelings when they were returning or leaving for the Cuban war.

In the field of classical music, Pau Casals, Montserrat Caballé or Josep Carreras represent the sensitivity of the Mediterranean people. Their music is full of emotive expression. The *Gran Teatro del Liceu* is regarded as one of Europe's most important opera houses.

Catalonia set the trend in modern music for the so-called *Nova Cançó.* In the latter years of Franco's rule, poets and musicians who openly rebelled against the state were part of this movement, by singing all their songs only in Catalan. Valencian artists like Raimón and Mallorcans like María del Mar Bonet also joined this movement, the first of its kind during the Spanish dictatorship. Soon groups of artists from other regions got together, but they never achieved the same musical or social significance that was associated with names like Lluis Llach or Joan Manuel Serrat – names which became symbols of resistance and the Catalan national feelings.

Literature: Barcelona has always been associated with the Spanish literary tradition. For quite a long time it took away the leading position from Madrid as the leading publishing city for a long time, especially in the years of the "Hispano-American boom", when the works of great South American writers like Cortázar or García Márquez were published here thanks to the Catalan wirter and publisher Carlos Barral. He published the kind of works that conventional publishing houses would have rejected.

There have been well-known writers who have written in Catalan since medieval times: the poets Joan Maragall, Josep María de Sagarra, J.V. Foix or Salvador Espriu; the novelists Mercé Rodoreda and Manuel de Pedrolo; or accomplished chroniclers and journalists like Josep Pla, regarded as the creator of the modern *Catalán.* Other Catalan writers have written their works in the Castilian language, the most famous among them are: the brothers Goytisolo, Manuel Vazquez, Montalbán, Juan Marsé.

Cinema: Catalonia set the trend for the experimental film genre brought forth in the sixties and seventies by the "Barcelona School", which produced extremely experimental films. Directors like Jordi Grau and Carlos Durán and actresses like Teresa Gimpera are just a few of the very many names associated with the school. These films were representative of the so-called *gauche divine* ideas which were being expressed by progressive intellectuals in places like the Boccacio Discoteque or on Barcelona's Tuset Street.

Theater: Thanks to a great number of Catalan personalities, like the author, actor and well-known director Adolfo Marsillach, and the actors Nuria Espert and Josep María Flotats, modern contemporary theater has made a name for itself. Barcelona's theaters have always had excellent ensembles. In recent years avantgarde ensembles like Dagoll Dagom, Els Joglars or Els Comediants have also established themselves in the world of contemporary theater.

SHERRY

The Jerez vineyards lie slightly above sea level, to the north of the bay of Cádiz. Spain's best-tasting wines are concentrated in the triangle between Sanlúcar de Barrameda, Puerto de Sta. María and Jerez de la Frontera. The proximity to the sea, the long hours of sunshine, the relatively abundant rainfall and the white *alberiza* soil which functions like a sponge during rainfall sucking up the water and reflecting the sun from underneath onto the grapes, makes this area ideal for producing large quantities of high-quality wine. The grapes are primarily the Palomino Fino kind.

The sherry-making process is unusal: the wine is matured in long tiers of oak barrels in the bodegas. The oldest wine is in the bottom barrels, collectively known as *soleras*. From time to time a third of

Above: A sherry bodega in Chiclana. Right: When out tasting the wines, a little food is recommended.

the wine is removed from the *soleras* and filled into bottles, leaving room in the barrel for the wine from the first *criadera* barrels, those above the *soleras*. In this way the younger wine slowly takes on the characteristics of the older.

The wine has to pass through up to six *criaderas* before it is considered properly aged. The barrels never get empted. The year in which the blending process began indicates the actual "age" of the wine. The minimum age is three years. This blending process, together with the wine-growers' long years of experience and skill, makes it possible to produce wine of a quality which is not in any way affected by changing weather conditions. The quantity of wine produced from one year to the next varies between one and two million hectoliters (26.5 to 53 million U.S. gallons), depending on the weather, among other factors.

Another feature of the wine-making process is the micro-organisms contained in the wine. Some must form a ferment-like substance in their first storage year

called *flor*. These wines are then categorized as *Fino*. Their most important classifications are: **Fino**: 15 - 17 per cent alcohol, light, slightly dry; **Amontillado**: 16 - 18 per cent, up to 24 per cent if left to mature longer at the must stage, darker and with a slight almond flavor; **Oloroso**: 18 - 20 per cent, gold-colored and somewhat heavier wine; **Cream**: from over-ripe grapes, slightly sweet, similar to Oloroso; **Moscatel**: rich, sweet, from Muscat grape raisins; **Manzanilla**, which also means camomile, is the name for the Sanlúcar Finos. They are very dry and taste slightly sour.

There are 13 villages that produce their harvests for sherry-making. But the wines form **Condado** (Niebla, Huelva Province), **Chiclana** or from **Montilla-Moriles** (Cordoba Province) are made by the same process, although the Montilla wines are produced from other grapes (Pedro Ximénez).

The history of the Jerez wines has been documented since Phoenecian times. The English took a supply to Plymouthin

1588 where Shakespeare has Falstaff praise it in *Henry IV.* He called it sherry, which sounded similar to the Arab name for the town, but by the same token was easier for English speakers to pronounce. The English began to commercialize the wine in the 19th century. Firms like Sandeman, Croft, Williams & Humbert, Terry, Osborne or Garvey invested a great deal of their capital in the highly lucrative sherry business.

Nearly all the bodegas are open to the public, and all of them have points of interest other than their wines. Many, especially the family-run businesses, have wine-tasting rooms and stands where you can purchase wine and a selection of souvenirs. All bodega visits end with generous wine-tasting. The traditional sherry glasses, or *catavinos*, can also be purchased. Sherry glasses all look similar. They are narrow at the top in order to preserve the bouquet. The bars in the area rarely serve other wines. Although it is not a table-wine, chilled Fino is just the right thing to have with a *tapa* snack.

FLAMENCO

Flamenco is poetry, music and rhythm wropped in one. These three elements are carefully combined to express man's innermost feelings. Traditional flamenco attempts to depict the individual with his feelings of joy, hate, hope, passion and jealousy, and his fears as well. Text and music, in this case, are as closely linked together as the two sides of a coin.

The guitar has accompanied flamenco song and dance since the 19th century. However, there are songs like the old *tonás* or *trilleras* which are performed without any instrumentalization. Rhythm plays a very important role in the so-called songs *de compás*. Sometimes the audience claps in time to the music, especially at festivals.

Although song is closely connected to Flamenco, the Flamenco dance is an ind-

Above and right: The flamenco can be danced in two contrasting fashions, re-strained, or unbounded and passionate.

pendent art form, expressing emotional states through body movements. Some academies have surfaced throughout the country recently teaching not only Flamenco in its genuine form, but also a popularized form that has become quite fashionable especially among members of the Yuppie generation. A more standard form of flamenco is taught at a school in Jerez de la Frontera.

The term "flamenco" was first used in Anadalusian folklore at the beginning of the 19th century. In the 18th century Argot it was a descriptive term for a braggart, and in Andalusia, gypsies were often referred to by it.

The gypsies had reached West Andalusia by the 15th century and were slowly becoming used to the way of life there. Sharing their place on the edge of society with peasants and Moriscos, they never fully integrated. They fused the musical forms they had brought with them with those of the Andalusian folk music. The flamenco song, with its Arab, Visigoth, Jewish, Gregorian and Byzantine roots developed from this fusion.

A great number of the flamenco songs were originally a personal form of expression. Eventually, they were sung in public and categorized as an art form. The first famous flamenco singer was the legendary Tío (uncle) Luis, at the end of the 18th century. He was followed by the personalities who set the tone for the flamenco tradition: El Planeta, Franco el Colorao, El Fillo, La Perla.

At the end of the 19th century came the people who went on to perfect the style of flamenco: María Borrico, Enrique El Mellizo, Loco Mateo, Diego el Marrurro, Joaquín el de la Paula and Silverio Franconetto, a key figure, born in Sevilla in 1830, and the only non-gypsy, he was founder of the *Cafés Cantantes*.

Manuel Torre, Tomás Pavón and Pastora Pavón, known as *la Niña de los Peines* (the comb girl) belong to the famous dancers of the 20th century.

In the second half of the 19th century, flamenco broke away from the intimacy of its Andalusian Gypsy environment and the small gatherings of those who loved this genre, to be presented in flamenco bars. The first was opened in Sevilla in 1842, but the most famous was undoubtedly Silverio Franconetti's, which opened in 1885. Soon there were also *Cafés Cantantes* in Madrid. They were frequented by those seeking entertainment and not consciously imbibing a vital aspect of Spanish culture. There was a great deal of controversy as to whether they made a positive contribution in the development of flamenco. Their audiences were made up of people from all walks of life – rich folks, toreros, the aristocracy and laborers.

Flamenco was no longer very popular in the 20th century and the *Cafés Cantantes* began to close down. Manuel de Falla, with the help of many other intellectuals like García Lorca, organized a flamenco singing competition in Granada. They wanted to re-establish this type of art form, but had little success with this endeavor. New competitions were organized in the fifties, this time with a great deal more success. The national Flamenco competition in Córdoba in 1956 brought forth a resurrected wave of popularity. Antonio Alcor deserves much praise for collecting traditional Flamenco songs, for his fastidious work in conversing the stylistic purity of the music and making various form of Flamenco known to the public.

All kinds of people attend Flamenco festivals and concerts today. Most of them belong to associations called *Peñas Flamencas*. They encourage artists interested in flamenco and spend a great deal of time examining and categorizing the various styles.

Peña Juan Breva in Malaga or the Peña de la Plantería in Granada are the most influential *Peñas*. Every tiny village in Andalusia has got a *Peña*. The intellectuals have also become interested in flamenco. Musicologists study its styles, publish anthologies and compendiums and make new releases of old records. West Andalusia was, and is, the very heart of flamenco country. Nowadays the most original Flamenco is performed in Utrera, Marchena, Carmona, Dos Hermanas, El Viso, Puente Genil, Estapa, Ronda, Jerez de la Frontera and San Fernando. But the famous Andalusian artists have also made it popular in Madrid by performing there in flamenco clubs. Flamenco has since become popular almost all over the world, and there are numerous experts in Paris, London, New York and Tokyo.

According to the "flamencologist" Ricardo Molina there are four main categories of Flamenco.

The Basic or Pure Flamenco

Siguiriyas: This is a tragic type of chant expressing a very deep sense of despair and pain often felt in sickness or at the loss of a loved one.

For example:

So great is my pain
It could grow no more
I'm dying insane
Without love's warmth
In the hospital,

Soleares: These generally consist of strophes of three lines that romanticize various topics ranging from love to death. They are intended for dancing and frequently require guitar accompaniment.

Tonás: It is a very old form of flamenco singing. It expresses the melancolic, miserable life of persecution and imprisonment that the Andalusian gypsies were subjected to.

Tangos: These are majestic, festive songs for the purpose of dancing. They have their own special rhythm which is accompanied by clapping. There are slower, ponderous tangos called *tientos*.

Variations of the Basic Style

Cañas: A type of song of Arabic origin, which was forgotten for a long time but has now been revived in conjunction with dance.

Saetas: These consist of religious songs performed in Andalusia during the Easter week, usually during the popular related processions, and without the accompaniment of guitars.

Bulerías: These arefestive songs accompanied by rhythmic clapping.

Other forms are: *polos, livianas, serranas, cantiñas, romances.*

Styles Related to the Fandango

Fandangos: These are quite widespread throughout the whole of Spain, and consist generally of strophes of five lines. They have no definite rhythm. There are styles of *fandango* that are particular to certain places or regions, and

Right: The paseillo, a small parade by the three cuadrillas before the bullfight begins.

there are what could be described as "art"-*fandangos*. The *fandango* has made its way into the classical repertoire. Worthy of note are: the famous *fandango* closing a quintet by Luigi Boccherini (who lived in Spain much of his life); Padre Antonio Soler also wrote a virtuosic *fandango* for harpsichord; and finally, one of the *Goyescas* by Enrique Granados consists of a sombre, romantic *fandango.*

Malagueñas: These are the type of *fandangos* from Málaga which have evolved into songs expressing strongly melancholic moods.

For example:

Your and my love
What will become of it, tell!
You try to hate me
And I still love you more
May the Lord bring me death!

Songs Derived from Flamenco

Tarantas: Miners' songs, primarily relating to Linares and La Unión. Probably the first form of musical protest about social conditions.

Sevillanas: Originally a variety of the simple La Mancha *seguidilla*, songs which complemented dancing. Today they are danced at all Andalusian festivals. The *sevillana rociera* is a variety performed at the El Rocío pilgrimage. It is accompanied by the flute and tambourin.

Peteneras: These have their roots in folk songs from the province of Cádiz. There are long and short *peteneras*. They were sung especially by Niña de los Peines. It is said that these songs tend to bring about bad luck.

Alboreás: They are sung at gypsy weddings. They have never really left their familiar surroundings and thus, by and large, retained their original form.

Other styles are: *Trilleras, manas, guajiras, rumbas, marianas, bambas, farrucas, garrotines.*

FIESTAS

There is no place in Spain without a fiesta and no fiesta without *verbena* (dance) on the marketplace, without the traditional annual market, without wine, high mass and processions, fireworks, and, above all, bullfighting. The whole village comes alive. The people are happy and relaxed, they stop whatever they are doing and enjoy the music. The pubs are overcrowded and groups of children run through the streets. A village festival is an ideal tourist attraction and a rare opportunity for visitors to mix with the locals.

Bullfighting

Bullfights are an integral part of every fiesta, even if they aren't well-liked by all Spaniards. Animal lovers find them cruel, others find them simply boring. Many find it immoral in a civilized country to turn brutal killing into a national festival. The fact remains that – although bull-

fighting is an expensive form of entertainment – the bullfighting stadiums are absolutely full, and for villagers a fiesta is not complete without a *corrida de toros*.

Bullfighting is an age-old tradition for most Spaniards. The first bullfights took place before the games on Crete and before the Roman circus, where the bull was taken by the horns in an attempt to force it to the ground. Figures representing bulls have been found on all prehistoric excavation sites. Many medieval *El Cid* legends, the illustrated texts of Alfonso the Wise and chronicles revolve around the bull. Golden Age drama contains many references to bullfighting.

Bullfighting in its present-day form dates to the 18th-century folk festivals. Before, it was an aristocratic sport carried out on horse-back. The mounted nobleman had helpers on either side of him. The beginning of Philip V's reign would have been less problematical if he hadn't made his boredom at the bullfights taking place at Madrid's Plaza Mayor so obvious. But the Bourbons brought new

customs to Madrid. Noblemen left the bullfighting arena, having found other forms of sport, and the equestrian form of bullfighting came to an end. The common people, however, remained full of enthusiasm for the sport they had been deprived of. Horses were no longer used for bullfighting, except by the *picadores*. As this form of bullfighting became more widespread, the first professional toreros emerged. Arenas were built solely for bullfighting. The oldest one in existence is the one in Ronda. It dates back to 1785 and is still in use today.

There were two different forms of bullfighting competing with each other at that time: one in Ronda, represented by the famous Pedro Romero, who practised a very rigid, serious and reserved form; the other form was practised in Sevilla and linked with the name of Pepe Hillo, and was more spontaneous and lively.

Above: The bull at the beginning is still full of vim and vigor. Right: He soon becomes the tool of the torero.

The first great bullfighters introduced the three distinct acts of the *corrida*, the *tercios* and developed various figures which the *torero* used to deceive the kill. They also perfected the art of the final blow. Pepe Hillo wrote a *Tauromaquia*, or " The Art of Bullfighting", similar to a rules and regulations handbook. Later, many artists dedicated their talents to this topic. One of the first to do so was Goya, who compiled a *Tauromaquia* series of etchings. He immortalised the names of many famous bullfighters in this series, including that of his friend Martincho. Goya also depicted Pepe Hillo's death in the arena like a detailed newspaper report. Picasso also created a famous series of pictures inspired by the *Tauromaquia*.

The art of bullfighting hasn't remained static. Many toreros have developed their own style and have created new customs like *gaoneras* or *chicuelinas*, which live on under their name. In time, the various matadors attracted their own supporters in a way that is comparable to present-day football stars. There have been op-

ponents who have been the subject of songs like Lagartijo and Frascuelo, Joselito and Belmonte, Arruza and Manolete or, closer to our time, El Cordobés and El Viti. They represent various styles of bullfighting and different preferences among the spectators.

Every year, 10,000 bulls or *novillos* (young bulls) are killed in the arena. Only 20 of the 500 toreros who participate are popular personalities. Naturally, every torero dreams about becoming famous in the same way as a soccer player in Brazil or Argentine dreams about becoming a Pelé. The toreros traditionally come from the rural working classes. They are enthusiastic youths seeking fame. Nowadays, there are training schools for intending bullfighters. In the old days, those wanting to become bullfighters had to, during the night, secretly climb over the fence of an estate where the *toros bravos*, the wild fighting bulls, were bred. This was, and still is, a dangerous venture as someone keeps guard on the bulls at all times. Once they have seen

through the *capa* trick, there is no way of knowing what they might do, and thus can no longer be used in the arena.

Bullfighters have a long way to go from the small village bullfights in arenas which can be dismantled to the big city arenas. It can take years before an agent discovers a young bullfighter and takes him under his wing. Many remain unknown. Those who are lucky begin their career as *novilleros*. Once they have proved themselves capable, they are given a permit by a *diestro* (experienced torero) and they become *matadores*. This allows them fight in arenas of the first category and to take on bulls weighing more than 450 kilos. An experienced *diestro* earns between one and five million Pesetas per *corrida*, whereby he kills two bulls. In all there are six bulls and three toreros at every *corrida*. Having earned enough money to breed bulls themselves, famous toreros are no longer obliged to endanger their lives, and they usually end their career at 40. It is a dangerous career and the toreros death is a frequent topic in literature. The most famous poem on this subject is by Federico García Lorca: *At five o'clock in the afternoon*. It laments the death of the torero Sanchez Mejías.

Special Festivities

Carneval is celebrated in Cádiz by the whole city, and in Sitges mainly by transvestites. A funeral procession of widows symbolizing the "Burial of Sardines" marks the end of the carneval and the beginning of the annual fiestas, celebrated in every village on their patron saint's day. The most frequent dates are San Juan (25.6.), San Pedro (29.6.), Santiago (25.7.), the Virgin del Carmen (16.7.), the Ascencion (15.8.), and the Feast of the Suffering Virgin (15.9.).

Easter Week: In addition, the Easter Week has a long-standing tradition in Andalusia. Figures (*pasos*) are carried through the streets at processions and whoever can roar out a *saeta*, at which the procession stops to pay tribute. This is a big event in cities like Sevilla and Málaga. Its religious character doesn't deter people from celebrating in the various bars which then remain open throughout the night. Processions in the smaller villages are also full of surprises (Ubeda, Ronda, Baena, Puente Genil, Jerez de los Caballeros). In Murcia, the *pasos* used in processions are made by the Baroque sculptor, Salzillo. In Jumilla and Lorca, the procession takes place on horseback. Passion plays are performed in many towns in the Levante (Moncada) and in Catalonia (Esparraguera, Olesa de Montserrat, Sant Vicent dels Horts, Ulldecona, Verges).

Andalusian Ferias: The Andalusian *ferias* are not religious festivals. When the orange trees are in bloom and before the intense summer heat decends on the

Right: Festivals and processions are an occasion to show oneself off in style.

city, people pour onto the Sevilla streets. Two weeks after Easter, sometimes earlier if Easter is too close to May, the **Feria de Abril** begins. This tradition began in 1846 when two strangers who had settled in the town, a Catalan and a Basque, received permission to start a cattle market in order to boost the town's crippled economy. The pleasure side of the market soon became its main attraction, turning the *feria* into a blaze of colour consisting of horses, music, dancing, and wine. The festive area is full of tents belonging to various clubs or institutions. Each has a bar, tables and a dance floor. The fun-fair is situated towards the end of the grounds. The various events are open at different times. The horse-show takes place in the morning, and there are family events in the afternoon. Dancing takes place throughout the night. *Ferias* are the same everywhere, but take place at different times and vary in size. The ones in small towns are usually more spontaneous. The second-largest is the **Feria del Caballo** with horses from Jerez. The *ferias* on the outskirts of Cádiz are especially interesting. They take place on the beach at Puerto de Sta. María, Puerto Real, Rota and Chipiona.

The dates of the various *ferias* change according to the church calendar. In Sanlucar, the **Feria de la Manzanilla** takes place during Whitsunday. In addition, there is horse-racing on the beach on Sundays during the summer months. The Jerez wine festival in September marks the end of the yearly cycle.

The Andalusian **pilgrimages** are based on ancient superstitions. García Lorca had his *Yerma* played in the ambience of the El Cristo del Paño pilgrimage in Moclín (Granada, 1.10.) Other festivals are regional in character: the Cascamorras of Baza and Guadix (6.9.) dates back to the time when the two towns were enemies. In Córdoba, the **Fiesta de los Patios** is celebrated by decorating the courtyards.

In Granada, there is a colorful festival of crosses at the beginning of May.

Festivals in the Levant: Valencian festivals are well-known for their fireworks displays and cannon fire. According to tradition, craftsmen apprentices used to burn wood-shavings and left-over bits of wood at the end of their apprenticeship. Nowadays, the streets and villages are full of gigantic cardboard figures at the San José Festival (19.3) which are then burned. Dancing and colorful costumes, as well as floral decorations, are part of these *fallas* (derived from the Latin word for torch). The San Juan Night bonfire on the 24.6., *nit del foc*, in Alicante has the same symbolic tradition as the St. John's bonfires in other parts of Europe. Many villages in the province of Alicante celebrate the *Moros y Cristianos* festivals. There, armies of Arabs and Christians dressed in colorful costumes simulate the *Reconquista* battles amid a deafening din. The grandest of these festivals take place in Alcoy and in Bañeres (22nd-25th Apr),

Biar (10.5.), Petrel (14.5.), Elda 27.5.), Villajoyosa (29.7.), Cocentaina (2nd Sunday in August), Onteniente (last Sunday in August), Castalla (1.9), Villena (4.9.), Caudete (Albacete 7.9.).

Bullfighting: Some festivals are based on special games and traditions with the bull in addition to the ordinary bullfight: El Toro Embolado (Castellón, 17.5.); El Toro de Fuego (El Grao, Castellón, 29.6.); Los Toros en el Mar (Denia, Alicante, 2nd Sunday in July); Las Vaquillas and Patos al Agua (Benicarló, Castellón, 24.8.); Corre de Bou (Cardona, Barcelona, 2nd Sunday in September); San Juan (Coria, Cáceres, 24.6.).

Corpus Christi Day: Corpus Christi celebrations in Granada and in Valencia are especially colorful and steeped in tradition. The streets are covered with flowers for this occasion in Sitges. Special events on this day are La Patum (Berga, Barcelona), La Degollá (Morella, Castellón), El Ball de la Matellina (San Sadurní d'Anoia) and the San Juan de las Abadesas pilgrimage. In Barcelona, an

egg dances on top of the fountain in the cathedral cloisters: *L'ou con balla*.

Folkloristic Festivals: Apart from the passion plays, other traditional theater events take place in many towns. The most famous is the *Elche Misteri* play (2nd Sunday in August). A medieval play *La Cura Fera*, is performed in Tortosa on the 8.9.

Festivals in Catalonia: The Catalan festivals are interspersed with folklore elements, making them especially attractive. *Sardanas* are danced everywhere, particularly at the following festivals: Calella (1st Sunday in July), San Feliú de Guixols (25.7.), Amer (Gerona, 16.8.), San Feliú de Pallarols (Gerona, Whitsun). In Gironella (Barcelona) people pay homage to the *botijo*, the drinking jug; in Ripoll to wool (mid May); and in Argentona to jugs in general (4.8.). The Festa delse Elois takes place on the last Sunday

Above: Costumes of the Inquisition during an Easter procession. Right: Departure from Granada on a pilgrimage to El Rocio.

in July in Berga. Human pyramids known as *torres humanas* are formed at nearly all the festivals. The most spectacular are found in Gerona on 29.10. at the San Narciso Festival, in Vilafranca del Penedés (30.9.) and Valls (23/24.6.). The Fiesta de San Jordi is celebrated in Barcelona, during which time it is customary to give flower and book as a present. The Gracia District Festival is celebrated on the third Sunday in August, on which the streets resemble banqueting halls and the people sing *habaneras*.

Baleares Festivals: The Cocadas y Jaleos have a long-standing tradition on Menorca: in Alayor (10.8.), in San Luis (25.8.) and in Mahón (8.9.). Horse-riding events and traditional sports events take place in Ciudadela (25.6.), in Mercadal (third Sunday in July), and in Ferrería (8.9.). There is the Diada del Lluc event in Escorga, Mallorca (2nd Sunday in September); the Butifarró Sausage Festival in San Juan (1st Sunday in October), and the Inca Folklore Festival on 30.7.

El Rocío

The virgin of **El Rocío** is the final destination of those taking part in the Whitsunday pilgrimage in which over a million people participate. In the middle of a flat part of land, with almost no restaurants, hotels, inns or toilets, the biggest festival in Andalusia, if not in Spain, takes place, lasting three days. This festival has an internally fixed program in which even the tourists are allocated a role. Crowds of people attend, and horses, ox carts and wine add to the chaos. There wasn't even a tarred road here until 1959 and the pilgrimage was a real folkloric event. Nowadays, over 70 brotherhoods from all over Andalusia, one from Madrid, one from Barcelona and one consisting of exile Spaniards attend. There are also thousands of onlookers who arrive by car, motorbike and bus.

Homage is paid to the statue of the virgin which dates back to the 13th century. The pilgrimage tradition only began 200 years ago. This chapel and the adjoining houses were erected in the present century. In recent years tourist facilities have been added.

The *hermandades*, or fraternities, organise the event according to age-old rituals and traditions. They travel from all over Andalusia in their ox carts, and are often on the road for three or four days, depending on where they live. They arrive in white covered wagons, bringing their provisions, pots, pans and blankets, as well as food for their horses and oxen with them.

Tractors and Land Rovers are beginning to replace the oxen. Proud Andalusian men ride alongside them. The route takes them over gravel and dirt roads, and they are even given special permission to cross the Coto Doñana National Park. In the midst of the trekkers' wagons there is the *simpecado*, a decorated wagon with a tiny shrine in which the fraternity's banner is kept.

All the groups are situated three kilometers from the pilgrims' chapel on by Friday evening. A troupe is sent out during the night to get things ready in the building belonging to the fraternity in question. The decorated wagons make their way to the chapel on Saturday and greet the virgin. The festivities last long into the night with music, *vino fino*, singing and *sevillanas rocieras*, solemn dances which are performed on hot sand. Mass is held on Sunday morning and more and more people arrive in cars, pushing their way to the virgin. Scenes of religious ecstasy take place in the chapel. Rosaries are said during the night and a procession takes place. Singing Ave Marias, the participants visit the places where the *hermandades* are staying. A fireworks display and an additional celebration end the day. The grand procession begins at sunrise on Whitmonday. Only the young

men belonging to the Almonte *hermandad* from the Rocío community have the privilege of carrying the virgin in the procession. The crowds are so dense that the virgin figure is rocked back and forth as if on a stormy sea.

Should someone who is not from Almonte attempt to touch the virgin, he is mercilessly punished. But this doesn't deter some people from trying, even if only for a second. After stopping at each of the fraternal houses, the procession ends in the midday heat, concluding the celebrations. The pilgrims are tired on the journey home, but the tumultuous welcome they are given when they arrive there soon livens them up again and they resume their dancing and singing.

The *Rocío* has become something of a national spectacle, televised each year. You have to be wealthy to be able to buy horses and expensive costumes and to take a week off work. The less privileged stand at the roadside, selling soft drinks and such. Although it is a time for celebrating, it is also a time for showing-off.

241

Nelles Maps ...the maps, that get you going.

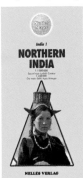

CRETE
Kreta

KENYA

THAILAND

NORTHERN INDIA

Nelles Maps

- Afghanistan
- Australia
- Bangkok
- Burma
- Caribbean Islands 1 / Bermuda, Bahamas, Greater Antilles
- Caribbean Islands 2 / Lesser Antilles
- China 1 / North-Eastern China
- China 2 / Northern China
- China 3 / Central China
- China 4 / Southern China
- Crete
- Egypt
- Hawaiian Islands
- Hawaiian Islands 1 / Kauai

- Hawaiian Islands 2 / Honolulu, Oahu
- Hawaiian Islands 3 / Maui, Molokai, Lanai
- Hawaiian Islands 4 / Hawaii
- Himalaya
- Hong Kong
- Indian Subcontinent
- India 1 / Northern India
- India 2 / Western India
- India 3 / Eastern India
- India 4 / Southern India
- India 5 / North-Eastern India
- Indonesia
- Indonesia 1 / Sumatra
- Indonesia 2 / Java + Nusa Tenggara
- Indonesia 3 / Bali
- Indonesia 4 / Kalimantan

- Indonesia 5 / Java + Bali
- Indonesia 6 / Sulawesi
- Indonesia 7 / Irian Jaya + Maluku
- Jakarta
- Japan
- Kenya
- Korea
- Malaysia
- West Malaysia
- Nepal
- New Zealand
- Pakistan
- Philippines
- Singapore
- South East Asia
- Sri Lanka
- Taiwan
- Thailand
- Vietnam, Laos Kampuchea

SPAIN SOUTH

©Nelles Verlag GmbH, München 45
  All rights reserved
  ISBN 3-88618-377-7

First Edition 1991
Co-Publisher for U.K.:
Robertson McCarta, London
ISBN 1-85365-255-5 (for U.K.)

Publisher:	Günter Nelles	**DTP-Exposure:**	Printshop Schimann, Pfaffenhofen
Chief Editor:	Dr. Heinz Vestner		
Project Editor:	Dr. S. Tzschaschel	**Cartography:**	Nelles Verlag GmbH;
Editor:	G. Knutson/C. Peyer		Freytag & Berndt, Wien;
Translation:	J. Clough		Ravenstein-Verlag,
	E. Goldmann		Lizenz-Nr. 1/139
Color Separation:	Scannerstudio Schaller, München	**Printed by:**	Gorenjski Tisk, Kranj, Yugoslavia

- 01 -

TRAVEL INFORMATION

PREPARATIONS

Spanish Tourist Offices

USA, Water Tower Place, Suite 955 East, 845 North Michigan Ave., Chicago, ILL 60611, Tel. (312)642-98-17.

USA, 8383 Wilshire Blvd., Suite 960, Los Angeles, CA 90211, Tel. (213)658-71-88.

USA, 1221 Brickell Ave., Miami, FLA 33131, Tel (305)358-19-92

USA, 665 Fifth Ave., New York, NY 10022, Tel. (212)759-88-22.

GREAT BRITAIN; 57-58 St. James Str., London SW1A1LD, Tel. 499-11-69.

CANADA, 102 Bloor Street West, Toronto, Ontario M5S 1M8, Tel. (416)96131-31.

AUSTRALIA, 203 Castlereagh Street, Suite 21, NSW 2000, Sidney South, Tel. (612)264-79-66.

Climate

Average daily temperatures in May, July and September, daily maximum in August (in °C):

	May	July	Sept	Aug
Catalonia	16	23	21	32
Baleares	17	24	22	36
Valencia	19	25	23	36
Almería	19	25	24	38
Granada,Jaén	17	26	22	40
Málaga	19	25	23	38
Cádiz	19	24	23	42
Sevilla,Córdoba	20	27	24	45
Extremadura	18	26	23	42
La Mancha	16	25	21	41
Madrid	16	24	20	38

These figures indicate high midday temperatures and relatively low evening temperatures for the entire inner region. As might be expected, the climate on the coast is humid, the midday temperatures are less extreme and the nights milder. This, of course, brings us straight to the next logical rubric.

Clothes

Summer temperatures are guaranteed during July and August. May/June and September/October are the ideal times to travel, but the weather can be very changeable. Raincoats are indispensable in mountain regions and warm clothing is necessary in northern parts of the country.

Currency

The Spanish peseta is a relatively stable currency since Spain's entry into the EC. You can either change money in your home country or use traveller's checks. A check card with a personal identification number is the best way to change money. Many banks displaying a Bureau de Change sign do not accept Eurochecks. Identification is always required when changing money. There are many money changing kiosks offering good exhange rates, but they charge a lot of commission. Most of the bigger hotels change their guests' money without any extra charge. You can draw money from your European post office savings account at the postal bank - *Caja Postal*.

There are 1,000, 2,000, 5,000 and 10,000 peseta notes and only very rarely 500 peseta notes. There are 1, 5, 10, 25, 50, 100, 200 and 500 peseta coins.

In a number of cases, new coins have been designed doubling those in circulation. the 100 pesetas coin does not bear the Arabic numbers only the word *cien*, meaning hundred.

Medical Precautions

Vaccinations are not required. The water can be drunk throughout Spain, also from public wells.

Documents Required

Visitors to Spain require a valid passport. EC residents can enter Spain with an EC identity card only.

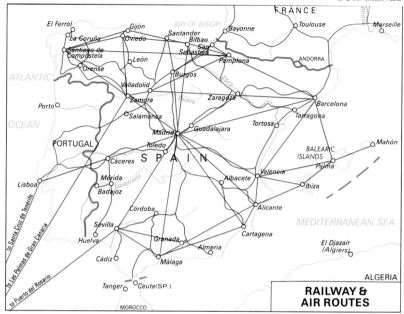

**RAILWAY &
AIR ROUTES**

TRAVELING TO SPAIN

The most convenient way to get to Spain is by air. Public transport is not the best. Flying is highly recommended for city holidays. Once you get there you can hire a car for short trips. Roads from France cross into Spain. The quickest way of getting there is on one of the two coastal motorways which twist around the Pyrenees. The Pyrenees can easily be crossed in one day, either by one of the passes or by using the Viella tunnel.

TRAVELING IN SPAIN

By Car
There are national roads, regional roads and communal roads. Conditions are usually good on all of them.

Autopistas (highways) are toll roads, and unlike *autovías* (without tolls) usually don't have traffic jams.

Most Spaniards get around by car. The major roads, N I to N VI from Madrid, which have partly been made into auto-

vías are very often overcrowded. Heavy traffic leaves the large cities in the morning in order to get to destinations in the afternoon. It is therefore advisable to use these routes either very early or considerably later than the locals do.

By Bicycle
Cycling is becoming more and more popular in Europe. Cyclists should know that Spain is a very hilly country. There are no cycle paths, but there are many country roads with very little traffic. It is possible to take your bicycle onto most trains. It is not advisable to transport bicycles on car roof racks as nobody would ever dream of leaving a packed car unattended anywhere in Spain.

By Plane
The national airline IBERIA has domestic flights from Madrid and Barcelona to 20 airports. There is an hourly shuttle service between the two major cities. Additional domestic flights are available from AVIACO.

By Train

Train connections in Spain are difficult because of the large number of mountains. There is not a complete railway network. There are good connections in Catalonia and in the Basque country. There are long distance trains in the following categories: Interurbano, Talgo, and Express. The last are more expensive.

The railway companys are called Renfe and Feve. Tickets for longer journeys should be bought in advance, and it is advisable to reserve seats.

There are special weekend trains called *trenes lince* offering cheaper return fares to León, Albacete, Jaén, Puertollano and Cáceres. In addition to this, there are a number of special offers in *trenes turisticos* to Andalucia, Salamanca, the Extremadura, Cuenca, Burgos or La Mancha. The fare includes sightseeing tours as well as overnight stays in good or very good hotels. These tours can be booked at the following address: IBER-RAIL C/Capitán Haya, 55 - Madrid, Tel: 91 - 2793605 / 3793200.

Overland Buses

Public transport connecting smaller towns and large cities is usually by bus. Information is available from travel agents or from the bus companies. In smaller towns there is a bus service to the nearest cities which usually departs twice daily from the town square.

PRACTICAL TIPS

Accommodation

An attempt has been made to select central and comfortable hotels in the towns.

The city tourist offices neither reserve nor allocate rooms. The following categories are available:

H . . . . Hotel
HR . . Hotel Residencia (Holiday Hotel
. . . . for longer stays)
HA . . . . Hotel Apartamentos
RA . . . . . Residencia Apartamentos
M . . . . Motel
Hs . . . . Hostal (basic hotel)
P . . Pension (often used as permanent
. . . . accommodation in cities)
HsR . . . . . Hostal Residencia (often
. . . . . . permanent acommodation)
F . . . . . . Fonda (very basic pension)

Hotels are usually clean; the beds, even in very good hotels, are uncomfortable. Noise is not accepted as grounds for complaint.

Paradores Nacionales are state owned hotels in the highest price category. These are nearly always in a pleasant area. *Paradores* catalogues are available from all tourist offices. It is advisable to book in advance during high season. Reservation office: C/ Velázquez, 18, 28001 Madrid, Tel: 4359700, Fax 4359944.

Business Hours

Shops usually open between 9 and 10 a.m., and close for lunch between 2 and 5 p.m. In winter, this may be half an hour earlier in the north. They close around 8 p.m. They are usually open on Saturday afternoons. City center shops often remain open at lunch time and close late in the evenings.

Museums and other public buildings follow the same plan. But they are also open on Sunday mornings and nearly always closed on Mondays. The opening hours vary a little from year to year and are much longer in summer than in winter. Many historic buildings in the country are completely closed during low season. It is always possible to obtain church keys from the caretaker.

Car Breakdowns

Call the royal automobile club, RACE, in case of an accident or breakdown. They have an arrangement with the following foreign automobile clubs: ADAC, DTC, AvD, AA, RAC, ACI, TCI. You can contact a national emergency service under Tel: 91- 5933333.

Cinemas

Some city cinemas show films in their original version with Spanish subtitles *(versión subtitulada)*.

Customs and Etiquette

Spain is Europe. But some things are different from elsewhere in Central and Northern Europe. Although there is a formal form of address *(usted)*, the familiar form *(tú)* is generally used in shops and restaurants.

It is quite normal to throw rubbish onto the floor in pubs. It is cleared away at regular intervals to avoid objectionable hygenic conditions. Unlike in other central European countries, it is not customary to make less noise after 10 p.m.

Things happen 2 hours later than in Northern European countries. Visitors have to get used to eating lunch at 2 p.m. and dinner at 9 p.m.

Daily Routine

The day begins slowly and late with a coffee and snack, preferably *churros*, at the bar. Office hours are from 10 a.m.to 2 p.m. If you don't get things done during these hours, you have to wait until the next day.

The main meal of the day in Spain is eaten between 2 and 4 p.m. Inexpensive meals are served at lunchtime in restaurants. Almost all the restaurants have very good lunches. Bread and wine is included in the price. Surprising as it may seems it's usually in the restaurants offering the cheapest meals that you can be sure of getting good home-made food.

The news is broadcast in English, French and German during the summer months at times that tend to change annually. The Spanish news headlines follow at 3 p.m., then there is *siesta* until 5 p.m. Evening entertainment and dinner don't start before 9 p.m. People don't usually go to bed before 1 a.m., not even the children.

Electric Current

Standard current is 220 volt (50 cycles AC). The majority of hotels have Europlugs. If they don't, adapters are available at all electrical shops.

Festivals

Every town has a local *fiesta* once or twice a year. Some only last for a weekend, others can last two weeks. Visitors will have to put up with more noise at this time. The answer is to join in the fun. Ticket reservations for the theater festival in Mérida: Viajes Emérita, C/Evaristo S.Miguel 17, Madrid, Tel: 91-2485854.

Museums and Art Galleries

Private galleries are often open on Sundays. Public galleries and museums are usually closed on Sunday afternoons and on Mondays. On one day a week, usually Wednesday, they often offer free entrance to EC nationals.

Pharmacies

There are pharmacies everywhere in towns and cities. They are well-equipped, and many medicines are available without prescription. Opening hours are the same as normal business hours.

Photography

Photography is allowed, except in museums. The use of a flash and video cameras is not permitted inside most monuments, however.

Postal Services

Many post offices *(correos)* are only open in the morning; stamps are available at every *estanco*, state-run cigarette kiosks. Letters and postcards to EC countries cost the same. Letters within the country vary acccording to destination.

Press

A large selection of foreign daily newspapers is available in large cities. Spanish papers have Sunday editions.

Public Holidays

1.1, New Year's Day and 6.1, Epiphany. Easter: Palm Thursday and Good Friday; in Catalonia Good Friday and Easter Monday. 1.5, May Day; 15.8, Ascension Day; 12.10, Virgen del Pilar and Columbus Day; 1.11, All Saints Day; 6.12, Constitution Day and 8.12, Day of the Immaculate Conception; 25.12, Christmas Day. There are also lots of regional and municipal holidays.

Renting a Car

A charge or credit card obviates the need for cash deposits. Passports and a driving licence at least one year old are required. Special weekend tarifs are available.

Telecommunications

When calling Spain from abroad, omit the 9 in the dialling code. You can make trunk calls from all public telephone booths. Dial 7 for international calls, wait for the signal and dial the dialling code of the country you are calling: (Germany 49, Austria 43, Switzerland 41, France 33, Holland 31, Italy 49, UK 44.) Directory enquiries: 003. Directory enquiries for Europe 008; International 005.

Theft

Even experienced tourists are recognizable as tourists. It is advisable not to carry a bag with you in large cities. Flight tickets, passports and traveller's checks are safer left in your suitcase at the hotel. Cars with foreign license plates are liable to be broken into, especially if your belongings are left in them. Cars with built-in radios are not safe in any Spanish town. Underground garages do not accept responsibility for anything left in the car. Cars are safer here, however, than on the streets.

Time Zones

Spain lies within a single time zone, 1 hour ahead of GMT, except between April and October when it is 2 hours ahead.

Tips

Tips are generally included in restaurant bills, but are gladly accepted. The IVA additional charge is VAT. In case of an accident it is not advisable to try and bribe traffic police or the Guardia Civil.

Tour Guides

Tour guides have a three-year training period and are usually highly qualified. Most tourist offices allocate English-, French-, or German-speaking guides.

A weekly calendar of events containing reliable information is available from newsagents' stands in Madrid and Barcelona. Tickets are often still available on the day of the performance.

Tourist Information

There are tourist offices in all the provincial capitals and in many tourist resorts (i = *informacíon* or *oficina de turismo*), where maps and brochures can be obtained. They have normal business hours. In the main tourist resorts they are also open on Sunday mornings.

Weights and Measures

Measurements, weights and sizes are the same as in central Europe.

USEFUL ADDRESSES

Embassies

(Madrid – Tel: - 91)

Austria, Paseo Castellana, 91; Tel: 5565315. **Belgium**, Paeso Castellana, 18; Tel: 4019558. **Canada**, C/ Nuñez de Balboa, 35; Tel: 4314300. **Denmark**, C/Claudio Coello, 91; Tel: 4318445. **Germany**, Fortuny, 8; Tel: 3199100. **Finland**, Paseo Castellana, 15; Tel: 3083427. **France**, C/ Salustinao Olozaga, 9, Tel: 4355560. **Ireland**, C/ Claudio Coello, 73; Tel: 5763500. **Israel**, C/Valázquez, 150; Tel: 4111357.

Italy, C/Lagasca, 98; Tel: 025436. **United Kingdom**, C/Fernando el Santo, 16; Tel: 3190200. **Netherlands**, Paseo Castellna, 31; Tel: 3083394. **Portugal**, C/Zurbano, 92; Tel:4411222. **Sweden**, C/ Zurbano, 27; Tel: 3086575. **Switzerland**, C/ Nunez Balboa, 35; Tel: 4313400. **USA**, C/ Serrano, 75; Tel: 3190200.

Horseback Riding

Horse-riding trips in the Catalan Pyrenees and to Andorra organized by Asociación de Marchas da Caballo de Catluna, Tel: Barcelona 93/2118448; Pireneos sin fronteras (Pyrenees), Tel: Huesca 974/551385; Alcarria al Caballo (to Alcaria), Tel: Madrid 91/2655375. Caballotour (in the Grendos mountains), Tel: Madrid 91/5634904; Centro de Recursos de Montana (in the Sierra Norte in Madrid), Tel: Madrid 91/8697058; Trastur (Asturian Valleys), Tel: Oviedo 985/ 806036; Equitour (Gerona, Castilla, Jacobs Way), Tel: Barcelona 93/4196272; Jesús Manuel Berna (Gredos, Castilla, Jacobs Way), Tel: Madrid: 91/5192644.

Information for Hunters

Federación Espanola de Caza, Av. Reina Victoria, 72, 1, Madrid, 28003.

Federación Espanola de Caza, Av. Reina Victoria, 72, 1 Madrid 28003.

CULTURE IN BRIEF

Visigótico = Visigothic, late classical (5-6th century).

Asturiano = Pre-Romanesque in Asturias, which escaped nearly all Arab raids (9th century).

Mozárabe = Mozarabic. Christian, but Moslem influenced art style – derived from Christians who fled to freed areas in the north from the Moorish areas in the south (10th century).

Omagyad = (8th/9th centuries), Arab ornamentation, transition to the Caliph style of Córdoba (10th century).

Mudéjar = Mudéjar – decorative style which evolved in the hands of Morisco masters working for Christians after the *Reconquista* (14th century).

Moriscos = Christian Arab converts.

Almohad = (12th/13th centuries), simple brick construction, predecessor to the Mudéjar.

Nazari = from the Nasrids, kings of Granada (14th/15th centuries).

Mocárabe = Almocárabe, wooden ceilings with broken prisms.

Artesonado = Arab and Mudéjar wood inlay ceilings (10th-16th centuries).

Flamboyant = stretched variant of the late Gothic style.

Modernismo = a type of Art Nouveau particular to Spain, especially in Barcelona.

Isabelino = Isabelline, late Gothic – intricate Renaissance style under Isabella I. (15th century).

Plateresco = Plateresque-decor style of the early Renaissance period. Has Gothic and Renaissance characteristics (16th century).

Herreriano = Herrera style. Classical style developed by Juan de Herrera, Philip II's architect. (16th century).

Hispano-flamenco = Flemish influenced style in the Habsburg period.

Churrigueresco = Churrigueresque style, late Baroque of the Churrigueras. (17th century).

A GUIDE TO SPANISH

In addition to Castilian, Catalan and Gallego are also spoken. In the Basque Country and Navarra, a large proportion of the population speaks Basque.
Pronunciation in Castilian:

ll as the lli in *million*; qu as the c in *cat*; and e as the e in *let*; v like b; z and c preceding, e and i; a, o and u like th; ñ as in *onion*; h is silent at the beginning of a word.

Basic Communication

Good day	*buenos días*
(as from 2.p.m.)	*buenas tardes*
Good night	*buenas noches*
hello	*hola*
please	*por favor*
thank-you	*gracias*
yes	*si*
no	*no*
goodbye	*adíos*
excuse me	*perdón*
How are you?	*Qué tal?*
good	*bién*
What time is it?	*Qué hora es?*
How much is it?	*Cuánto cuesta ésto?*
Where is..?	*Dónde está...?*
to the right	*a la derecha*
to the left	*a la izquierda*

Numbers

one	*uno, un*
two	*dos*
three	*tres*
four	*cuatro*
five	*cinco*
six	*seis*
seven	*siete*
eight	*ocho*
nine	*nueve*
ten	*diez*
eleven	*once*
twelve	*doce*
twenty	*veinte*
a hundred	*cien*
five hundred	*quinenta*s
a thousand	*mil*

Times

today	*hoy*
tomorrow	*mañana*
yesterday	*ayer*
minute	*minuto*
hour	*hora*
day	*día*
week	*semana*
month	*mes*
year	*ao*

Days of the Week

Monday	*Lunes*
Tuesday	*Martes*
Wednesday	*Miércoles*
Thursday	*Jueves*
Friday	*Viernes*
Saturday	*Sábado*
Sunday	*Domingo*
Public Holiday	*Festivo*

Booking a Room

Have you got a room?	*Hay habitación libre?*
double room	*habitación dople*
single room	*habitación sencilla*
with breakfast	*con desayuno*
quiet	*tranquilo*

Ordering a Meal

menu	*menú del día*
dessert	*postre*
bread	*pan*
drink	*bebida*
wine	*vino*
beer	*cerveza*
mineral water	*agua mineral*
sparkling/still	*con/sin gas*
black coffee	*café solo*
coffee with a little milk	*cortado*
milk coffee	*cafe con leche*
breakfast pastry	*churros*
omlette	*tortilla*
potato omlette	*tortilla espanola*
fish	*pescado*
soup	*sopa*
meat	*carne*
pork	*cerdo*
veal	*ternera*
chicken	*pollo*
lamb	*cordero*
steamed	*guisado*
fried	*frito*
grilled	*a la plancha*
baked	*asado*
salad	*ensalada*
vegetables	*verdura*
The bill please!	*La cuenta, por favor!*

Fish

hake	merluza
trout	trucha
salmon	salmón
tuna	bonito
swordfish	emperador
sea bream	besugo
monfish	rape

AUTHORS

Borcha Folch is an architect and a dyed-in-the-wool Catalan. He lives in Barcelona and writes free-lance about the city and its surrounding area.

Gabriel Calvo Lopez-Guerrero is a professor of language and literature, a journalist and an author of film scripts. He spent ten years in Germany, followed by several years at the University of Cádiz. Today he lives and writes in Madrid.

Eliseo Fernandez Cuesta is an anthropologist specializing in Arab culture in Andalusia. He lives in Granada together with Francisca Barrionuevo Arrevalo, a teacher. The two have published a number of articles on the lives and destinies of the people of Andalusia.

Carlos Garrido Torres comes from Barcelona, and is a writer and journalist. He has been living on Mallorca since 1976, where he worked as an editor for the daily *Diario de Mallorc* and as director of the magazine *Brisas*. Furthermore, he has written books on the magic of Mallorca and Menorca, and on the secret paths to the beaches and into the mountains of Calviá.

Pio Moa is a free-lance journalist and volunteer director of the Atheneum Library of Madrid, the oldest, Liberal intellectual organization of Spain. He has also concerned himself with the sciences, notably with the publication of the journal *Ayeres*.

Dr. Sabine Tzschaschel, project editor of this book, studied Spain, Latin America and the European Community during her university years. She lives in Madrid where she works as an independent journalist.

Mercedes de la Cruz, who lives in Ubeda, is a professor of literature and a "flamencologist".

Maria Reyes Agudo has, as an art historian, accumulated a wealth of knowledge on Spanish architecture. Besides her work in an archive in Madrid, she also writes articles for the press in her field.

PHOTOGRAPHERS

Archiv für Kunst und Geschichte, Berlin   43, 48L, 48R
Academia de San Fernando, Madrid   31, 39
Brosse, Werner   2, 164/165
Calvo, Gabriel   15, 25, 28, 97, 144, 154, 171, 176, 178, 190, 195, 230
Durazzo, Michelangelo (Viesti Associates)   66, 76, 81, 229
Fischer, Peter   152
Hartl, Helene   21, 51, 155
Hospital de la Caridad, Sevilla   36
Jurado, Bernardo   17, 19, 20, 41, 65, 104, 127R, 146, 168, 188, 223, 226, 237
Kanzler, Thomas   8/9, 60, 70, 83, 84, 86, 89, 101, 153, 220/221, 227
Kneuer, Henry   1, 12/13, 42, 54/55, 56, 113, 122, 125, 133, 142, 148, 173, 180, 182, 233, 239, 240, 241
Kunert, Rainer   116, 131
Kürzinger, Georg   23, 94, 96, 132, 218/219, 236
Museo ArqueologicoNacional, Madrid   14
Museo de America, Madrid   33
Museo del Prado, Madrid   29, 34, 40
Müller-Moewes, Ulf   102, 202, 207L, 212, 215
Paraíso Gonzales, Angeles   62, 147, 161, 127L, 200/201
Prieto, José Ignacio   10/11, 24, 35, 63, 67, 72, 187, 224, 235
Ramos Blanco, Manuel   169
Reuther, Jörg   cover, 45, 95, 108, 109, 111, 121, 138, 214, 225, 231
Schiffl-Deiler, Marianne   115, 118
Skupy, Jitka   207R, 208, 209, 211, 217
Thiele, Klaus   232
Vestner, Rainer   49, 69, 119, 123, 136/137, 196, 197, 222
Viesti Associates   78, 80, 175
Zielcke, Hildegard   52/53